SOUTH BUFFALO

Life of the Baby Boomers in the 40's, 50's, 60's, 70's

The Way It Was

photo by R.R.Rainville

Featuring:

Old First Ward, Valley, Seneca/Babcock, McKinley Parkway, South Park Avenue, Abbott Road, Seneca Street

By:

Roger Roberge Rainville

South Buffalo

A Portion of the proceeds of this book will be donated to Harvest House of Buffalo NY.
https://www.harvesthouse.ws

5 Stones Publishing

randyjohnson@ilncenter.com

5 Stones is part of www.ilncenter.com

Updated 4-19-2017

Unless otherwise indicated all images courtesy of Roger Roberge Rainville

Contents

A South Buffalo resident once made the following statement:

"You can take the boy out of South Buffalo, but you can't take South Buffalo out of the boy"

Comments from Contributors

As you read, you'll bump into the following comments made by some of my interviewees about South Buffalo on the subject of life in the 40's, 50's, 60's, 70's and the present.

"What makes South Buffalo great?"It's not events, places or buildings, it's the people."
George Tutuska

"The 50s and 60's were magical, possibly the best times of my life"
Jim Anthony

"I'm proud as the Lord to have been born in the Old First Ward. It still means a lot to me."
Tim Fitzgerald

"South Park Avenue (OFW) was once a booming area with all kinds of businesses. It was great!"
Bert Guise Hyde

"Even after leaving this area, a lot of people I know come back to visit. It's still their home! Even me! I like coming back here now and then. My heart is definitively still here."
Joe Lucenti (Valley)

"I think if you talked to any of the members from the 50's and 60's, they would all agree that some of the best times of their lives were spent at The Club (Boys Club).
Dan Neaverth (Seneca/Babcock)

"Growing up in South Buffalo was a great experience! It was a blast growing up on Olcott and Choate Ave."
Pete Hermann

"I wouldn't want to have lived anywhere else. So sad Seneca Street isn't what it was. "It's really sad to see so much of what we had is gone. It was great growing up there."
Iva Miller

"It was great living here! I have many fond memories of this area."
Mr. Ed Miller (Seneca area)

"There was always something going on in that park." (Caz Park)
Gerry Regan

"Seneca Street will always be special to me, lots of great times and many good memories."
Ralph Batchelor

"It was one of the best neighborhoods because of friends, locally, and from other neighborhoods and other schools. There was a strong camaraderie."
Roger Pasqurella (South Buffalo)

"I never regretted being from South Buffalo. There's no other place like it and never will be. Oh, the memories!"
James "Butch" Wilson

"If I could, I'd go back and live in the Abbott Road area in a heartbeat. I loved the camaraderie we had."
Tom Best

"The role of George Hermann in the lives of many young men in the South Buffalo area can't be overstated. Men like George (at Mulroy Playground) and Paul Head (at Hillery Playground on Mineral Springs), went way beyond the call of their profession and really impacted our lives."
Steve Banko II

"There's no other place we would rather live than right here in South Buffalo. It's a wonderful place, close to theatres, green space, and our awesome waterfront. We even like the winters."
Ed and Lori Cudney (McKinley Parkway)

"It's the most wonderful place you can live in. The people here are magnificent."
Jack Heitzhaus (McKinley Parkway)

"It's really sad to see how much of what we had, is now gone. It was great growing up in the Abbott Road area."
James Mahoney

"I was always proud to say I was born and raised in South Buffalo. We had deep roots and a sense of pride in the neighborhood. Good old South Buffalo! It was sacred!"
Dan Shea

"It was a great life. I established long friendships. It was a time and place of close knit families and safe neighborhoods to grow up in."
Kevin Caffery (Abbott Road area)

"South Buffalo was a strong community with strong family values and family ties. It was a place where everyone had numerous friends from diverse nationalities."
Dave Caruso (Triangle area)

"Lifelong friendships were developed with real community spirit, and pride in being able to say 'I'm from South Buffalo'. It was a place, and a time that is hard to explain. It had to be experienced."
Pat Nightengale

"It was great living in South Buffalo. It wasn't a perfect place, but all the different aspects of it made it special. A lot of the memories of people, places and events have not faded with time."
Roger Rainville

"South Buffalo was one of a kind in the 50's, 60's and 70's. There was no place like it back then. It was very special. As I get older and talk to other guys from that time, the feeling is, we wish the old neighborhoods could be the way they were. Younger people today have no idea how great it was. It can't be put into words. It was something that had to be lived to understand. It was awesome!"
Bobby Greene

Work Dedicated To...

I'd like to dedicate this project to all of the South Buffalo folks who built South Buffalo. To the living and deceased from the Old First Ward, the Valley, the Seneca/Babcock area, Elk Street, Abbott Road, McKinley Parkway, South Park and Seneca Street areas - you are the reason South Buffalo was the special place it was from the 1940's-1970's.

Also, very fitting and most importantly, I dedicate this to the Greatest Generation; those who lived through World War I, the Depression, World War II, and the Korean War. A special section is dedicated to you, our war heroes. You raised families and created strong communities in South Buffalo. Special kudos to all the grandmas, grandpas, moms and dads who raised the Baby Boomers. You were the backbone of the families, communities and cities.

It is said that a generation is twenty years. This work will feature two generations, from the 1940's-1970's. Wikipedia states that the start of the Baby Boomers was 1946, the year after World War II ended and lasted until around 1964. I was born right at the start, November 1946. It's probably a good idea to include people born a bit earlier than 1946 and those born a bit later than 1964. My oldest brother, Gilles, was born in 1942 and considers himself a Baby Boomer. For that matter, I had three siblings born before 1946 and five siblings born after 1946. We're all Baby Boomers.

Section 1

Recognition and Tribute

Introduction

One of the reasons I wanted to undertake the task of documenting people, places and events of the Old First Ward, the Valley, the Seneca/Babcock area and, South Buffalo proper is because the old neighborhoods have changed so drastically from their glory days. The Baby Boomers and their extended families who lived there during the 40's, 50's, 60's, and 70's enjoy remembering *the way it was.*

It's important to preserve in print, the history of that generation. This book is at least ten years in the making. Besides my own memories, I spent untold hours doing research, spoke to over a hundred individuals, made dozens of trips through the neighborhoods, and took hundreds of photos. Through this journey, I was able to gather many neat facts, comments and stories about the life and times of the Baby Boomers.

There was something special about being part of the these neighborhoods, whether one was from the First Ward, the Valley/ Little Hollywood, Seneca/Babcock, or areas connected to Elk Street, Abbott Road, Seneca Street, McKinley Parkway or South Park Avenue. Those areas, except McKinley Parkway, were much, much different than they are today. When folks who used to live in the old neighborhoods drive through or visit there, they readily see what and how much has changed. Their hearts are genuinely saddened.

"A lot of that 'special something' is now gone and will never, can never return."

In order to understand you would have to have lived there during the years that are presented in this book. Pat Nightengale, a former South Buffalonian, said it very well.

"It was a place, and a time that   is hard to explain. It had to be experienced."

This project is a documentation of people who shared an immense array of unforgettable experiences while living in South Buffalo during the Baby Boomer decades, and the hope of keeping alive, memories of a unique time and place.

When people who lived there meet on occasion after a time of not seeing each other, the conversations usually goes something like this:

"How long has it been since the last time we saw each other?"

"Whatever happened to Scrooge? Is he still around?"

"Do you remember Crystal Beach when Mikey nearly fell out of the Comet ride?"

"Do you remember hopping garages and Bobby falling through the roof?"

"Do you remember Sister Mary Augustine and how she controlled her class?"

"Do you remember going to the Timon and Fazio dances?"

"Do you remember Caz pool, Joey Keane, and guys belly-floppin' off the high board?"

"Do you remember the Rocks and Squeaks, and the way they looked?"

"Do you remember when we had our first drink at Michler's Bar?"

"Did you go to the Woodstock concert back in '69?" It was far out, man."

For those of you who lived then, put on your mental walking shoes and reminisce.

For those of you who didn't, you might find it interesting, amusing and informative.

As my buddy George Rodriguez might say, *Vámonos.* "Let's go, y'all."

Chapter One
A Tribute to America's War Heroes

I hate to start our trip down memory lane on a sad note but, America experienced a lot of hardships and great losses from the 1940's-1970's because of wars. So many members of the Greatest Generation and Baby Boomers lost their lives or loved ones in those wars. It's only right to remember those who sacrificed their lives as well as the survivors who fought for our freedom. Because of these great men and women we can enjoy a strong, safe and free America.

World War II

From September 1, 1939 through Sept 2, 1945, the United States was involved in World War II. It was fought by what came to be known as the "Greatest Generation". Those were the men and

women who came through the Great Depression of the 30's. I salute those who gave their all on the battle fields. One out of every four married women entered the work force in factories and provided materials needed for our military men. Representing the female workers in a government campaign ad to draw women into the work force for munition factories and shipyards was the iconic *Rosie the Riveter*. Rosie was represented by a young lady with a red and white bandana on her head, wearing blue overalls and flexing her bicep proclaiming: *"We Can Do It!"* It was a good thing for America but not for the ladies. They rarely earned more than 50% of what men did. Those great ladies pressed on - for America.

Franklin D. Roosevelt was our president during that war which was the deadliest conflict in history. It is said that worldwide, over 60 million people died from direct combat, collateral casualties, sickness, diseases or famine. The United States with a population of 131,021,000 at the time, lost nearly 420,000 brave men. Most of our American WWII veterans have now gone to their eternal rest. America salutes you!

Korean War

Only 5 years after WWII the United States became embroiled in another war on June 25, 1950. In 1951 US News & World Report called the Korean conflict. It was sometimes referred to as "The Forgotten War" due in part to the fact it was never a declared war and it ended in an unsatisfactory stalemate. America sent 1.8 million soldiers into combat. It isn't forgotten. America lost 37,000 of its brave soldiers who never got to see their families again. Over 100,000 were wounded, both physically and emotionally. War is war, no matter the length, reason or location. No one really wins and the losses are terrible.

You'll see those still living from both WWII and Korea march proudly in parades or meet up at the many VFW posts throughout the United States. If there is a veteran in your family, take time to sit with him, thank him and see if he'll talk about his combat experiences. Once he's gone, all that he could have shared with you will also be gone. It would be good to write down anything that can be passed on to his children, grandchildren, great grandchildren and beyond. Just something to think about.

Jean Aures, (my father-in-law) a World War II and Korean War veteran shared how he made an unbelievable 52 trips back and forth across the Atlantic during WWII on the U.S. Smart, a destroyer escort ship. During one attack on the ship, he shot down a German plane that came so close that he was able to clearly see the pilot's face. America salutes you!

Vietnam War

Not too long after Korea, the United States joined the Viet Nam War. This war was fought by Baby Boomers, as well as men who fought during WWII and the Korean War. Of these three wars, this one proved to be our lengthiest. To many folks it was our most unpopular and misunderstood war. American soldiers were involved in it for sixteen years, from March 1959 through April 30, 1975. The United States lost more than 58,000 brave men and over 304,000 wounded. The country of Viet Nam between 1954 and 1975 lost 3.8 million of its own. It was the first televised war reported on the news every night with recent footage; much of it, very graphic. America salutes you!

Here's a poem I wrote sometime after having escorted the Viet Nam Movable Wall in a nearly 2,000 strong motorcycle procession that ended in East Aurora, New York.

The Wall Says It All

We are a country who says - in God we trust!
With men who went to serve and died for US
Our nation stands because we dare to take a stand
Standing against enemies from any foreign land .... The Wall says it all

We all love this country - land of the free
But you know the cost of freedom isn't free
It's been paid by all who went and stood tall
So our nation and others would not fall ....The Wall says it all

Look at the names of sons written in stone
Brave and valiant souls who are now gone
It's the wall of those who fell, courageous men
Who laid down their lives like faithful friends.........The Wall says it all

They left their loved ones and their beloved land
Many never returned, they fought to the very end
Folks come to see the names of those heroes gone above
The sons of mothers and fathers, who were so loved..The Wall says it all

Those who returned told stories and remembered well
How they and so many others went through hell
Serving their country with honor and great pride
Honoring especially the thousands of men who died..The Wall says it all

We are a country who says - in God we trust!
With men who went to serve and died for US
Our nation stands because we dare to take a stand
Standing against enemies from any foreign land ...... The Wall says it all
RRRainville (10/31/12)

16

So many families from the Buffalo area had to say good-bye to someone who served our country during Nam and previous wars. We salute you all.

Near War

Backing up just a bit to 1962, during Kennedy's presidency, it must be noted that a war between the United States and Russia nearly erupted during what was called, the "Cuban Missile Crisis". It began on October 15 and ended October 28, 1962. That stretch of time was dubbed the "13 Day Crisis." Russia's leader, Nikita Khrushchev had entered into an agreement with Fidel Castro to place nuclear arms on Cuban soil and positioned submarines armed with missiles aimed at the United States. Key West was only 80 miles away and the mainland, 90 miles away.

The reason for the offensive had to do with the "Bay of Pigs" attack on Cuba with CIA-financed and trained Cuban refugees who wanted to overthrow the Castro regime. It was a failure. Castro then welcomed Khrushchev to bring in armaments.

This was the first time in our modern era that the United States mainland was directly threatened with war. The Baby Boomers had never experienced war. It was extremely scary for them. The threat of war was at their doorstep with the very real possibility they could see America devastated.

With Russia threatening nuclear war, the government recommended that people build bomb shelters in their backyards. I remember a South Buffalo family took in some of their young relatives from Florida so they would be safer in the event Russia launched missiles. It wouldn't have taken long for missiles to cover the 90 mile distance. It wasn't only Florida that was in danger, Russia had several other major United States cities targeted as well.

Thank God it never escalated to the point of nuclear war. Had it happened, one can't imagine the immense devastation our country would have suffered. We would have been involved in a war that would have resulted in unimaginable destruction.

President John F. Kennedy Assassinated

May 29, 1917 – November 22, 1963

The year following the Cuban Missile Crisis America received a terrible blow at the hands of an assassin or assassins.

John F. Kennedy was a World War II hero who became our 35th president. News that he was assassinated came as I was sitting in my Social Studies class at South Park High School. Our president was in Dallas, Texas on November 22, 1963 at 12:30 PM when he was shot while sitting in an open-top convertible. Dr. Hayes, our school principal, came over the loud-speaker to announced the sad news. He asked that everyone quietly gather their books and leave the school. The students were in shock. Many girls and some guys wept, while others just walked out in a daze as the reality of it sunk into their heads. The United States had lost its leader. It was a terrible day for our country.

The debate as to whether or not there were one or more shooters is still active today. Personally, as do a great number of people, I believe others besides Lee Harvey Oswald were involved. Those in power who maintain that Oswald was the sole gunman will never admit that it is more believable that there were at least two shooters, possibly three. It would be very interesting to finally find out what actually happened on November 22, 1963.

Bobby Kennedy Assassinated

November 25, 1925 - June 6, 1968

President Kennedy's younger brother Robert "Bobby" Kennedy served in the Navy and followed in his older brother's footsteps by campaigning for the presidency. Bobby had served his brother in the White House as Attorney General. On June 5, 1968, he was shot and killed by 24 year old Palestinian immigrant, Sirhan Sirhan, at the Ambassador Hotel in Los Angeles California, using a .22 caliber pistol. After a three hour surgery at the Good Samaritan Hospital in Los Angeles, Bobby lay in intensive care but never recovered. He died at 1:44 AM on June 6, 1968.

Section 2

The Areas
of South Buffalo

The Sections of South Buffalo

South Park Avenue goes through the center of the Old First Ward, by the Valley and into South Buffalo-south. Here is a list of the streets to help you as you read along:

OLD FIRST WARD

Washington	Moore	Hamburg
Illinois	Marvin	Sidway
Mississippi	Chicago	Illinois
Baltimore	Louisiana	Red Jacket
Columbia	Hayward	Katherine
Michigan	Alabama	Fitzgerald

THE VALLEY

Van Rensselaer	Harvey Place	St. Stephens Place
Elk	Bolton Place	Smith St.
Leddy	Euclid	

ALL THE REST

Owahn's Pl	Alamo	Crystal
Lee St.	Remolino	Bloomfield
Bertha	Macamley	Amber
Abby	Keoster	Choate
Germania	Trowbridge	Lockwood
Boone	Josie	Whitefield
Hopkins	Pries	Altruria
Payson	Coronada	Sheffield
Lilac	Como	West Woodside
Buffalo	Olcott	Woodside
Bailey	Columbia	Ladner
Verona	Tifft	Mariemont
Good	Richfield	Reading

Harding	Ashton/Eden	Dorrance
Colgate	Dalas	Parkview
Culver	Cantwell	McKinley Pkwy
Ridgewood	Downing	Nason Pkwy
Okell	Leland	(Lackawanna)
Marilla	Aldrich	

The Coffee Pot on Nason Parkway next to Botanical Gardens.

Chapter Two

The Old First Ward, The Cradle and Gateway to South Buffalo

The Borders, its People and a bit of History

To speak or write about South Buffalo and not start with the Old First Ward would be - unpardonable. It is the cradle of South Buffalo. That's where the spirit of Buffalo was born. The other neighborhoods all branched off from there. The importance of its location is that it is close to downtown Buffalo and the waterfront. Buffalo was first settled in 1789 and the city itself was founded in 1801.

The Old First Ward (OFW) covers about one square mile. It has Fuhrman Blvd and Lake Erie to the west, Michigan Street to the north, South Park Avenue as its center, the I-190 Thruway to the east and next to the tracks to the south is Fitzgerald Street. Today the average age there is 43. Sixty percent of residents own their own home in a population of about 1,485 people. Back in the 50's and 60's, according to Joan Graham at the museum, the OFW had between 5,000 and 6,000 residents. The demise of the grain mills and other industries has caused the population to significantly decrease. I remember in the '60's when there were residential buildings as well as bars and restaurants on the lower part of Washington Street which is on the fringe of the First Ward

In 1950 construction began on our 100 foot high Skyway and can certainly be considered part of OFW territory. It was completed in 1955. If the wind is blowing just right when I drive over the Skyway on my motorcycle, I get filled up on the smell of Cheerios cereal when I crest the top near General Mills. The I-190 Thruway was built in the late 50's and completed in 1964.

If you go toward the lake at South Park and Michigan to get to Fuhrman Boulevard, some Baby Boomers might remember a small bridge right next to General Mills on Michigan Avenue near Ganson Street and connected directly with Fuhrman Boulevard. It was called the South Michigan Street Bridge. An article on the removal of that bridge stated: *"It was rendered inoperable and was removed by the City of Buffalo in 1964."* Where it states, "inoperable" brings me to what Steve Banko said to me about that bridge.

"I believe it was taken down because it was rammed by a barge on the river."

I guess that'll do it! It linked Kelly Island to Fuhrman Boulevard. I remember driving over it in the early 60's. Too bad it's gone.

As a point of interest - Dug's Dive's address and the Small Boat Harbor is (one, one, one, one) 1111 Fuhrman Blvd.

Old First Ward Community Center

To begin my research, I went to the Old First Ward Community Center and met Laura Kelly, the center's director. She guided me to the 1st Ward's museum on Hamburg Street so I could gather material for this project. That proved to be a very good start. There, I met Bertha "Bert" Guise-Hyde, Peggy May-Szczygiel and Joan Graham Scahill who run Waterfront Memories and More. They told me that the first settlers in the area were called "Beachers" because they lived along the beaches of Lake Erie which included the Small Boat Harbor area along with Times Beach and the Marine Drive area. Two Beachers families were the Lattimers and the Freitas.

Bert Guise-Hyde said:

> *"As time went on and the city grew larger and larger.*
> *Catholic Churches were set up throughout Buffalo and the*
> *different communities were referred to as parishes. People were*
> *connected to specific Catholic churches that revealed what part*
> *of the city they were from."*

The waterfront was where ships came and went and a great number of Irish people settled there around 1842. They came to work the grain elevators, emptying ships of their grain. They worked the docks, rail lines, and other industries. By 1850, Buffalo had a population of around 80,000 people with many, residing in the Old First Ward. The grain elevators were a major industry and grain was shipped out via the Erie Canal (built 1817-1825) and by rail to many parts of New York and other eastern states. By 1850, the city of Buffalo was ranked 10th in the United States for population growth and commerce.

Grain Elevators

The first steam-powered storage grain elevator was built in Buffalo in 1842 at the foot of Commercial Street and named "Dart's Elevator" after its inventor Joseph Dart. The elevator had a capacity of 55,000 bushels of grain. Dart's elevator had a leather conveyor with buckets [scoops] attached to it. Ships were now able to unload grain at a rate of 2,000 bushels per hour instead of 2,000 per day when it was all done manually.

The Old First Ward became known as "Elevator Alley" after several more grain elevators were built. A great number of the Old First Warders worked the grain mills and elevators. It was arduous work with dangerous conditions for the scoopers. A scoop was a large four foot wide, metal shovel hooked to pulleys by ropes and chains to a conveyer contraption used to empty ships of their grain cargo. A "Grain Shoveler" or "Scooper" was the man responsible for filling the scoops. The grain dust was explosive and suffocating. In early times, the men wore make-shift paper masks to filter the air they breathed. Some First Ward old timers who worked there, are:

Jimmy Griffin – former Buffalo mayor

Tom Griffin - his father and grand-father did the same work

Jack Suto - was a second generation scooper. His father was a former president of Local 109 Scoopers Union.

Robert Metevia was the oldest scooper to give it up at age 68. He spent 48 years in holds emptying ships. At the end of his career, he was quoted as saying:

"This is it. This is the last. It's going to be weird after 48 years not having to come in here. It's been good."

To honor our Scoopers, here's a statement made by Lorraine Pierro of the city's Industrial Heritage Commission.

"In the early afternoon with the ships' holds empty, the scoopers gathered in a tavern named McCarthy's, a bar proud of its Irish heritage. A trait shared by the scoopers who have always been almost exclusively Irish is they were boisterous behind bottles of beer and their memories. They drank to the end of an era."

By 1863 Buffalo had 27 grain elevators. You may think your job doesn't pay much, but in 1895 a scooper worked long, hard hours and only made around $300 a year; about a dollar a day based on a five-day week. The elevators are still there today as a reminder of Buffalo's glory days. Take a ride through the Old First Ward by the Buffalo Creek and Buffalo River areas to get a glimpse of those massive structures. They are awesome!

As I went through some of the streets in the Old First Ward on the west side of South Park I could sense the pride of the community. Bert from the Hamburg Street museum stated that the Old First Ward was once, *"very family oriented."* Although it is a very old neighborhood with aging houses, I did not get the sense that it was rundown. I noticed quite the opposite. A great many houses were refurbished with new siding, new porches and steps. I thought to myself,

"These folks are keeping up their houses. They take pride in the way the neighborhood looks."

On average, houses today in the OFW are worth around $140,000. Not bad for an old neighborhood, eh? Many of the houses have been handed down to family members as parents passed away. Many have lived there all their life. The people there value where they live, family ties, and Irish culture. They have great community pride.

As I turned from South Park onto Hamburg Street, I noticed how many American flags were flying from porches or flag poles. The pride they demonstrate is not only for their neighborhood and their Irish heritage,but also, for their country, the United States of America. I salute you Old First Ward

The OFW, as previously mentioned, had a lot more people several decades back. It has shrunk greatly in number, and most of the businesses are gone. As far as schools go, PS #4 at South Park and Louisiana is still active. Saint Valentine Church and school on South Park, as well as Saint Brigid on Michigan Avenue have closed. The only Catholic Church still active is Our Lady of Perpetual Help on the corners of O'Connell and Alabama streets. Its elementary school closed years ago. That particular area with the church and the houses all around it reminded me of the 1944 movie "Going My Way" with Bing Crosby as Father O'Malley, Ingrid Bergman as Sister Mary and Barry Fitzgerald, the elder priest with the thick Irish brogue, as Father Fitzgibbon.

Driving through there, I could imagine what it was like in the Ward with all the families, docks, rail lines, grain mill activities and businesses up and down South Park. So much of it is now gone. Like other areas throughout Buffalo, the Old First Ward can never be what it once was. A good portion of the east side of South Park's First Ward is where the Commodore Perry Projects are located as well as quite a few homes. The OFW had a concentration of Irish that occupied the homes there. But the east side of the Ward in the projects has had a mix of nationalities for many years now. I was told by the folks at the museum that the Commodore Perry Housing Project was the first of its kind in the United States.

Bill Nicholson was a Baby Boomer born and raised in the Old First Ward and lived in the projects from the late forties till 1961 when his family moved further south to Lockwood Avenue. While on Lockwood, he attended Holy Family. He did his stint in Nam, got married and retired in Boston, New York.

Old First Ward Irish Pride and Events

There are two big events that need to be mentioned: the Shamrock Run and the Saint Patrick's Day Parade. The Shamrock 8K Run has been a springtime event in the Old First Ward for 38 years as of 2016. According to Kenny Castillo (an OFW resident) Jimmy Griffin was part of starting this event. It draws over 5,000 runners which includes people from the Ward for sure, but also from many other parts of the city and beyond. A young lady named Pam Greene, originally from Florida and living in West Seneca, took part in 2015 and 2016, and a family from East Aurora made it a yearly event.

At the end of the run it's party time with Irish gusto. One of the sayings about those who partake in the event is:

"No matter what your heritage is, everyone is Irish at the Shamrock Run."

There's that Irish pride. Erin go Bragh. (actually Éirinn go Brách) "Ireland Forever."

The Saint Patrick's Day Parade is an event where you see Irish pride in full bloom.

The City of Buffalo had Saint Patrick's Day Parades starting mid-March 1848 which continued for 19 years. It was put on by the "Friendly Sons of the Saint Patrick Society." The largest parade in the city was held in 1876. There were other parades but the trend didn't last. There were breaks from 1917 to 1935, and more breaks during the World War II years of 1942–1945.

Saint Patrick's Day Parade Revival

Peg Overdorf is Executive Director of the Valley Community Association. She founded the "Old Neighborhood" Saint Patrick's Day Parade in 1994 as a way of bringing back that much missed event the folks of that area loved. The parade makes its way through the Valley and Old First Ward neighborhoods. Peg said:

"I grew up in a household where my parents put a lot of emphasis on our Irish heritage. It was always a huge part of our lives. St. Patrick's Day was special. It brought everyone in the family and everyone in the neighborhood, together. That's what I wanted to recreate with the parade."

In 2016 the Ward and Valley celebrated its 23rd parade. It started at the Valley Community Center on Leddy Street. From the Center it went down Harvey Place, Saint Stephens Place, over to Elk Street, then to South Park and over the bridge until it got to Hamburg Street. It took a left and went to South Street. It used to turn down O'Connell, but was rerouted to South Street which is wider and a better fit for the parade.

In 1969, the Valley Community Association was formed. The community center building at the corner of South Park and Liddy Street was completed in 1971 and named the Fr. Carmichael Center.

28

McCarthy's Bar

As you travel down Hamburg Street, you come across the well-known McCarthy's Bar and Tavern at 73 Hamburg Street. Gene McCarthy opened it in 1963 and around 2012 new owners Bill Metzger and Matt Conran took over. It has the cozy feel of Cheers (popular 1980's sitcom) restaurant and pub with its regulars - retired folks and workers from the General Mills plant, business people who come to have lunch or dinner and drinks, and to hear good live music. McCarthy's owners also operate the Old First Ward Brewery that is right next door to the bar.

While visiting McCarthy's, I asked bartender Hannah Lowman if there was anyone around who I could speak to about the area. She pointed to 81 year old John "Jackie" Donnelly from the Tennessee-O'Connell area who was sitting by the window having a brew.

"I'm here every day," he told me.

When I asked Jackie what was special to him about the Old First Ward his response was:

"I just love it here. I'll never move out. People stay in the neighborhood. They don't move away. I've been in the same house here in the Ward for 81 years. When parents pass away, most of the kids keep the houses instead of selling them off and moving elsewhere."

I asked him what difference he's seen that he's not pleased with.

"In the old days, being Irish was very strong. People back then used to practice being Irish and you knew who was Irish in the neighborhood and who wasn't. People used Irish terms and even spoke it. Today, it's hard to tell who's Irish. But, there are still a lot of us here. It's still a great place to live."

Jackie mentioned a few of the guys he knew back in the day:

Jim "Boy" Smith and his brothers, Pete and Joe. Also, Mike Miller. *"Most of the guys I hung with are gone."*

The Other Side of the Tracks and Names of some of the OFW Residents

When you get to McCarthy's Bar you'll see a set of railroad tracks a stone's throw from there. The other side of the tracks takes you into another portion of the Old First Ward. It's still the OFW but those tracks made a distinction between its residents.

It seems that at one time, the tracks were a line of demarcation. Pre-Baby Boomer Joan Graham Scahill told me that the folks residing on the side of the tracks nearest the Buffalo Creek were referred to by a, "pet name" that many today would find offensive. If you would like to know the exact term go to the museum and ask Joan. She was one of them. Although it sounded negative, she clarified:

"The term wasn't necessarily a derogatory one. It was just meant to give a location for those who lived closest to the creek. All the folks, whichever side of the tracks they were from, were all Old First Ward people. No one was above the other. We were all equal."

I don't know which side of the tracks he was from, but Tim Fitzgerald who was born in the OFW in the early 50's and later lived on Whitfield told me:

"I'm proud as the Lord to have been born in the Old First Ward. It still means a lot to me."

I've yet to meet a person who was born or lived in that area ever say that he or she regretted having lived there. There's that pride of being part of a people and place.

It's something that imbeds itself in the soul of a person or group of people. It stays with them all of their life.

Some of the people Tim came to know or was acquainted with in the OFW are:

Scud and Vi Mann, Marty Mann Danny Bodkin, Jim Flood (owner of Floody's Tavern), Corky Connors, Tim and Mike Connors, Jack and Mary Fitzgerald, Jack Montando, the Keneficks, Francis, Bob and Joe. Also, the Hofstetters, Travis', Catanzaros, Mullens, Horrigans, and the Simoniks.

Bert from the museum and OFW, a Baby Boomer herself, recalled others. Some of the people I knew as well are noted by an asterisk.

31

John Cummings, *William "Whitey" Guise, Pete May, *Mike Flood, Pat Stilt, Beau Korek, Duke Holland, *Mike "Cats" Catanzaro, Gene Dunbar, Betty Stack, Sue Griffin, Tom Szczygiel, Richy Hoar, Cindy Morris, Sue Eynow, Moe Hassett, Shela Hassett, Kenny Zabawa, Ace Hassett, Val Galanti, *Tommy, Jack and Jimmy Shine), and *Jimmy O'Connor.

I spoke to Dan Concheiro at Tully's Bar in the Valley who had the following acquaintances in the Old First Ward back in the day:

Frank and Beth Badaszewski, Tom, Joe, Maryann, and Paul Heidinger, Doug Beltram, Jim and Angelo Bouquard, Bob Rodgik, Ray and Ellen Conchiero, Tom and Peg Wahl, Ted, Gene and Peg Overdorf.

Old First Ward, South Park Avenue Businesses

"You don't know what you've got till it's gone!"

I asked Bert Hyde what the South Park strip of the First Ward was like with regards to businesses, stores and other tenants in the 40's, 50's, 60's and 70's. She said,

"South Park Avenue was once a booming area with all kinds of businesses. Not anymore."

She gave me a chart with a host of stores and businesses. Here are several that existed on South Park Avenue in the years above. Bert made sure I noted the 19th century tavern known as the Swannie House at 170 Ohio and Michigan. As of 2016, it's a 120 year old establishment run by Tim Wiles.

Swannie house

Businesses

Along South Park Avenue was Louie's Masque Theatre. One of the ladies at the museum said that it was nicknamed "The Rat Hole Theatre."

The Malamute Pub at South Park and Michigan.

321-27 South Park there was the Harris Lumber Yard

357 Previty Groceries.

384 Lanigan's Park

Loblaw's near Louisianana Street

397 McGrath's Restaurant

399 Desiderio's Restaurant.

400 Dublin Restaurant

402 a gas station at Louisiana

403 Liberty Wine and Liquor

405 Market

408 Marine Trust Bank,

418 Speakman's Hardware Store

410 Starr Credit Jewelers

423 Turk Max Variety Store.

430 Pantera's Cut Rate Drugs Store

528 Saint Valentine's School and Church

543 Mazurek's Bakery (formerly South Park Bakery) across from Saint Valentine's and next door to Mazurek's is the Old First Ward Tavern at 555 South Park. It became Mazurek's Bakery

in 1933 under Frank and Jean Mazurek, then son Jack and his wife Carol and finally, Ty Reynolds and Nick Smith. It has been in business for 83 years as of 2016. They sell a variety of pastries and the very popular "Paczki" (ponch–kees) before Lent. In case you're not familiar with Paczkis, they are delicious doughnuts typically filled with strawberry or raspberry jelly. Current employee Angie, has worked at the bakery for nearly 30 years at this writing and still lives in the Old First Ward. Mazurek's was one of the most sought out stores at Easter time. Joe Lucenti from the Valley said:

> *"People from all over would come to Mazurek's Bakery. One of the most desired items was their rye bread. There used to be a line out the door all the way to Hamburg Street."*

Another special food item for Easter was sausage. Joe told me:

> *"For that, people would go to Kurzanski's Meats on Fulton Street. What could be better than kielbasa from Kurzanski's and rye bread from Mazurek's Bakery?"*

Below are places located on the Western most part of the Old First Ward, some of which remain to this day.

- The Malamute Bar - 211 South Park Tim and Morgan Stevens purchased it and renamed it Ballyhoo Links & Drinks Sept. 28, 2014.

- The Swannie House - 170 Michigan at Ohio is 120 years old and was originally called Swanerski House is the second oldest bar in the city.

- Milt's Tavern/Carmen's Tavern, now gone was on the corner of Ohio and Louisiana

- General Mills - foot of Michigan Street

- The Bison City Rod and Gun Club on Ohio

- Advantage Trim & Lumber on Ohio

- The defunct grain elevators that made Buffalo world known

- Great Lakes Fibers Corporation on Ohio

- Two bridges: one that crossed the Buffalo River at Ohio Street and the bridge connecting Ganson and Michigan near General Mills (Michigan Street Bridge).

- Saint Mary's Cement Co. on Ganson Street

- Lafarge North American concrete company on Ohio and Ganson Streets.

- Rigidize Metals Corp on Ohio Street.

- Gerdeau Ameristeel on Ohio Street.

- A bit removed from the Old First Ward but very close neighbors are:

- Site of the old Freezer Queen Foods Company on Fuhrman Blvd. was started by businessman Paul Snyder in 1958. Snyder also started Darian Lake Amusement Park in 1964. I worked at Freezer Queen as a forklift driver in '68 and '69.

- The Small Boat Harbor - 1111 Fuhrman Blvd

- Dug's Dive – 1111 Fuhrman Blvd. at the Small Boat Harbor

- Another grain silo at the Gallagher Beach site Fuhrman Blvd near the foot of Tifft Street.

- Tifft Street Nature Preserve which covers 264 acres 1200 Fuhrman Blvd

Some Thoughts about the OFW

As I was driving down South Street in the OFW, I saw four teenage girls walking and thought I would get their views of the Ward. Two were Ward girls and two others were guests from streets off South Park (south of Tifft Street). I asked the two who lived in the Ward. *"How do you like living in the Old First Ward?"*

One responded: *"I love it. Love living here."* The other added: *"There are no conflicts here."*

I asked the other two girls if they liked where they live in South Buffalo. One said *"There's too much drama where I live; too many fights and drugs."*

The other said: *"I like it here better. It feels friendlier than in the South Park area where I live."*

I asked mailman Chris Mulvaney on his route on South Street his feelings about the Ward. He said: *"It's friendly here. I like the 'old school' effect, the people, houses, neighborhoods and the vintage look and feel."*

I encountered Tim Dickman at the Master Market at Louisiana and South streets. He's been an Old First Ward resident for years. I asked about a bar I used to go to in the late 60s that was located at Ohio and Louisiana streets. He said:

"Oh yeah. That was Milt's Tavern. It became Carmen's Tavern. Around the 4th of July in 1998 it caught fire. People near the place were setting off fireworks and something lit up the place. It was destroyed. When the police investigated, it was funny; a whole bunch of guys turned themselves in at Precinct 7 at Louisiana and Miami. There was no way of knowing who did it. The cops let 'em all go."

Tim added: *"All of those guys I knew are no longer around."*

I personally remember that Milt's had great hamburgers back in the 60s, where me and a lot of the guys who worked at Freezer Queen used to go to cash our paychecks, order a hamburger and down a couple of beers.

Notable Persons from the Old First Ward and South Buffalo William "Wild Bill" J. Donovan

The Old First Ward had several people who were born there or had a connection to it and made a name for themselves. The most illustrious was William "Wild Bill" J. Donovan. He was born in January of 1883 and lived on Michigan Street. He attended Saint Bridget's on Louisiana and Fulton streets then transferred to Nardin Academy and finally, attended Columbia University Law School. Donovan died in February of 1959. The university erected a bronze statue in his honor in 1979.

Writer Richrard Dunlop said of him, *"He was the most renowned person to come out of the Old First Ward"*

Dunlop wrote about Donovan's part in World War II as the director of what was called, the OSS (Office of Strategic Services). That office was the precursor of the CIA and Donovan is regarded as being the *"Father of the CIA."* Dunlop said this concerning Donovan: *"Hitler feared and hated him more than any other American."*

Many of you remember the building across from the old War Memorial Auditorium on lower Main Street (The Aud, as we called it). Right across the street stood the General William J. Donovan Building, which was built in 1962 and used for 45 years.

Donovan was a highly decorated U.S. soldier, a lawyer, intelligence director, and diplomat.

By the time he finished his service duties, he amassed an incredible number of service medals:

Congress Medal of Honor

American Campaign Medal

The Distinguish Service Medal

Asiatic-Pacific Campaign Medal

2 Oak Leaf clusters
European-African/Mid-Eastern

The Distinguished Security Medal

Campaign Medal

Silver Star
WWII Victory Medal

Purple Heart with 2 Oak Leaf clusters

American Occupation Medal

Security Medal

Germany Clasp

Mexican Border Service Medal

Armed Forces Reserve Medal

WWI Victory Medal with 5 Campaign Bars
Army of Occupation of Germany Medal

Jimmy "Six Pack" Griffin (June 1929 - May 2008)

Hizzoner Jimmy Griffin, one of our *"older"* sons came from the Old First Ward then moved to Dorrance Avenue near Abbott Road. He worked as a scooper in the grain mills, a railroad engineer and bar owner. His greatest achievement was becoming the 56th mayor of Buffalo January 1, 1978, serving 16 years as mayor. Everyone who knew him remembers the slogan *Gimme Jimmy* as a political campaign slogan. During his office as mayor, he was instrumental in erasing the city's $19 million deficit and was part of the resurgence of Buffalo with new development and construction. The downtown baseball stadium known as Pilot Field was one of his pet projects. I remember when I worked for International Cable and Mayor Griffin was a guest on Paul McGuire's Sportsline Show. He brought a model of the stadium to the TV studio and spoke excitedly about building it right in the middle of downtown Buffalo. Built in 1979, this was big news. Besides the stadium, many other improvements took place in the city under Griffin's leadership.

He was also known for a statement he made on radio and TV when the infamous blizzard of 1985 hit Buffalo. His suggestion to get through the foul weather was:

"Stay inside. Grab a six-pack and watch a good football game."

Hence the nick-name *"Jimmy Six Pack"* was born.

Feisty Jimmy Griffin was a different kind of candidate and mayor. There is no denying that he ruffled more than a few feathers. He never minced words. He shot straight-from-the-hip when it came to certain issues and publicly spoke his mind on more than one occasion. Sometimes things got pretty heated. I believe he even got into a bit of fisticuff with someone who pushed his button by using foul language in front of his wife. That opponent lost the match.

He got himself kicked off Channel 7's AM Buffalo show with host Brian Kahle in 1987 over a discussion about allegations that federal money was mishandled by his brother Tommy. Some subjects were better left alone while in the company of the Mayor. If you wanted to get into a verbal battle with him, he wasn't shy about telling you off or getting his point across. A lot of folks loved to hate him while many truly loved him. Whatever side you were on, you must admit that he was an unforgettable character

First Ward Giant, "Big Red" Carroll

John Francis "Big Red" Carroll of the Old First Ward was one of the tallest men in the world at 8 feet 7.75 inches. Born in 1932 at 9 pounds 5 ounces, he was five and a half feet tall by the time he reached age 12. At the age of sixteen, he shot up to six foot, two inches and wore size 16EEEE shoes. He attended Bishop Timon High School where he was a definite asset to the basketball team. By the age of twenty, he was over seven and a half feet tall. In his younger days, he was able to pick up one end of a car; the back end I'm sure.

As an adult he served as a local park supervisor, superintendant of Isle View Park in the Town of Tonawanda and county parks. John served as Republican committeeman and ran unsuccessfully for county supervisor in 1955 and 1957. He died in 1969 at the age of thirty-seven.

The Tutuskas

While researching my book, I stopped at the Old Triangle Tavern at South Park and Abby. I spoke to bartender George Tutuska and learned he had ties with the Old First Ward. I also found out the tavern had several names before becoming the Old Triangle Tavern. It once was Talty's, the 19th Hole and Burke's Tavern.

George began talking to me about his background and who he was connected to. His grandfather was B. John Tutska, a First Warder who once held the offices of Erie County Sherriff and Erie County executive.

Another connection George had to the OFW was his uncle, Bill Conway. Conway got into the Guinness World Record Book for having been the youngest man to obtain a ship's Master Pilot license, he was 21. He came in first on the list of those who took the test for the license.

George himself has a claim to fame. In 1986 he formed the Buffalo based group the "Goo Goo Dolls", along with John Joseph Theodore "Johnny" Rzeznik and Robby Takac. He was the drummer for the band and played on the group's triple platinum album, *Dizzy Up the Girl.* He was with the band until 1996.

While talking with George about South Buffalo, he wanted to stress what made South Buffalo great. He said, *"It's not events, places or buildings, it's the people."*

39

Boxers Tied to the Old First Ward

Jimmy Edward "Shamus" "Slats" Slattery was an Old First Ward and Valley idol. He was born on Fulton Street and bought a house for his mom on Bolton Street in the Valley with his first boxing winnings. Slats was born in 1904 and died in 1960. He was one of former Mayor Griffin's four top heroes.

As the story goes, Slats' start in boxing stemmed from a fight he had with a 210 pound thug who snatched a box of chocolates out of his hands that he bought for his mother on Valentine's Day. He didn't let the matter slide. According to details given by writer Timothy Bohen, author of "Against the Grain," the story went like this:

> *"There were about two hundred people watching the match where young Slats beat the bully in about 30 minutes. His father saw his son's potential as a fighter and brought him to the First Ward Athletic Club. Jimmy's boxing career started when he was 16 years old."*

He turned pro in 1923 at age 17. At 175 pounds, Slats fought as a light-heavy weight. He had 129 fights and was inducted into the Buffalo Sports Hall of Fame in 1992 and the International Boxing Hall of fame in 2006. He had 114 wins, 51 knockouts, 13 losses and 0 draws. One of his best weapons was his left punch. He retired in 1931.

One story about this OFW son was that he'd throw money out of his car window as he drove through the Ward streets to help poor children buy shoes for school. He was honored in 2006 by having a sign placed with the Bolton Street sign of his childhood residence that reads *"Jimmy's Place."* Going north on South Park, Bolton is a couple of streets on your left just before the curve leading to the bridge going toward the Old First Ward.

I found out that I am connected to Slats through marriage. Kathy Byrnes Aures is my sister-in-law, married to my wife's brother, Gary Aures. Slats is her distant cousin. She explained the lineage like this: *"My dad was Patrick Byrnes. His mom was Agnes Byrnes Hickey who was my grandmother. Her father was Michael Hickey who was my great- grandfather. Her father's sister was Mary Hickey. Mary Hickey Slattery was Jimmy Slattery's mom. That makes his mom, my dad's great aunt and my great, great aunt making Jimmy my distant cousin.*

40

Richard "Rocky" Fumerelle The Blond Bomber"

South Buffalo-born Rocky Fumerelle, "The Blond Bomber" who attended South Park High fought as a middleweight from 1955 to 1963. In 1955, he won the Buffalo Golden Glove novice middleweight title and repeated that title the following year. He went undefeated in 19 amateur bouts. He was taken to San Francisco along with Bobby Scanlon by manager Mike Scanlon. He retired in 1963 because, *"It wasn't fun anymore."*

Rocky settled down and studied communications and property management at Canisius College for a few years. He married Rita Cafarella.

Bobby Scanlon

Another boxer from the OFW was Bobby Scanlon. He was born in 1936. He spent part of his life at the Father Baker Orphanage. He started off in Golden Gloves and went on to fight as a pro lightweight at 5 foot 6 inches.

Excerpt from Art Benjamin, Nick Kobseff and Lou Sabella's writings, one statement about Bobby went like this:

"Because of his choirboy looks, he was frequently a target of bigger and tougher kids. He turned to boxing and became the orphanage's champion."

He turned pro in 1954 and fought, primarily, in Buffalo, Rochester, New York, Syracuse and Erie PA. Part of his record was that he was undefeated in 22 fights. Eventually, that number rose to 32 fights ending in wins. Between 1958 and 1960, his career had run its course. By the end of his fighting days, his record stood at: 42-12-1. During his career, he fought 412 rounds in 55 fights. He retired in 1966. After his boxing days were over, his life went downhill. Bobby's buddy Rocky Fumerelle said this:

"Bobby Scanlon was his own worst enemy. Had he taken better care of himself, I have little doubt that he would have been the Lightweight Champion of the world."

One source stated that Bobby struggled to find meaning to his life after his career. His life was boxing. After a while, his health started to diminish. Sadly, he died in a fire in the Lackawanna Hotel on June 23, 1975 at the young age of 39

Jimmy Ralston

Although not a Ward guy, Jimmy Ralston, born in Riverside, was another Buffalo-born boxer. He knew Bobby and most of the other Buffalo fighters. He told me:

"I liked Bobby a lot. He was a nice guy. He wasn't flashy and never played the role. He was a quiet, nice guy. I was very sad when he passed away."

Ralston was rated 6th in the world. Like Bobby, he too fought in the Aud in Buffalo. His career record was 19-1-1. I spoke to Jimmy in November of 2015 at Talty's. He told me about a match in he had in 1969 where he knocked out a guy in 7 seconds of the first round. WOW!

Bobby Aldridge

I'd like to slip in a story about a Lackawanna/South Buffalo Golden Glove New York State Champ by the name of Bobby Aldridge. He was involved in an incident outside South Buffalo's South Park Deco 22. First of all, you have to know from what I knew of Bobby, he seemed nice; not a wise guy or menacing in any way. Every time I saw him he was joking and laughing with his friends or engaged in some conversation. I never saw him being aggressive or unruly. If I'd say "hi" to him, a pleasant "hi" came right back. A friend of his, Ray Colpoys, reinforced that:

"I always saw Bobby as a guy who was mild mannered and humble. He never looked for trouble or instigated bad situations. But, if trouble came along, he'd take care of business. Not once did I ever hear him tell people in bars that he was a boxer."

One night, some outsider came by the Deco and for some reason, messed with Bobby. He began taunting him by walking around him; maybe gave him a little push and said something to the effect of:

"Soooo - boxer eh? I hear you're good. I hear you're bad. Come on, show me something. Let's see what you can do."

Bobby could have let it go, but you have to understand that for some people, a challenge is a challenge. He felt that backing down was not an option. After all, his buddies were watching and he just couldn't let it go. There was pride and reputation at stake - New York State Champ and all. According to one of the boys who saw it, Bobby threw a series of explosive rapid-fire punches and put the guy down.

End of story. Now everyone knew what he could do. No real damage done to challenger beyond a few bruises to both his body and his ego.

Years later, Bobby lost his life from a gunshot to the stomach. I never got the details as to what happened exactly; only that he was shot and drove himself to the hospital. The police were called and when they asked who shot him, Bobby wouldn't give up the shooter's name. He simply answered *"John Wayne."*

Chapter Three

Intro to South Buffalo (South)

Next in line as we go down South Park is the Valley. It is a brother to the Old First Ward. There are many connections between these two areas of South Buffalo. So as not to stray from South Park Avenue, I'll continue traveling south and returned to the Valley in a bit.

A portion of South Park Avenue makes up part of Route #62. It is very unique because of its length. It begins north of us in Niagara Falls, New York, continues through Wheatfield and is part of Niagara Falls Boulevard and Bailey Avenue. After that, it makes a left at Bailey and South Park and goes through Lackawanna, Blasdell, Hamburg, Eden, Collins Center and Gowanda. It continues through Amish country near Randolph and then on to Jamestown, New York. You will need to travel much further south before you run out of route 62, through such cities as Oil City, PA, – Columbus, Ohio, Buffalo, Ohio, Bradstown, Kentucky, New Madrid, Missouri, Corning, Arkansas and then pass through Matador, Texas, through Hobbs, New MX and finally El Paso, Texas at the Mexican border of Juarez, Mexico. With that bit of information, let's get back to the streets.

From the foot of Main Street and South Park to the Lackawanna bus turn-around at the old Coffee Pot which touts a picture of Jackie Gleason on a bus, there are seventy-six or seventy-seven streets.

South Buffalo Baby Boomers

Samples of Who Wound up Doing What - Careers, Jobs

As you read, you'll find that some of the characters were not top of the class types nor did they mind their moms and dads all the time. A few ended up making very bad choices with some even doing a bit of jail time. Most guys and girls were better focused and more or less knew where they might be heading in the future. Kevin Caffery for instance, knew at the age of five.

Here are names and careers of a few of the Baby Boomers who came from South Buffalo.

Clergy

Fred Betti and James Higgins became priests.

Law Enforcement

John and Tom Thurston from Crystal - FBI agents

Police officers

Jim "Jet" Jackson

George Amplement

Joe Prendergast

Joe and Lenny Weber

David Caruso, from police officer to inspector

Kevin Caffery from Milford Street - Sheriff's Department

Ernest P. Masullo became Evans Town Chief of Police

Tom Best and Dan Shea were promoted from police officer to detective in Hamburg

Officer George Battaglia became the first active member on Buffalo's Swat Team in 1966 serving around thirty years.

Firefighters

Neil Keane, *Mike Catanzaro, John Tevington and Carl Villalobos.

*Mike Catanzaro, From the Old First Ward lost his life in an immense propane blast December 27, 1983 at 191 N. Division & Grosvenor streets.

Lawyers

Billy Bond
(same family as Mary Bond's Deli at the corner of Harding)

Tom and Kevin Brinkworth

Will Curtin

John McGee

Mike Caffery

Teachers

Joe Lucenti - became a principal

Adele Petrilli - became a language teacher

Medical Field

Margie Morrison

Karen Lobuglio

Marcia Miniri

Businessmen

Roger Pasquarella

Dennis Dargavel

Billy Held

Billy West

John Mugas

Politics

Jimmy "Six-Pack" Griffin - mayor of Buffalo 1978 to 1993

Richard and James Keane

Brian Higgins

Tony Orsini

Mickey Kearns

Tim Kennedy

Mark Schroeder

Carl Paladino

If you listened to WKBW AM Radio in the 60s and beyond, DJ Dan "Smiling Dan" Neaverth from the Seneca/Babcock area was one of the most well-known radio and TV personalities in Buffalo and beyond.

Most of the guys and gals we came to know got decent paying jobs in offices, large companies or manufacturing plants in the Buffalo area. Remember the steel plants and all other companies Buffalo once had? Here are some that employed hundreds and even thousands of people.

All of the Grain Elevators, Old First Ward area

General Mills/Gold Medal Flour on Michigan and Ganson streets

Bethlehem Steel, Lackawanna all along Route #5

Buffalo Tank Division, Lake Avenue in Blasdell

Republic Steel, South Park near Buffalo Creek

Buffalo Forge, 490 Broadway

Donner Hanner Coke off South Park Avenue, Abby and Mystic

Buffalo Train Terminal - Central Terminal, Paderewski Dr. 1929-1979

Courier Express Newspaper, Main Street

Westinghouse Electric, Genesee Street, Cheektowaga

Worthington Pump, Kaisertown area, off Clinton near Bailey

Buffalo China, Seneca Street near Bailey

Trico Plant #1, 817 Washington St.

Trico Plant #2, 2495 Main Street

Trico Plant #3, 500 Elk Street

Mobile Refinery 625 Elk Street

National Aniline Chemical Company/Dye Plant, South Park and Lee Streets

Nabisco Bakery Company - 243 Urban Street (East Side)

There were very few men and women in the area who did not do well. Most people landed somewhere between making a decent living and making a great living.

South Park (south) Businesses and People

The South Buffalo neighborhoods were so different from what we see of them now with regards to the commerce that once existed. People with their heart still there are saddened as they ride through the area because of what they see or don't see. Gone are the many specialty shops and stores. It would be safe to say that from the good old days of my time there, at least 90% to 95% of the establishments and businesses that existed on South Park are now gone. That's how much it has changed. As you read the lists, you'll easily see what we once had.

Bob Regan who moved from Scranton PA to 149 Ladner Street in November of 1955 was a fountain of information concerning what once existed all along the southern part of South Park Avenue. You'll read more about him as you make your way through this trip. Other contributors along with Bob were: Butch Wilson, Roger Pasquerella, Joe Parisi, Ray Mattingly, Tim and Ann Fitzgerald, Billy McEwen, Bob Greene, Barbara Buckley, Margie Miller, Bob Domzalski and Jimmy (Crystal Avenue) Miller.

The list starts at Abbott and South Park and makes its way to Dorrance Avenue at the Buffalo/Lackawanna railroad trestle. There may be a few places missing, but most will be listed.

Although the following list of stores and businesses may be a bit boring, I felt it was very important to make it as complete as possible as a keepsake and to remember just how many businesses were there. I've weaved in personal memories, statements and stories from individuals. There were a few other businesses a bit north of South Park and Abbott Road, but, I'll start the list at that location. Some of the locations of the businesses as I head south may not be in order, but they existed in that general area. Forgive me if I missed any or misspelled the names of any person or stores.

Walk With Me and see what was, and no longer is ...

At South Park and Abbott was: The South Buffalo Cab Company a Marine Midland branch that became an M&T branch and PS #28. Then, there was Hal Casey dealer, Dick Kratz Chevrolet which eventually moved to South Park and Okell Street. Russo's Trophy Room bar, Ray Lak's Chevrolet, Campbell's Drug Store, Strohm's Bakery, S & P, Sirett, Koch's Department Store and Dry Goods Store, McPartlan's Bar, the Red Brick Inn, the Villa Pizzeria which is now the Bread of Life Church, Sheehan Ford dealer at the corner of Koester and Holfinger's Delicatessen. Across from that is Taylor Park next to South Park High School where one of the crews that hung out there included:

Nino Petrilli, Bob Rabitore, the Bunch brothers (Dave and Chuck), the Bugmans, John Faliero, Ron Wendtland, Sam Giritano, Joe Nappo, Joe Avolio, Vito Bovo, John Ademy, and Tony Skoviak.

Going further south there was a soda shop, the Capital Theater which became Fazio's Hall, and for a short time Fazio's Peppermint Lounge. Then there was Crehan's Club Como, The Phone Booth Lounge, the OK Inn, Shea's Triangle Bar, Como Deli, Coster's Transmission, a liquor store, the old Post Office, an A & P Super Market, Phone Company, Sterlace Bar/Blarney Castle, Hector's Hardware, Nightingale's Funeral Home near the corner of 920 Tifft Street, Holy Family School and the church at 1885 South Park.

Note: the school closed around 2004. I am told that this was the original site of Mercy Hospital until they moved to Abbott and Lorraine.

Across from Holy Family on the same side of the South Park was Joe Corto's Barber Shop and across the street from Joe's there was Sinclair's gas station. There were a couple more businesses on both sides of South Park before Crystal. There was Biday's Delicatessen near Tifft, a hobby shop and auto parts store.

From Tifft Street to Choate my contributors remembered places like Morrison's Delicatessen, NU-WAY Supermarket at Richfield, Hempling's Pharmacy on the corner of Crystal. Then, there was Paul Wiles Texaco station (still there at this writing now Dick O'Neil's Garage). Next to the gas station was Murray's Delicatessen and next to that, the Chat and Nibble's Soda Bar. Across the street on the corner of Bloomfield was a little diner called Laddy Boys and on the other side of Bloomfield was Mueller's Tavern which first became Ann's Inn and later the Nine-Eleven Inn. Across the street at Amber is Mr. Submarine and on the other corner was Gene Wahl's Tavern which became Pal Tony's bar and then was demolished. Crossing again, there was the Star Liquor store and next to that Louie's Hat, Shoe Repair and Shine Shop. Later, I will tell you a bit more about Louie's Shop.

A few steps from Louie's was our beloved poolroom run by Harry Aldridge where representatives from every generation came in to shoot pool.

Harry Aldridge's Pool Hall (a.k.a. Monk)

Everybody who hung out somewhere on the strips (South Park Abbott Road, McKinley and Seneca Street) had special places they liked to go. For me and many others, it was Harry's Poolroom, two doors down from Nick's Texas Red Hots near Choate. We played such games as; eight ball, straight pool, oddball, five/nine, pea-pool and so on. The pool hall brought in people from all the neighborhoods. We had guys from Lackawanna, Blasdell, Seneca Street, Abbott Road, McKinley, the First Ward, the Valley and other areas.

From time to time, someone would get yelled at by Harry "Monk" Aldridge. Even 'Sis," Harry's wife, who was there almost as much as Harry was, would sometimes light into some young buck who got out of hand and would chastise him like a mom would. All the boys respected her. If anyone dared go over the line against Sis, it was the wrong thing to do. All the regulars had her back and they made sure she was safe. She was like a mom or better yet, a grandma. Disrespect was not an option at Harry's pool hall.

No one can forget the way Monk would sit in his comfortable stuffed chair near the little office area with the cash register behind him. He smoked quite a bit. Both he and Sis used a cigarette holder when they smoked. We thought it was unique. It was *"Harry and Sis unique"*. You know what I mean. Sometimes, he didn't get to enjoy his smoke very long. It's interesting that even with all the noise in the pool room he'd often fall asleep after he lit up. Watching to see how long the ash at the end of his cigarette would get before it fell right into the ten inch round, two inch high can, became a thing for us to do as we played pool. It was right below the arm rest. He'd sleep and the cigarette would burn out completely. When he woke up he'd look at his cigarette holder, take out the burned butt and simply insert a fresh one. I believe his cigarette brand was Raleigh.

Pool Room Story

One night Angelo "Sonny" Ferrari was ready to sink a ball in the corner pocket. It was a "berry" as we called them; an easy shot. Mike Smith was at the end of the table, face level with the table and urging Sonny to nail it! He hit the ball really hard. I mean hard! He sank the target ball but the cue ball kept going and knocked out two of Mike's front teeth. Ouch! I saw Mike in the spring of 2016. We talked about that incident and had a good laugh.

Harry had eleven tables in his pool hall. They were the old types from the twenties or thirties maybe. They were neat. His best table, number 4, was right near the cash register and his soft chair. From time to time he'd show the guys in the place a few trick shots. He always used that pool table, fourth from the door as you walked in. There was also one upstairs at the end of the hall. From there, we could look down at most of the other tables and catch the action.

Speaking of catching the action, the pool hall had elevated seats against the left side that were on platforms like downtown at the Hippodrome Pool Hall. They were good seats to watch some of the money games and the really good players who would take on any comers. There were some very good shooters who came by. Harry had known many of the greats like William Joseph "Willie" Mosconi (1913-1993) from Pennsylvania, world champ in the 40s and 50s; and Rudolph Walter Wanderrone Jr. "Minnesota Fats" (1913-1996) from New York, NY. Some of Buffalo's top players graced his tables. It was truly a classic pool hall in the grandest sense. At the time, we didn't fully appreciate what we had there. This is one of the things you needed to have experienced to get a true sense of what the place was like and what it offered. Those of you who played there know what I'm talking about.

One of the top players was Joe McGir from Lockwood Avenue. I remember playing eight ball with him one time for $1 a game in 1964. In the first game, he destroyed me. For the second game, he spotted me three balls. Lost that one too. Joe, knowing how good he was, gave me a fighting chance that would give me hope for winning at least one game. In the next game he spotted me five balls. Nobody ever spots anyone five balls in an eight ball game. That's ridiculous! I wasn't a bad pool player, but five balls!

"I said; *"Okay, let's do it."* All I had to do was sink two balls and the eight ball. No problem. He even let me break. I thought, *"That's good. I get to break. Alright. I gotta win this one."* Do I even have to tell you what happened? Yep. I missed my first shot. He ran that table and just laughed. I didn't. I smiled, but I was totally demoralized. Do you think I ever played any more money games with Joe? I may be dumb at times, but I'm not stupid.

Bob Regan was also one of the top shooters there. I didn't play pool too often with him. He could run a table and pull off shots I couldn't dream of pulling off. I remember one day when John Harmon from Crystal Avenue was home on leave from the Navy and Regan was on leave from the Army. Both had been regulars at the pool hall. With his usual wit, Bob said:

"Hey John, how about you and me have an Army-Navy game?"

It got a good laugh out of everyone. We knew Bob was better than most of the guys he hung out with but we didn't know how well John would do against him. Anyway, John laughed and took on the challenge. Bob won.

Classic Whit

Dan Mattingly, another one of the Baby Boomer poolroom boys had a little run-in one day with Harry. He told me how Harry had chastised him for doing something that had upset him. He said that he lashed out at him with a tongue twister that went something like this:

"You don't know how little you know of how much you know, and that's all you know of how little you know of what you know - that's how much you know of how little you know of all you know."

I would have loved to have been there for that one. That is pure Monk classic stuff.

By the way, in the 1965 South Park High senior yearbook, the quote that accompanied Dan's name was; "Born Comedian." He was very amicable and - funny.

The pool room under Harry's command lasted until a bit beyond the mid-sixties. Bernie Blanchard took it over for a while and then Larry Martinez from Blasdell ran it in the late sixties. I even took a shot at running it in 1971. I think it only lasted from August till December.

Moving On

Next to the poolroom was Schere's Market which became Alexander's Lounge and next to that was Nick's Texas Hots. Right next to that at Choate was Ralph's Delicatessen. On the same side of South Park across the street was Donovan's Five and Ten Store which later became Jack Bonner's Lounge. Liberty Bank was across the street which is now a Key Bank.

Nick's was really unique. For starters, is was so small that maybe ten or twelve people could fit in there at one time semi-comfortably. On their limited menu was basic breakfasts, cheeseburgers, a few different types of sandwiches and of course their specialty, hot dogs. The price back then was 25 cents each. I'm told that in the late fifties, you could get five for a dollar. The thing that made them special was the sauce. You know, that spicy brown gravy meat sauce. It made the hot dog very different from hot dogs one ate at a back yard Bar-B-Q. It wasn't only the sauce but also the wieners and the buns. Nick's used one of the top wiener brands in the city. I don't know if they were Wardynski's or Sahlen's, but they were always

54

good. The buns were kept in a little container where they were slightly steamed which gave them a fresh taste. That, combined with the sauce, made for a treat anytime. Abbott Road and Seneca Street had their own hot dog restaurants too. They were all great places to enjoy - Texas Red Hots.

On your left as you walked in to Nick's was the "take-out" section by the front window and grill. Behind the man working the grill, there would be (one or two other Greek owners). Obviously, one of them was Nick and another by the name of Johnny.

One man worked the grill and the other two worked the French fry pit, made sandwiches, served the coffee, tea, milkshakes, soft drinks, and cashed out customers. There was a counter with four or five stools, and I think, three two-person tables against the right side wall. That was it. They were busy from opening until closing. You would walk in and give your order to the counterman. You would hear orders being called out, in a Greek accent as follows;

"Order to go. I need one chi-burger, one fry and one Pepsi"

"I need chocolate shake, 'two up' and one fry." (two up meant hot dogs with everything on them)

"Order for table 3. Two up, one chi-burger, one Pepsi, one tuna sandwich and one coffee."

The orders kept getting filled like that all day. Everything would only take a few minutes to make. A lot of the food was for "take-out" orders. When Saturday Night Live did a skit on a Greek short-order restaurant back in the 70s, anyone who went to Nick's immediately related to it. It was almost as if the skit writers of SNL had eaten there and got their idea from them. The way the comedians on that show went through their material was a lot like being - at Nick's. They have been closed for years. No more Greek grill and countermen. Great memories.

After Nick's Texas Hots around the corner from South Park was an important part of the community, Spoonley The Train Man" at 37 Choate. Everybody knew Chester Spoonley, and many went there to get their first train set or purchase items to add on to their existing sets.

A slight aside here. I was told that Jim Morgan of the famed 1957 Ford Fairlane 500 with a 427 engine lived above Mr. Spoonley back in the 60s.

Across from Choate was the Liberty Bank and next door, Koch's Shoe, Spark's Bakery and Horrigan's Meat Market, then, Daisey's Deli and a Coal Company. At Lockwood was Parson's & Judd's Pharmacy with a classic soda fountain. Who can forget that? About everyone on the strip went there and enjoyed a soda, a sundae or

an ice cream cone. Crossing the street at Whitfield was Bob Mallon's Men's Store and the Dudley Library. Crossing again, there's the Black Dog Saloon -still active, then there was Bell's Market which I believe was an IGA Market at one time, next was the Woodside Furniture store on the corner of Altruria Street. I could never understand why it was called "Woodside Furniture" when it wasn't on Woodside.

Marge Weber stated that before it became Mike Scrip's Woodside Furniture, it was the original South Park Presbyterian Church. A new church was built on McKinley between Lorraine and Alsace.

Right across from the furniture store was Precinct 15 followed by Belvedere Cleaners where I got my sharkskin pants cleaned and pressed. On the other side of Altruria Street from Woodside Furniture was Lou Bielli's Dodge dealer. Along with the car dealership, there was a tavern named Agaro's Italian Restaurant which then became Sperduti's and Bill's Manor was next and lastly, before it burned down, the Barber Shop owned by Tony Orsini. Back across the street there was a shoemaker and another delicatessen. Next to that was Felong's Tavern. Across from Felong's at the corner of Sheffield on the same side of South Park was the Sheffield Inn which later became O'Conner's and is currently Talty's Bar owned by Dennis Talty. A few feet next to Talty's, there were trampolines during the summer of 1963. Across the street from Talty's, according to Sam Fassari, it was Broker Motors and a Studebaker/Packard dealership. Ullenbruck's Delicatessen, Cadet's dry-cleaner shop were at the corner of Woodside.

Across from Ullenbruck's was La Hacienda Pizzeria on the corner of West Woodside. It was initially owned by Sam Coro. I remember Mary Marcucci and her mother were waitresses

In the 70's, Gary Schintzius and Doug Alessandra took it over and added submarine sandwiches to the menu. Next to that was a Helpee-Selfee coin laundromat where I and a lot of other guys remember ducking in during some cold winter days to get a little relief from the cold before continuing on to wherever we were going. Next to the laundromat was Gannon's Delicatessen. I went to Holy Family with Paul F. Gannon, one of Mr. Gannon's ten kids. By the way, Paul invented the "Pegxco Spotter Club." It's a modified golf club for disabled golfers to sink their "T" and spot their golf ball.

Across from the delicatessen at Woodside was a Texaco service station. Across the street from the Texaco station, you would find Tony and Johnny Orsini's Barber Shop. Next to that Drapper's Jewelers and Power's Drug Store. On the corner of Mariemont a garage on one corner and some other business on the other corner. Across from Mariemont was Fachko's, which later became the South Park Grill, owned by Ron Delano. Next, Buffalo Builder's and Aberdine Glass. And behind them a beer distributing company that lost a few cases of beer at the hands of some unscrupulous young men from the area.

On the same side of the street was Bob Senco's Sonoco station. He was well-liked and respected. He would allow some of the boys who frequented the Deco Restaurant across the street to put a few dollars of gas on a tab. I can remember him spotting a few delinquent patrons hanging around the restaurant. He'd go over and put the squeeze on them. Only kidding! He was a great man. He would simply walk over to remind them it was time to settle their tab. Most guys did the right thing and settled their debt. Bob heard a lot of stories from delinquent debtors. It was like a cop stopping them for a traffic violation. Bob heard 'em all. Anyway, they'd eventually take care of what they owed. As of 2016, Bob is still with us in his 90s.

Deco Restaurants

The Deco restaurant in our neighborhood was known as Deco 22 in the Buffalo area. Along South Park there were three and Seneca Street had five. Few people may know this, but there were 50 Decos in the Buffalo area at one time that were open 24 hours a day. Below is a list of which street and number they were located.

Deco Restaurants Locations

- Bailey Ave. at 856, 1834, 2855 & 3144
- Best St. at 393
- Broadway Ave. at 171, 901 & 1650
- West Chippewa St. at 29 & 142
- Clinton St. at 1437
- Delaware Ave. at 2320 & 2944
- East Delavan Ave. at 1040
- West eagle St. at 24
- Ellicott St. at 169
- Elmwood Ave. at 516
- West Ferry St. (Commissary) at 935
- Fillmore Ave. at 385, 1387 & 2385

- Genesee St. at 599 & 808
- Hertel Ave. at 1338
- Jefferson Ave. at 1316
- Main St. at 248, 1001, 1390, 1528(offices), 1578, 1857, 1955, 2948 & 3292
- Michigan Ave. at 403
- Military Road at 340
- Niagara St. at 219, 1116, 1159, 1615 & 2801
- Seneca St. at 60, 741, 1670, 2222, 2447
- South Park Ave. at 48, 309 & 2132 (DECO #22 see next page)
- Washington St. at 389 (last one in Buffalo at 609 behind the Ellicott Square Bldg.)
- Williams St. 426 & 771 (This last one was right near the site for road tests)

An awful lot of the South Park young adults and adults spent time there. It had a lot of regulars, day and night. Harry's pool room owner would often take a walk down South Park to have his supper there.

Bombing at Deco 22

There were numerous incidents that occurred in and around Deco 22. One of our fine young men miscalculated as he backed up his car toward the side of the restaurant and ran into it with sufficient force that it knocked over the large milk machine and numerous other items off the wall.

Another time Dennis McDonald and I were sitting in a booth by the window on the Harding Street side when we saw an individual come by, open the sliding window and then walk away. Moments later, in came this canister which landed on the floor and began spewing out bright, thick orange smoke. At first, we thought it would only let out a little smoke and stop. Nope! It poured out bright orange smoke until the entire restaurant was completely filled with it. Elsie, one of the waitresses freaked out and screamed,

"It's a bomb, it's a bomb. Get out... Get out..."

Denny and I realized it was only a smoke bomb. We got out anyway just in case. Shucks! We didn't get to finish our coffee. True to their claim, Deco did serve the best cup of coffee in Buffalo.

Deco's founder was Gregory Deck who was born around 1900 and died in 1969. He started his business at the age of 18, as a hot dog stand back in 1918. He went to Canisius College but dropped out to expand his business. His first enclosed restaurant was situated on Eagle and Pearl Street in 1921 and the last one was locate at 389 Washington Street which stayed open until 1979. For those of you who remember and frequented the Deco restaurants way back then, I urge you to read Gregory Deck's amazing success story online.

In my life I've made a lot of connections, and would you believe I have one with the Deck family. I taught French to Gregory Deck's grandson, Paul Deck, at Canisius School in the early 1990s. Several years after Paul was done with school and began working, he remembered me and sent me a Christmas card, which I still have.

That Deco site subsequently became Peter and Pauls Pockets.

On the other corner from the Deco was Mary Bond's delicatessen at Harding Street with its own crew of guys who would gather there to pass time. Across the street was Vanott Machine Corp. owned by Jimmy Mungovan's father and across from that was the Poplar Inn. Then there was Murphy's Insurance and Dr. Sullivan's Office. At Culver and South Park was a gas station and across from that still going south on South Park was Loblaw's Food Market where you got S &H Green Stamps with your purchases.

Green Stamps

S & H Green Stamps were popular from 1930's till the 1980's started by a couple of guys by the name of Sperry and Hutchinson.

Customers would receive stamps at the checkout counter of supermarkets, department stores, gasoline stations and other retailers, which could be redeemed for products in the S & H catalog. Businesses supplied booklets in which to paste your stamps. The downside of that process was that you had to lick all the stamps unless you did it the smart way by using a sponge. The glue tasted terrible. The amount of stamps given for each purchase was up to the business owners. Customers got one stamp for each 10 cents spent. The books contained 24 pages and filling a page required 50. Each book contained 1,200 points

More Businesses

After Loblaw's closed, it became the NU-way Market. At the edge of the parking lot going south was the second location of Tony Orsini's Barber Shop.

Tony had a door at the back of his shop that led to who knows where. While waiting to get my haircut one day I saw guys come in and disappear into that room. I asked *"What are those guys doing back there?*

Johnny and Tony replied: *"Oh, they're playing cards - Pinochle. They love Pinochle"* Hmmm, I'm not sure about that.

At South Park and Ridgewood was Cuthbert's delicatessen. There was an average of twelve to fifteen delicatessens along the strip between the triangle at South Park and Abbott to Dorrance. Getting bread, milk, coffee, cigarettes and beer was never a problem. Cuthbert's was a place where some of the guys would get three quarts of Topper Beer for a dollar according to one of my sources. Folks, that's three quarts, not regular size bottles.

Across from the deli was PS #29 where many from that area hung out playing handball, shot dice and past time away.

Next, depending on who I spoke to, I got varying lists of the names of car dealers that occupied the following site:

Across from school #29 at 2600 South Park and Okell was Schwartz Buick a car dealership that covered both corners. This is where Jimmy (Crystal Avenue) Miller bought his first car after he came out of the service in the late 60s.

At the corner of Marilla and South Park was another site for hanging out. On the corner was South Park Electric and across the street was DePottey's Pharmacy which later became McNearney's Pharmacy. Across the street, McLaughlin's Delicatessen, owned by Vic McLaughlin's dad. Marilla and South Park was full of Baby Boomers. Some of the people in the crew that hung out in that area were:

John Ranne, Billy Held, Mike Knezevic, Bob Fulmer (one of the first on the strip to ride a motorcycle), Louie Clouden with a couple of his brothers, Vinny Catanzaro and several more.

The next group was primarily from the area of Eden and Aldrich streets. Some of the names that come up in that crew were:

Doug Kroll, Doug Kelly, Jack and Dennis Sixt, Mike and Shawn Smith, Ted and Mike Pasiecznik, Dan Riordan and several others.

On the same side of the street was Murphy's Funeral Home. There were two or three more small businesses after the funeral home.

Across from Muphy's, South Park United Methodist Church, the Wayside Restaurant, Dave's Service Station and then Sorrento Lactalis Milk Products followed in line.

The next businesses were a Mobile Station on one corner of Aldrich and Cutinelli's Delicatessen on the other corner. Next to Cutinelli's was the Mr. Softy Ice Cream trucks' home base.

The only places of interest between Aldrich and Dorrance (city line) were Recckio's Bowling Alleys and the famous Mangano's Bakery. There weren't many of us who were who were interested in bowling. It was for the older crowd, married couples and fans of bowling who were into bowling leagues. I don't remember anyone in any of the groups ever saying; *"Let's go bowling Friday night."* It wasn't our thing although some of the young people did bowl now and then.

The second to last business before the railroad trestle/bridge was Mangano's Bakery where you could actually see all the baked goods being prepared as you looked through huge windows. You could get a dozen doughnuts for 75 cents back then. Today at Wegmans they're 85 cents each. The last business I remember before the bridge was a scrap yard called Metalico.

There used to be over 100 businesses and establishments from Abbott and South Park to the city line. Today you'd be lucky to find a handful of the original places. This gives you an idea of what South Park had. Sorry for any I missed. Some of the people I asked to furnish the names of businesses couldn't recall every single one. Remember this covers a span of over 50 to 60 years. I hope it brought back some neat and interesting memories.

South Park/Lackawanna Border

The next point of reference was the railroad bridge beyond Dorrance - the South Buffalo-Lackawanna border. We had little interest in going beyond that point. The only attraction was South Park Lake and the Botanical Gardens. Sometimes, we would go into Lackawanna to attend Friday night dances at OLV High School or go to a carnival on Ridge Road. As we got older, there was the Astro-Light night club on Ridge Road where we'd go to hear some of the best bands in the area and hang out with friends. One of our guys, Ray Colpoys, tended bar there. Again, eighteen was the legal drinking age then. It was pretty cool getting your Sheriff's Card as a picture ID to get into bars. Our driver's license in those days didn't have our picture and was only a thin card with basic information. It stated ones name, address, birth date, height, weight and eye and hair color. To get into bars a lot of underage guys and girls would simply get someone's license that had matching height, color of eyes and hair and a birth date making them eighteen. I still have my Sheriff's Card.

Bars Were Our Social Network System

One thing about bars everywhere in the neighborhoods is that people from various groups came to socialize. Some bars were frequented by mostly older people in the neighborhoods while other bars were mostly for the younger crowd.

Inside the bars there would be the different crews who hung and drank together. From time to time guys from one crew would walk over to another group and talk about any number of subjects from up-coming get-togethers for ball games, parties or sometimes someone had a question that needed an answer from guys of another crew. Someone might have heard that so and so did this or that and there was the curiosity to find out exactly what happened and get as many details as possible concerning the hero or culprit.

Example: *"Who cut down the tall pine tree at the McKinley-Red Jacket circle?"* or *"What started the fire at Pal Tony's at the corner of Amber?"*

Somebody knew. Some laughed at the downed tree incident on McKinley, but a lot of folks took it personal, feeling as though someone messed with their neighborhood and they didn't like it!

Today some of those active social networking bars in South Buffalo are:

Swannie House on Ohio, McCarthy's on Hamburg Street, The Triangle Saloon, Black Dog Saloon on South Park, Nine-Eleven on Bloomfield Hop Inn on Hopkins, Doc Sullivan's on Abbott, Ballyhoo at South Park and Michigan (was the Malamute), Avenue Pub on South Park, Buffalo Irish Center on Abbott , Blackthorn on Seneca, Rush Inn on Seneca, Daly's on Seneca Street, Talty's on South Park

The Reunion at Talty's - Baby Boomers Reminiscing

It was at a reunion at Talty's Night Club in 1999 that inspired me to wite this book. I heard many of the guys talking about what South Buffalo used to be like, all the guys they knew, the stores and businesses that were there and what the neighborhoods were like. They talked a lot about what they remembered and missed. I thought it would be great to have a book that would feature a lot of what we Baby Boomers once shared back in the 40s, 50s, 60s and 70s.

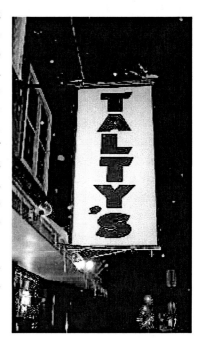

The idea of a South Buffalo reunion was sparked by Lockwood son, Kevin McCarthy's death in January 1999. Joe McGir (deceased 2007, Lockwood boy) was in town from Florida. Dennis Talty, Danny Jordan, Joe Nappo (deceased 2006 from the Taylor Park crew) and several others from the South Park area were at a concert at the Buffalo Marina in August of 1999. We asked those who were there to spread the word that we would do an impromptu reunion of the South Buffalo crews at Talty's Bar at Sheffield and South Park. I told everyone present to call anyone they knew and tell them to meet there August 27, 1999.

Besides myself, Bob Regan and Butch Wilson were very instrumental in spreading the word about the reunion. The night arrived and at least thirty-five to forty people showed up. It was mostly guys who came from several crews of different neighborhoods and age groups. It was certainly, a guys' night. It wasn't a large number considering the couple of hundred guys or more everybody knew up and down the strips of South Park Avenue, McKinley, Abbott and Seneca Street. But it wasn't disappointing at all. We had a great time and held at least two a year for several years from then on. At this writing, the hope is that it continues. We had the second reunion in December of '99 and about seventy-five guys and some ladies showed up. What a gathering it was. Every time we were together since, we would see someone new popping in. One of the guys who finally made an appearance was Bob Domzalski from Amber Street. I remember coming in to Talty's and Roger Pasquerella asked me, *"Do you remember this guy?"*

I took a good look but I didn't recognize him. He looked like one of the guys from ZZ-Top with long grayish hair and a long beard, but that smile was the same one I remembered from when he walked the neighborhood as a young man. It took me a little while and then it hit me. "Bob Domzalski!"

It was great seeing him and chatting a bit. Some guys hadn't seen each other in over 40 years. It was fun going over events, memories, and stories about our lives there. At our first reunion, some of us sat down and started counting guys who had passed on. We came up with nearly 40 names. From that first reunion until 2016 we lost between 15 to 20 or more people. That brings the total to more than 50 of our Baby Boomers, gone.

Dennis Talty from Lockwood Street has been a great promoter of South Buffalo and Irish Pride. I was told that his family has been in the "pub business" for about 100 years. His bar at South Park and Shefield provides his patrons with great atmosphere and top shelf music by some of Buffalo's best.

Billy McEwen, Joe Head, Jim Brucato

Bob McConnell from Lockwood was partners with Dennis Talty for twelve or thirteen years. Jimmy (Crystal Ave) Miller bartends on occasion, and Bobby Hartman is still in charge of scheduling bands that come in to play.

Contributors' Memories of South Buffalo

The following individuals contributed to this book with some of their memories of the way it was in South Buffalo. They provided names of friends, places they hung out at and activities that occupied their time.

Butch Wilson

Butch and his crew came from the area near PS #29. Several guys he hung with were:

Jack Gallagher, Billy Held, Bob Fulmer, the Burketts, Robert Clouden, Joe O'Holloren, Gerry Hurly, Ed "Stosh" Mendefik, Charley Pierce, Horst Sanders, Tommy Best, Jack "Jet" Jackson, Doug Kroll, John Ranne, Doug Alessandra, Tom Hurley, Dan Shea, Vinny Catanzaro, and Tom Rogers.

As teens, their hang outs were in front of Marge's Deli and Mary Bond's delicatessen. He remembers sledding at Lockwood Hill and playing Relievio at the Latona Court Apartments' playground. In his late teens he often patronized the Deco and Harry Aldridge's poolroom. Butch concluded his contribution to this project by stating, *"I never regretted being from South Buffalo. There's no other place like it and never will be." Oh, the memories!"*

Bobby Greene

Bob lived on Harding near the Deco#22 Restaurant. He treasures the memories of the old neighborhood; the stores, the playgrounds, the old pool room, the bars, but most importantly, all the people he came to know and hang around with. The total number of people he actually knew and hung out with are well over 100 individuals. He knew and hung out with people from all of the four main South Buffalo streets. One name he mentioned to me several times is "Jeff Taylor" from Seneca Street.

His close circle of friends included: John Maxim, Dan Griffin, John Woodman, Allen Yox, Jim McCrory, Ray Wade, Mike Sperduti, Jerry Quinlan, Skip Ganger, the Cunningham and Jordan brothers, Ed Baun, and Billy Hillman.

When asked what he loved most about being a South Buffalo son, he said:

"South Buffalo was one of a kind in the 50's, 60's and 70's. There was no place like it back then. It was very special. As I get older

and talk to other guys from that time, the feeling is, we wish the old neighborhoods could be the way they were. Younger people today have no idea how great it was. It can't be put into words. It was something that had to be lived to understand. It was awesome!"

Ray Mattingly

Ray remembers a lot of the same things Butch remembered. He added that the guys would play steam ball behind the NU-Way Market and took swimming lessons at South Park High School on Saturday mornings. He gave me a neat bit of information about the purchase power of items costing less than 50 cents. For instance, he said that at Mary Bond's delicatessen he could buy a peanut stick, a small coke and a Superman comic for 25 cents and a liverwurst sandwich for 15 cents. *"When you got to smoke cigarettes, you could get a pack for 26 cents."*

Pat Nightengale

I was the fourth of seven children. It was more common in the fifties and sixties to have large families. South Buffalo had distinctive neighborhoods where the older kids looked after the younger ones. In my case, the neighborhood was South Park Avenue from Tifft Street and going south to about Ladner Street.

It was a time of families. Fathers worked and mothers were home taking care of everything. For better or worse, the older kids were in their own way, mentors. There was a stair-step approach from the older kids to the younger ones. Handed down were; the rules of ice hockey on frozen ponds, street games such as relievio, and kick the ricket. There were always pickup basketball, football and baseball games in the street and at Mulroy playground. Teams were picked by the older captains; the younger ones hoped not to be selected last. Paper routes were handed down from older kids getting their first real jobs. They got jobs at the Park Edge Market, or one the local pizzerias or other neighborhood shops. Many of us learned to smoke our first cigarettes as young as 13 years of age, to look cool.

These were happy times where simple victories were acknowledged, and losses were comforted by moms and dads. Lifelong friendships were developed with real community spirit and pride in being able to say, "I'm from South Buffalo." Although many have stayed and others moved away, we continue to embrace and share our learned values of community, respect, patriotism, honesty, and fairness.

This was a place and a time that is hard to explain. It had to be experienced.

Billy McEwen and the Neighborhood

Billy remembered many things about the old neighborhood such as going to Ullenbruch's Delicatessen between Sheffield and Woodside on South Park as a teen. He mentioned that he never saw Norm Ullenbruch without a cigarette in his mouth. *"He would treat all the kids as if they were his own."*

If the boys perused the comic books too long, he'd say to them:

"Hey you! Gonna buy those comic books? This ain't no library you know."

He remembered Broeker Motors at the corner of West Woodside that sold Ford Edsel cars in 1958 and 1959 as well as Studebakers and other used cars. Also, "Joe the Butcher" from Food Land at South Park near Altruria.

"At noon, Joe would run across the street to Felong's Saloon for his liquid lunch. It was amazing that he never lost any fingers while cutting meat after coming back from those lunch breaks."

Another unique business Billy remembered was Cook's Shoe Store between West Woodside and Ladner. He said that he and others would go in and put our feet under a gizmo called a fluoroscope. It was an X-ray device *"We'd put our feet under the scope, push the button and we could see the bones. I'm surprised after all the X-ray exposures we got that any of us are still alive."*

He recalled Powers Drug Store between Ladner and Reading. He said Mr. Powers used to sell Wing cigarettes for 23 cents a pack. Billy would fib and score some smokes for himself, he would say *"Yeah, they're for my father."*

He also remembered La Hacienda Pizzeria at the corner of South Park and West Woodside. He said that he'd go in there, split a small pizza and two cokes with a buddy for 55 cents each. Speaking of good prices, he remembered Mangano's Bakery next to the railroad bridge before Lackawanna where you could get a dozen donut for 60 cents. That's five cents a donut. Today, the average costs of a donut is 75-85 cent each. At $9.00 a dozen, that's an increase of 675% from the old days. Doesn't it make you a little sick? That's inflation gone nuts. It's kind of scary when you look at it that way. By the

69

way, there was no sales tax on foodstuff like that, not even at the restaurants.

Joe Parisi

Joe is a former Holy Family school student who, with his older brother Sam, lived right across the street from the school. He still lives in South Buffalo not far from where he grew up.

One of the first things he mentioned was Harry's Pool Hall. *"This is where all the young guys learned to play pool."* He also mentioned a rival pool hall owner, Joe Licatta. As Parisi remembers, *"That's where the big money games were played."* He too, remembers Mulroy playground with George Hermann, where all who went there learned to play sports. He recalled the Sunday dice games as one of the less glamorous uses of the park. Besides the poolrooms and Mulroy Park, Joe spoke about the forts in the Tifft Street fields. Another fond memory was Fazio's Capital Hall where he went to Friday night dances. He talked about the sandlot tackle football games every weekend at Mulroy playground. He bragged that the *"South Park boys never lost to any of the other neighborhoods."*

He brought up South Park and Timon High noting that the people from those schools all meshed together from South Park, Abbott Road and Seneca Street. He remembered that there were a few fights between the neighborhoods. *"There was nothing new about that. I think people from different neighborhoods always had some sort of territorial thing going on."*

He noted that most of the guys from all areas of South Buffalo served in the Viet Nam War during that time.

Terry and Joan (Colern) Shanahan

Terry and Joan, both from the South Park area, talked about many of the same places already mentioned in the list of businesses along South Park. Some that came to their minds:

The old Post Office and Pat's Shoe Store at the corner of Olcott with an A & P Market across the street. Horrigan's Meat Market at Choate, Sputniks Bakery, Abirigo's Pizzeria at the corner of Altruria where Joan's big brother Joe Colern worked. She did her Christmas shopping at Donovan's Five and Ten Store on the corner of Choate. She remembers the soda fountain at Parson's and Judd's Pharmacy and Biddies Candy Store next to the Neighborhood House #3 not far from Tifft Street. At the Neighborhood House, they offered music lessons to Girls Scouts as an after school activity. Then, there was Murray's Deli, Chat Nibbles and next to that, Gene Wahl's Tavern at the corner of Amber. Joan and Terry remember Precinct 15 with Officer McDee being a favorite neighborhood officer on the beat.

Pete Herman

Pete is the nephew of our beloved George Hermann, bar owner, Mulroy playground director/coach/overseer/sergeant-at-arms and "father" to all the boys who hung out there.

Pete had this to say:

"Growing up in South Buffalo was a great experience. All of us were so competitive. This brought out a fierce a sense of pride in our part of the city. I was taught how to play ball at the Caz diamonds and Mulroy Playground. Holy Family and Bishop Timon High set me up for a future in coaching. Lifelong friendships are always there. It was a blast growing up on Olcott and Choate streets.

Sam Accordino

Sam Accordino was born in the early 40s and lived on Heussy Street near Saint Agatha's. He went to school 28 elementary adjacent to South Park/Abbott. After eighth grade, he enrolled at Burgard High. After High School, he enlisted in the Army and did a stint from 1961 to 1963.

When he and his friends were around fifteen they hung out mostly at the Greek's and Taylor Park on South Park. He and his friends formed a gang with about fifteen to twenty members called the "Gators" with the gang's emblem on their black and powder blue jackets. The girls connected to them wore pink gang jackets.

"We weren't the kind of gang that got involved in typical hard gang activities. It was just a thing to do; to hang out together and have an identity as a group. We weren't in competition with other gangs, frats or clubs and we weren't into gang fights. Seneca Street also had a couple of gangs; the Cougars and the Rebels I believe. Anyway, we hung out as a group to have fun."

The spellings might not all be correct but some of the people Sam remembered hanging out with were:

Gussy Carmani or Carmanis, Vinnie Antonelli, Chuck Rambino, Gerald Marchain, Carmen Sabastian, Joe Simmons, Tom Gombush,

Diane Charlton, Sandy Nappo, Jeanne Shank, Pat Balonio, Rosie Backman, and Bob Moffitt,

He attended Burgard High where a lot of Baby Boomers learned to work on cars and many became top mechanics. Sam and I got on the subject of cars he had. He said that his first was a 1950 Mercury. His favorite was a 1956 Ford two door automatic with a Continental kit which is that awesome looking shelf and spare tire accessory at the back of many classic cars of the forties, fifties and sixties. It was first seen on Ford's Edsel Lincoln Continental in 1942.

Below is a 1956 Ford with a Continental Kit. .

One of my Memories

The South Buffalo "Beatle"

The guys on our strip got a preview of what was to become a fad all over South Buffalo and beyond. One of the neighborhood's young men, Dennis "Smokey" Wojciechowski went to see barber Tony Orsini for a regular haircut. His hair was long but always neatly combed. Tony thought he'd like to see what Smokey would look like with the mop head Beatle look. He commenced to cut and shape the hair, combing it down and blow-drying it in Beatle style. A side view of Smokey instantly reminded us of one of the Beatles. Before I give it away, for those who knew Smokey, guess which Beatle he resembled? John, Paul, George or Ringo? You'll need to read on to find out. Tony even bent Smokey's nose down a bit to get a striking side view resemblance. He left the barbershop after the cut and walked down South Park showing off his new hairdo. People took a look, made comments, laughed and made fun of it. It was only a joke at the time, but later, a lot the guys put away their Brylcreem and grew their hair long and added mustaches.

So.... which Beatle did Smokey resemble? It was Ringo. He never got the nickname "Ringo" though. To his friends, Smokey is still Smokey to this day.

Trivia: Ringo was the oldest of the Fab Four.

Richard "Ringo" Starkey, born July 7, 1940

John Winston Lennon, born October 9, 1940

James Paul McCartney, born June 18, 1942

George Harrison, born February 25, 1943

Chapter Four
Valley in Baby Boomer Days and Little Hollywood

Naming the Valley

A section of South Buffalo which is a neighbor to the Old First Ward and the Seneca Babcock area was first called the Valley in 1956 by a friend of former Sherriff Higgins. It stuck ever since. Because of the way it was situated, with five bridges being the only way in or out of the area, it made sense calling it that. The bridge at Smith and Seneca was removed during the years 1990 and 1991. The others are still very active with traffic.

Tour Guide

I connected with a man named Joe Lucenti who grew up in the Valley at 785 Perry Street. He graduated from Canisius High School in 1973. After college, he worked there for 19 years in several capacities; his last position there was assistant principal. He then went on to become principal of Akron High School in 1999.

We took a tour of the Valley for this project on January 18, 2015. As we made our way through, a thousand memories flooded Joe's head. I wrote things down as fast as I could. I could sense that although he no longer lived there, he's still a Valley son and very proud of it.

The Valley had a large number of Polish people as well as Irish. The greater number was the Polish folks who dominated Perry, Fulton and adjoining streets located between Elk and Seneca streets. The Valley is bordered by Seneca Street, Smith Street, the

Buffalo River and Van Rensselaer. At the Selkirk Street area side of the Valley, there are numerous sets of tracks behind the houses. Joe said:

> *"You could not get in or out of the Valley without going over a bridge that went over tracks. Hence, the 'Valley.' In its hay day, there were probably a dozen sets of railroad tracks on the south side of Selkirk Street with rail activity on every track."*

One could argue that Buffalo Creek and the lift bridge near Lee Street and South Park is the actual southern border of the Valley area since there were several factories and plants where a lot of the Valley men and women used to work. But technically, it is the rail lines that mark the southern border.

Three Valley Areas

The Valley covers an area of about one square mile with three distinct areas:

1. The western-most section left of South Park as you head north which ends at Buffalo River

2. The section from Smith Street to Elk Street and South Park where you find St. Clare's Church (Used to be St. Stephen's), PS. School #33, and beyond that, the old St. Stephen's Catholic School, built in 1893. It is three stories high and had about 20 classrooms in it.

3. Then, there's the area they call "Little Hollywood." It takes in Smith, Milton, Clifford, Selkirk, Sordyl and Andrew Alley. I asked Joe if he knew how the section they call Little Hollywood got its name. *"No one really knows for sure,"* he replied.

Little Hollywood

Curious, I continued to inquire how Little Hollywood got its name while on solo visits back to the area. I asked a younger man, Joe Dilivio, who lives on Minton Street right in Little Hollywood. He didn't know. I asked a postman who had delivered mail there for a long time. He wasn't really sure. *"I don't really know. It might have something to do with the bridges the Valley has."*

With that explanation, I didn't see the connection to Hollywood. I then asked Smith Street resident Rich Golden who has lived in the Valley for over 60 years. He didn't know either.

"That's a good question. I never thought much about it. I really don't know how it got the name. Now that you mention it, I'm kind of curious to find out."

It wasn't until I went to the Seneca/Babcock Community Center and spoke to some people that I got an answer that made some sense. I was talking to Lynn Salomon, Jack Wagner, and Pat (Green) Lovern. I asked them the same question about Little Hollywood. Pat and Lynn from the Community Center didn't know, but Jack said that there are several stories as to how it got the name, but he wasn't sure. He told me;

"It is believed that there were several silent film stars from the 20's that were Buffalo natives or were Buffalo-connected and ended up living there. That was the connection with Hollywood."

I couldn't be sure that it was *the* story so I did more research by following up on Jack's statement *"...there are several stories as to how it got the name."*

I called Peg Overdorf, Executive Director at the Valley Community Association Center on Leddy Street to see if she knew. I figured if anybody would know, it would be Peg. Here's the account of what she heard about the origin of the name.

"There are several stories about that area of the Valley. I'm not sure how true this is, but one of the stories I heard was

that Andrew Sordyl owned property near the present site of the Larkin complex, and they (Larkin people) bought the land and moved the people (28 houses) over to the other side of Exchange Street in the area of Smith, Milton, Clifford, Andrew Alley, Sordyl Alley and Selkirk streets. Sordyl placed the houses in such a way (on Andrew Alley and Sordyl Alley) that the backsides of the houses from both streets formed a courtyard, and the way the staircases were built reminded people of Hollywood movie sets. So, for that reason, the area became known as Little Hollywood."

During interviews at Tilly's Bar several weeks after I spoke to Peg, Cheri Dolan who is associated with Peg, agreed with her story via a cell phone interview. Cheri added;

"When people went over the Smith Street Bridge near the Little Hollywood area and looked down, the view of the buildings reminded them of the West Side Story movie set."

This story sounded pretty good to me but to check further, Peg gave me the phone number for Marge Starzynski so I could get another explanation about the area in question. She told me;

"Marge and many people in her family lived a long time in the Valley. She might know how Little Hollywood got its name."

I called Marge, asked her the question and without any hesitation, she said, *"I don't know."*

After a very short conversation, with a laugh in her voice, she said;

"Maybe it was because so many of us 'Starz-ynskis' lived there during that time."

And, there were indeed, a lot of Starzynskis who lived there at one time." Get it? Starz...ynski, as in movie stars - Hollywood.

So far none of the four people who gave me an answer were absolutely sure about the true story of Little Hollywood. I phoned Art Robinson, who is familiar with the Valley, and has lived in the Seneca/Babcock community some 60 years. He didn't know either. I told him, *"I won't rest until I get the answer."*

He laughed and said, *"When you find out, let me know. I'd love to know the answer to that question, myself."*

77

Ken Seifert, a former Seneca Babcock resident thought it could be because not far from that area, *"There were several movie theatres."* I could accept that somewhat but the area he spoke about was a bit removed from Little Hollywood to make a direct connection.

On January 30, 2016, I returned to the Old First Ward's museum,- Waterfront Memories & More to dig up more information on the Valley, specifically, Little Hollywood. I was given a binder on Little Hollywood with a lot of newspaper clippings about it but there was nothing in it that talked about the origin of the name of the area in question. There were several older gentlemen looking over material on the Old First Ward who were somewhat familiar with the Valley. I asked them about Little Hollywood, but none of them had the answer. I figured that I had come to a dead end. If the museum didn't have the answer, local residents of the area didn't know nor did all those other people I talked to, then that was that.

I took a few notes about the Valley that I could add to the book and packed up. I made my way to the Larkin Complex (Larkinville) on Seneca Street where they were holding a winter-type festival and happened to park next to the fire station at Seneca and Swan streets. I thought to myself,

> *"While I'm here, I'll slip into the fire station to see if there's an older fireman here who might know something about the Valley from the old days."*

Remember reading about Marge Starzynski a little bit ago? Well, by chance, the man in charge was Tony Starzynski. It took a while but then it hit me. I asked Tony:

"What's your mother's name?" He answered: *"Marge Starzynsky."*

What a fluke! I told him that I spoke to his mom the night before and recounted the conversation we had. He laughed. I got to the point and asked him if he knew how Little Hollywood got its name. He told me that he had asked his father a long time ago how that came about and here's what he said.

> *"My dad told me that way back when, in the area of Smith and Exchange streets, there used to be a bunch of younger guys in their late teens to early twenties that used to dress up real nice, wearing leather coats with the collars turned up, and slick hair. They had a kind of Hollywood look about them. So, people came to refer to them as the 'Hollywood Boys.' From the Hollywood Boys, the area became known as Little Hollywood."*

The last people I spoke to about this topic, for the sake of getting to the truth of the matter were officers Jim Shea and Dan Redmond. (Both South Buffalo sons) As soon as I asked the question: *"How did Little Hollywood in the Valley get that name?"* Dan jumped in right away.

"My dad told me about that years ago. It had to do with young people during the Depression raiding box cars that were stopped on the tracks near Selkirk Street on the southern edge of the Valley. The rail cars contained new dress clothes and suddenly, a lot of young people turned up wearing very nice looking outfits. They were so well dressed that the folks in that area called the classy looking guys, 'movie stars.' From that, the area came to be known as Little Hollywood."

Dan called his father on a cell phone to confirm the story. Dan's dad told the same tale about brand new clothes stolen from rail cars by youths in the Valley during the Depression.

Jim Shea added, *"It was also noted that several young blond ladies from that same area were seen all decked out in new clothes, probably clothes the guys got from the box cars. Their sharp good looks added to the whole movie star thing of Little Hollywood."*

There you have it folks, accounts of how the name may have come about.

- Bridges
- Retired silent Film Stars settling in the area
- Staircases of houses reminding people of Hollywood movie sets
- The Star...zynskis
- Several movie theatres in the area
- Well-dressed, leather coat sporting youths with slick-hair looking like *"Hollywood boys"*
- Depression era youths raiding rail cars for brand new clothes, being called, *"Movie Stars"*

Which one of the stories gets your vote?

Tony Starzynski

When I spoke to Tony Starzynski in the firehouse, he told me that he was a good athlete in his younger days and that he would be invited over the bridge from the Valley to the Seneca Babcock neighborhood to play sports against the guys over there. Normally, the Valley guys didn't mix it up with the Babcock area boys and vice versa. People stayed on their own turf. Tony was an exception. As a matter of fact, Danny Neaverth, once from the Seneca Babcock area himself, reinforced that unwritten turf law. Dan said:

> *"We didn't go over to the Valley and the Valley guys didn't come on our side of town. But, if they came to the "club, the Babcock Boys Club, there were no problems."*

Both Tony and Dan alluded to the fact that stepping onto each other's turf could be taking a chance. Interestingly enough, Tony told me that Mr. Neaverth had coached him for intramurals at the Boys Club when he was younger. Small world isn't it?

Valley Community Center

At South Park and Leddy streets, there is a facility known as the Father Carmichael Community Center. It is a day-care and senior center facility, headed by Executive Director, Peg Overdorf. The Valley has a public elementary school on Elk Street (PS #33) and next to it, Saint Clare RC Church (Used to be Saint Stephen's). The only businesses left in that neighborhood are a few bars and delicatessens. In the 40's 50's, 60's and 70's, the Valley was a lot more active with school, church activities, plants, factories and bars. For its small size, it once had a population of about 5,000 people; a mixture of people; Irish, Polish and Italians. Joe Lucenti is half Polish and half Italian.

Joe said he used to walk to St. Valentine Elementary School on South Park from his house on Perry Street. There, he served as an altar boy and in later years, played the organ for church services and events. The church itself was on the first floor and had around eight classrooms on the second floor. St. Valentine's was built in 1920 as a temporary church and school. Joe said:

> *"They were going to build a larger church and school, but, because of the Depression, there wasn't enough money to do it. So, a new church and school were never built."*

The original building is still there but not used as a Catholic Church and school anymore. Like so many parishes in Buffalo and outlying towns, the parishioners and school children had to find other churches and schools.

Common Living Arrangements and Telescopic Houses

Joe stated that when he lived at 785 Perry Street, out of six houses in a row, four of them were occupied by his own family, grandparents, aunts, uncles and cousins. He stated that his parents lived there 49½ years; from 1953 till 2003. None of his family or relatives live there now. He said:

> *"Even after leaving this area, a lot of people I know come back to visit. It's still their home. Even me. I like coming back here now and then. My heart is definitively - still here."*

He also mentioned how many dwellings throughout his area and the old sections of Buffalo have what he called, "telescopic houses."

"As families grew bigger and bigger, one thing they did was, build additions to the existing homes to accommodate extra kids or for someone who got married and wanted to stay in the neighborhood near mom and dad. Some additions were built to take care of aging parents or grandparents so they would be near family in their final days."

When you drive down the I-190, take a look at the older houses on either side as you pass through South Buffalo and Kaisertown, you'll see a great number of telescopic houses. For a lot of people, back in the day, the idea of putting ma or pa, grandma or grandpa in an old folks' home was not an option.

In the Valley for Baby Boomers: work was a short walk away

Joe remembered when he was young, most of the people in the Valley worked the local mills and plants. He said that his dad worked at General Mills in the Old First Ward for 38 years and that his brother John Lucenti is still there (2016) as well as his brother-in-law, Steve Spima. Other Valley people worked at Republic Steel, the Mobile Refinery on Elk Street and at National Aniline, Trico or other plants nearby. All were within walking distance.

Joe said, *"Back in the 40's, 50's, 60's, and 70's, a lot of people I knew who lived in the Valley and worked the local places of employment didn't have a car. A lot of the workers could and would walk to work. It was so common back then."*

He mentioned that there was a running joke about the Valley and its bars.

"People used to say that in the Valley, there was a bar on every corner. Not really, but there were a lot, that's for sure. Some of them were in the middle of residential blocks... not only on the corners."

Most of the nearby industries that hired many people from the Valley closed. When that started happening, many bars closed too. The clientele just wasn't there. In its hay day, the large work force supported the bars. Many of the local blue-collar workers were on one of three shifts in the grain mills, production plants and Republic Steel. Joe said:

"You have to realize that for many of the men working the 11PM to 7 AM shift, the bars would open at 8 AM and a lot of men ended up in there. That was their dinner time and a time to socialize."

He listed most of the bars that are or were in the Valley:

Tilly's Bar at Fulton and Smith, used to be Matikas and then Tuney's.

Other bars were:

Tippie's Bar owned by the Kasowski's

Boot-Nose Bar at Perry and Van Rensselaer

Kelly's Bar

Johnny Hoar's Bar at South Park and Harvey

The Roaring 20's bar was a stone's throw south of Kelly's. At Tilly's Bar I found several very friendly people who were more than happy to help me gather material for this book. Cheers to Dave and Bernedette Concheiro and Robin Sanly.

John's Tavern on Perry Street was open from 7AM to 3AM. The whole family ran it and took turns working to accommodate the plant shift workers. Those who worked from 3 PM to 11 PM could go out and stay at the bar till 3 AM to meet up with friends who worked that same shift.

Joe's family owned John's Tavern for 55 years. First, his grandparents owned it then his aunt and uncle on his mother's side. His grandparents, his mom, aunts and uncles lived above the bar. He literally grew up there.

He reflected back to his younger days:

"I remember listening to the jukebox, live music in the back room, and eventually bartending at the age of eighteen. My first experience playing in a Polka band (accordion) was in the back room when I was twelve years old. I remember my grandmother with tears in her eyes. She was so proud of me because she bought me the accordion. I still have it almost fifty years later. I dazzle my nieces and nephews when I play it."

Valley Youth Activities

Joe talked about life in the Valley and some of the things the boys did to pass time away. We went down Perry Street and stopped at the old Niagara Mohawk Plant. Across the street is the embankment to the I-190 which was built around 1957 when Joe was a baby. He pointed to the near ground level windows on the Niagara Mohawk building where they painted a batter's box on the brick part of the wall. It served as the strike zone. Using a four foot long, one inch round stick and a small, hard rubber ball, they'd have at it. There was no catcher. The pitcher would throw the ball within the strike zone and if the batter hit it to the edge of the grassy area of the Thruway slope, it counted as a base hit. If the ball was hit to the middle of the slope, it was a second base hit and if the ball made it to the top part of the slope, it was a homerun. Joe never did say if they beaned any cars on the I-190 as folks zoomed by. What do you think folks? Should nailing a car zooming by on the Thruway have been a grand slam?

Joe went on to tell me:

"Around the 4th of July, we would get fireworks and go over to the old Niagara Mohawk Sub Station on Perry Street. It was a huge brick shell with an incredible echo. Well, we'd drop a cherry bomb or an M-80 through an open window. It sounded like an atomic bomb. We were just boys being boys."

Joe and the neighborhood boys would play touch football in the streets or on several grassy areas. One such place was near the Swift Meat Processing plant on Perry Street, west of Van Rensselaer next to the I-190. He said:

"The slope of the Thruway had these huge boulders and one day during a play, one of the guys knocked me into one of them, face first. I got fourteen stitches on my upper lips."

Joe said that they also played street hockey and basketball in a little park they called Best Field, across from the Swift plant. Besides Best Field, there was also Collin's Park where young people played the usual good weather sports and in the winter, they had toboggan chutes.

People and Places in the Valley

Steve Cichon and his family have been part of Buffalo for eight generations, and is connected to the Valley, the Seneca Babcock neighborhood and Seneca Street (south). He is very well-known in the Buffalo area as a former radio newsman, historian, author, adjunct professor at Medaille College and producer at WNED-TV. He provided the following for this project.

"The Cichons were in the Valley on Fulton Street until 1966 when they moved to Fairview off Seneca (near Caz Park)... *And the Coyles were on Orlando Street* (Sen/Bab area) *until they moved at Hayden off Seneca in 1957* (St. Teresa Parish)."

"My grandpa, Jim Coyle, was one of the guys who ran the (Babcock) Boys Club while Danny Neaverth, Joey Reynolds, Bill Masters Danny McBride were going there.

On our tour around the Valley area, Joe pointed out where Allen Kaspersak, the Mayor of East Aurora used to live on Fulton Street and where former Buffalo Mayor Stan Makowski (1974-1977) lived on Roseville Street. We went to another street where the Smardz family lived. Joe said they raised chickens, pigeons, and had bee-hives.

Speaking of animals, this story was heard throughout Buffalo; so it's worth dropping it in here. Joe told me that his brother John woke him up one morning to tell him there was a cow in the street. (on Perry). He got up to take a looked for himself, and sure enough, there was a cow right in the middle of the street.

On May 16, 1980, an old 2,000 pound gal along with a host of other bovines escaped from the P. Brennan Meat Packing Plant at 1010 Clinton near Fillmore, not too far from the Valley. I remember that event and that I had worked at that plant in 1964. It was Togg's Meat Packing Company then. The great escape made for a very funny 6 o'clock news item with Irv Weinstein at WKBW-TV. Cops and locals all joined in to gather the scattered herd. They got 'em all back to the meat company.

Valley Businesses

Joe said besides the many bars there was Ricota's (Rix's) Deli on the corner of Elk and Smith streets and Frank's Barber Shop a little ways north and a deli at Fulton and Smith. At Elk and South Park, there used to be a Mobile gas station. On the corner of Smith Street and Elk was Dudois' Hardware and next to, it a Pittsburg Paint store and Ortiz's Deli at Milton and Smith. Tucked in the backside of Little Hollywood was Basil Skorupski's Deli on Clifford and Selkirk. He added:

"We even had a 'bookie' down on Elk Street," and no deli was more famous than Kurzanski's in the middle of Fulton Street run by Eddy and Sophie Kurzanski. It was from an era long gone when everyone knew each other."

We continued our tour down Smith Street toward Buffalo Creek at the westernmost part of the Valley where it ends. We turned down Saint Stephen Place and headed toward a bright yellow house at 16 St. Stephen Place and could see the Coyne Seed Plant over the house.

In the Seneca/Smith Street area, there was Minton's Café and Beer Garden owned by John Pierszynski and a billiard parlor owned by Joseph Jagodzynski. You may have noticed several Polish names. It backs up the fact that there were a lot of Polish folks living in the Valley.

Joe said that at one time going down Seneca towards Main, there was a barber shop with apartments above it, an Overall Laundry, Boradzyk's Tavern, a soda shop, a shoe maker and Gladkowski's Bowling Alleys. He added:

"For basic necessities, we didn't have to leave the neighborhood. We had pretty much everything for our daily needs."

Chapter Five
Seneca Street (Route 16)

Seneca Street (Route 16) is not as long as South Park's connection to Route 62, but goes a fair distance. It starts near Lower Terrace in downtown Buffalo, becomes Route #16 and goes south through Buffalo, Elma, East Aurora and continues to Olean, New York. I found that there are several Route Sixteens in the United States. One is in Georgia which crosses that state and ends up at the city of Savanah

Buffalo Streets Connected to Seneca Street

If I've missed any streets, my apologies. I believe most are there.

Lower Terrace	Winona	Knoerl
Delaware	Oakdale	Haden
Franklin	Troupe	Ryan
Pearl	Bradford	Geary
Main Street	Milton	Yale
Washington	Harrison	Weyand
Ellicott	Lester	Kemper
Oak	Hayes	Princeton
Elm	Keating	Norman
Michigan	Mergenhagen	Kingston
Butler	Bailey	Zittle
Elmira	Keppel	Peremont
Chicago	Archer	Cazenovia
Louisiana	Pomeroy	Buffum
Cedar	Avon	Seneca Parkside
Spring	Southside	Theresa
Hamburg	Leamington	Indian Church
Larkin	Avondale	Fairview
Van Rensselaer	Remington	Durstein
Hageman	Juanita	Cazenovia Parkway
Hydraulic	Unger	*Warren Spahn Way*
Griffin	Sage	Newman
Smith	Riverview	Edson
Peabody	Pomona	Mt. Vernon
Walter	Hammerschmidt	Greymont
Maurice	Armin	Maywood
Orlando	Paul	Manhasset
Wassor	Roanoke	Burch
Babcock	Stephenson	Wildwood
Gorham	Mineral Springs	Chamberlin
Imson	Melrose	City Line

Seneca Street (North)
Custom Canvas, Chuck Guido

Going north on Seneca Street, I came to a business that's been there for decades: Custom Canvas at 775 Seneca. I stopped in to speak to the owner, Anthony "Chuck" Guido, a friendly older man close to 80. As of 2016, the business had been in operation for 55 years. He told me, *"I opened on January 12, 1961."*

He flashed back with me about the old days when he lived in the Spring-Swan Street area. He brought up that the old neighborhoods were so different from today and that most neighborhood folks in the baby boomer days didn't lock their doors.

"I never had a key for my house as a kid. Most of our neighbors didn't lock their doors either. I remember once when it was raining pretty hard, my mom said to me,

'Go across the street to Tripi's house and shut all their windows so the rain don't get in.'

I didn't need a key. They always kept the doors unlocked. Neighbors took care of each other back then."
Sound familiar?

He also told me about the bars that used to operate back in the day. He said:

"Once, you could hit each bar going south, have one drink and by the time you hit 'em all, you'd be drunk. You'd start behind the firehouse at Swan and Seneca, go into Lee's Lounge, have one drink and continue south on Seneca to the next one, the Swan Lounge. Then cross the street to the Horse Head and afterward go to Big Joe Dudzik's place. Next, there was a bowling alley where you'd have another, and finally, you'd end up at Julia's Bar. By then, you felt really good!"

The Larkin Square Area and Hydraulic Street

Continuing toward downtown, I passed Larkin Square at 745 Seneca Street where buildings in the area go back to 1827. There is a street down there called Hydraulic Street between Exchange and Swan streets. I wondered why it was called that. I learned that around 1827, the Hydraulic Canal was built which provided hydraulic power for factories and mills located in the Larkin complex and Exchange Street area. By 1832, there were several mills and factories, all run by the hydraulic power from the canal.

Located there was a saw mill, a gristmill (mill for grinding grain into flour), a brewery, a hat, pail and shoe factory. In 1867 John Larkin built a factory called, "Plain and Fancy Soaps." By 1902 there were 87 businesses in that area of Seneca Street.

Seneca Street (North)

DiTondo's, a Great Family Restaurant

I credit Robin from Chef's Restaurant for guiding me over to DiTondo's family restaurant which has been in business at 370 Seneca Street since 1904. Robin told me that it was the second oldest restaurant in Western New York. But, present owner, Alan Rohloff corrected that by saying:

"It's the oldest continuing restaurant in Buffalo and has been operated by the same family for 113 years."

I'm not completely sure, but the Swannie House (originally called The Swanerski House) at 170 Michigan and Ohio Streets could hold the record for being the oldest bar/restaurant in Buffalo at 120 years old. It has changed hands a few times, though.

DiTondo's had no break in ownership. No one else in the city has this distinction. It was started by Sabastiano DiTondo in 1904 and run by himself with the help of his sons Amedeo, Armando, John and Joseph. Alan's wife Rose Mary DiTondo, is the granddaughter of the original owner.

She and husband Alan have a fairly simple menu that offers several very tasty Italian dishes at very reasonable prices: Spaghetti for $6.75 or Stuffed Eggplant Parmesan for $5.95. It's a great place to eat. The only drawback is that they are only open for lunch Monday through Friday 11 AM to 2 PM; no weekends. On Fridays after a three hour break, they re-open from 5 PM till 9 PM.

By the way, it's a cash only kitchen.

Chef's Restaurant

Chef's Restaurant at 291 Seneca at the corner of Chicago is renowned in Buffalo as one of the city's best restaurants. It's been frequented by folks from all walks of life from blue-collar workers to lawyers businessmen, entertainers, and a hoard of professional athletes. It was opened as a bar in 1910 by Gino Silverstrini and Lee Federconi, and in 1923 as a restaurant.

Lou Billittier started out under Silverstrini and Federconi as dishwasher. He worked as a busboy, a waiter, and later became the restaurant's manager. In 1950, he was half owner and by 1954 became full owner. Today, it is run by his daughter Mary Beth and son Louis John Billittier.

Pierce Arrow Museum

The Pierce Arrow Museum located at 263 Michigan and Seneca Street was founded by James Sandoro and his wife Mary Ann. It is an absolute must see day-trip destination for all antique and classic car lovers. They have some of the most outstanding cars of days gone by. As one ad says, *It traces Buffalo's transportation history.* To get more information go online. Also check out a great article written by Buffalo News writer Mark Sommer.

Chapter Six
Seneca/Babcock Area Baby Boomers and More. What was this neighborhood like from the late 40s to the 70s?

Little City

The Seneca Babcock area, about one square mile, is close in size to its neighbor, the Valley. It once was known as the "Little City within the City." Not anymore. The many changes have taken away the title. It got that name because it contained pretty much everything the people needed. *"It was self-sufficient,"* as Lynn Salomon said. So much is gone now, and it doesn't look like it's going to return to its former glory anytime soon. The same goes for so many other parts of the city.

The Seneca Babcock area was more family-oriented a few decades back. A lot of families not only had their own home on a given street, but many had grandparents, aunts, uncles and cousins living on that same street or only a couple of streets away. There was greater unity among families. There was also the stay-at-home mom factor that proved to be a great thing in raising the Baby Boomers. There were indeed lots of children in the neighborhoods back then. It was a different time family-wise and socially.

It was common for families to be much bigger than in today's culture. The McCabe family had 16 kids, the Sitarski's with at least 12, and the Green's with 12.

Connecting With the S/B Community

I made a phone call to the Seneca Babcock Community Center and spoke to Community Center volunteer Carrie Sitarski in order to connect with people from that neighborhood who have been part of it. I told her I wanted information about the area; names of people, stores, and activities that made the Seneca/Babcock area what it was. She connected me with volunteer Lynn Salomon and a couple of other people who could help with my project.

I set up a date with Lynn for a Wednesday afternoon January 2016. As soon as I walked in and introduced myself, she led me to Pat (Green) Lovern and Jack Wagner who began unloading a ton of information about their beloved community.

I began by asking, "What was this neighborhood like from the late 40s to the 70s?"

Lynn said:

"It was a great neighborhood. We knew everybody. If I wandered off four blocks from home as a kid, somebody would yell at me to get back home or they'd tell my mom. People looked out for each other, especially the kids. It once was a family oriented neighborhood.' It certainly isn't like it was. It's changed a whole lot."

We had everything anyone needed in this neighborhood. We didn't really have to go anywhere else for; food, clothing, barber and beauty shops, bakery, delicatessens, bars, entertainment, schools, churches, playgrounds or youth centers. We had it all."

I spoke of unity before. This also applied to the bars. Lynn and the others said that all the bars in the Seneca Babcock area used to get together and have a yearly vote to elect what they called the "Little Mayor" of the Seneca/Babcock area. I don't know why they used the word "little" but I surmised it was because of the small area that it represented; the Little City within a City thing. At any rate, this went on for a good while.

Community Center and Boys and Girls Club

This community had a ton of people who have either lived there for years or still live there and have great pride in their old neighborhood. They have a very strong connection to it and are involved in maintaining as much of the integrity of the neighborhood as possible. They are committed to keeping alive a community that has seen its best years go by. That's one of the reasons the Seneca Babcock Community Center and the Boys and Girls Club exist and are still going strong. They want to train the young people to "take over" and make it a better place, now, and for the future. There is a feeling of great loss among the older folks who lived there when it was vibrant. They wish it could be the way it was. For sure, they absolutely still feel great pride in being or having been, part of the Seneca Babcock neighborhood.

95

Leaders

Some individuals whose names I was given that are or have been involved and committed to keeping the community alive and well are:

Dr. Daniel Alexander, longtime supporter and benefactor

Bob Kurtz, Director of the Boys Club until the 80's

Dennis Phillips, Director of the Boys and Girls Club

Carrie Sitarski, Community Center's Director

Brian Pilarski, Director of the Community Center

Peg Bougucki, Senior Director

Jodi Briggs-Garcia works at the Boys Club

Dan Neaverth, volunteer for intramural sports

Jack Wagner, Volunteered in various capacities.

Kari Colon, Youth Director of After School Programs

Rita Carluccio, Food and Pantry and Child Clothing

Lynn Salomon, After School Activities Coordinator

Carol Sylvia, ceramics class

Jackie Green is the cook for the kids' program

Another player who had an important role in nurturing the youths of the neighborhood was Dr. Richard Quinn (Principal of PS #26 on Harrison and Milton streets (the school no longer exists.) A special thanks to all of the administrators and teachers at PS #26.

Pat Lovern and Jack Wagner wanted me to mention some of people who were part of School #26:

Rita Victoria, school cook

Betty Salomon and a lady named Joyce - cafeteria monitors

Helen Dibbles was a crossing guard for 60 years and a Brownie Leader.

Florence Mathers, crossing guard, whose house was a Buffalo Evening News newspaper drop point for the boys and girls with paper routes in the neighborhood.

Other community members and supporters of the area whose names came up as being part of the Seneca Babcock neighborhood are:

Greg Vaughn, Jim McCabe, John Keller, Nelson Hughes, Dave Kleinesmith, Larry Soloman, Victor Victori, Pat Green, Moe Cochran, Eddy Cudney, the Sytarski family.

Seneca/Babcock Businesses
"You don't know what you've got till it's gone."

The following will give you a look at what once was. Then, maybe you'll understand what was lost, and you'll gain a better appreciation of why the older folks are saddened with the condition of the neighborhood today. It's not the same with so much gone.

I asked my interviewees, *"What about businesses in the Seneca/ Babcock area in the 40's, 50's, 60's and 70's? What do you remember? What did you have here?"*

Lynn Salomon, with the help of Pat Lovern and Jack Wagner, and a couple of people they phoned while I was doing the interview, did the best they could to provide me with information about their old neighborhood, the way it was. Starting north of the Buffalo Creek area they went up to the point where you come to the bridge that leads to Smith Street. Here is the list of places, stores, shops, bars and other businesses that used to be. Very few remain from the old days.

Not all sites will be in order and forgive me for any that are missing. I only noted the ones given to me.

97

From Bailey

Hangert's Auto Parts, Len-Co Lumber, Buffalo China and Ebb Plumbing Supplies on Hayes Street, the Thruway Inn, Tobin's Bar, a barber shop, Slim Boots Deli, a trailer lot, a gas station on the corner of Troupe, a credit union at Inson, a Methodist Church, Ford's Deli, Quality Bakery with a doctor's office upstairs, Teen Haven and a pizzeria.

There were a few Pizzerias that Existed

Vic Victori's Pizzeria, Rita Maria's Pizzeria and, Moe Cochran's Pizzeria.

We Continue....

There was a dry cleaner's shop, a butcher shop, Chicks Hair Salon, Michael's Deli, the Boys Club, A & P Grocery, Cudney's Bar, Tobin's Bar at Harrison, Savris' Deli which later became a fast food place, Babcock Grill, Bradley's Bar & Bowling, Hank & Stell's Bar between Morris and Walters, Kentucky Cabin, Napoleon's and Cigars, a liquor store, Old Sod, Jean Machine (a pants store). Down Backcock Street going toward Elk Street, there was a bar that had a few other names: [1] Sally's [2] Sally's Split Decision [3] Sally's Daughter [4] Porkey's [5] Porky's II [6] Tigs and [7] Froggy's... WOW!!! AND then, there was Pristach's Bar on the street behind Froggy's Bar.

Still in the Seneca Babcock Area

Saint Monica's Elementary School on Orlando Street, Ernie & Vy's Bar, South Side Club, Trico #3 Plant, South Buffalo Junk Yard, Woop-P-Doo's Bar and the Babcock Grill which later became Betty Boop's at the corner of Babcock. Other businesses were: a restaurant supply company, Quinn's Liquor Store, Bradley's Bar and Bowling Lanes, the Oakdale Theatre at Seneca and Babcock, the Atlantic Lumber Yard, Casey's Junk Yard, the Mullen Playground which is attached to the now demolished P.S. #26 on Harrison Street.

Youth Activities

I asked Lynn Salomon, Pat Lovern and Jack Wagner about activities that used to be a part of life in their community. Lynn stated that, aside from school and church activities, the youth played organized and non-organized sports of all kinds. A lot of these activities revolved around the Seneca/Babcock Community Center and the Babcock Boys Club which was known as "The Club."

For outside recreation young people in the neighborhood did pretty much the same things as other youths everywhere else. A lot of the young males played baseball, football and basketball in the playgrounds or on some sand lot. Many outdoor games were played such as hide and seek, kick the can, chestnut wars, steam ball, relievio and so on. Jack said that in the summer, one of the dares was to hop garages and in the winter it was, hitching on the backs of cars, trucks or busses. He said that hitching cars was called "Pogoing" and hitching busses was called "Jarving." I never knew there were names attached to that activity.

It must be assumed that adults did their adult things: working to make a living and taking care of their families and homes, backyard B-B-Q's, birthday parties, bowling, mingling with neighbors and tipping a few pints at the many local gin mills. For many, there were Sunday dinners at grandma's house; an after church gathering that started around noontime and lasted into the late afternoon. It gave a chance for families to come together. This included aunts, uncles, cousins and some close friends. Thanksgiving, Christmas, Easter and the 4th of July were great times for big family get-togethers that kept families close.

By the way, the names of the meals used to be: breakfast, dinner, and supper. Somewhere along the line, dinner got replaced with lunch and dinner went to the supper slot. Kids were told by moms:

"Don't be late or you'll go to bed without your supper."

Hardly anyone uses supper any more to refer to the last meal of the day. If you speak to older folks, many will tell you,

"That's right. Supper was the last meal of the day. It was always around 5 PM."

Dan Neaverth Memories

I connected with former resident of the Seneca Babcock area, radio and TV personality, Dan Neaverth. We first met at WKBW Radio back in 1966 and 1967 when I worked there as a mail clerk. There was never a dull moment at the radio station when Dan took to the mike. As some of you may know, he got his feet wet in radio broadcasting at the Seneca Babcock Boys Club.

I asked if he'd tell me about his memories of the old neighborhood when he was young. Here's what he had to say.

"I attended St. Monica's grammar school on Orlando Street which was a few blocks from the Boys Club of Buffalo. I lived on Keppel Street. From the sixth grade on I would normally go directly to the Club. That's what we called it, 'the Club. After school we'd get into some spirited games of Dodge Ball; a sport so violent that today's anxious parents would have forbidden it. In the scaled down area used for basketball, boxing, and other less violent indoor activities, we would stand with our backs to the brick wall, which was padded only in the area directly behind the basket. A ball was placed on the floor at half court and Mr. Kelly, who seemed to be about 100 years old, would throw a second ball at the one on the floor. Then all hell broke loose as we would scramble for the loose balls. If you were hit by a thrown ball you were out, but, if while holding a ball, you could deflect the thrown ball, you were not out and you continued to play. After a while it usually came down to a few guys left.

The most feared dodge ball player was Louie Saviano. He was left handed and if he hit you in the head with the ball, your head would bounce off the brick wall. The object was to slap your hand back and stop the ball so you could go after him if you were fortunate and he missed you, If in your excitement you crossed the center line, Mr. Kelly would call you out. He always referred to me as Smiling Dan. The Club colors were blue and orange inside a Pennsylvania keystone.

During Easter breaks from school we had a tournament called the Blue and Orange. It was ideal for building relationships because you were teamed with guys you either didn't know very well, or didn't like at all. Now, you were on the same team. The event lasted almost a week and results of each day's events were posted and we anxiously checked them out. It was a competition of everything; basketball, dodge ball, shuffleboard, checkers. You played whatever you felt you were good at and could help the team you signed up for.

One of the highlights of being a team member was riding to other clubs in the Club car. It was a stretch Desoto that held about 12 kids. You felt so proud arriving at another club in that vehicle. On Friday nights we would watch movies and serials. I loved the "Fighting Marines." Each week, an impossible escape would arise and the following week they would escape.

Several guys decided we should start a radio station at the club. Danny McBride was the lead person and convinced Mr. Jenkins, club director, to let us broadcast from the third floor over the intercom to the other floors. We had a turntable and brought our own records to play. We even had a sponsor. Well, not quite a sponsor, but we did commercials for Vi and Emil's Casa di Pizza. We would occasionally get a free pizza. Later, Danny McBride convinced a local radio station to give us some newer records to play.

Also on our staff, were Joey Reynolds, Bill Masters and John Sezpanik. We all had fake names for our shows; I was Joe DeMarco, Joey Pinto was Joey Reynolds, Danny McBride was Mickey Bride and John Sezpanik, was Jack Kelly. Only Bill Masters used his real name. At the Club we MC'd dances and did play by play of football games while leaning

101

*out the window of the third floor that overlooked the playing
field. We all went on to careers in Broadcasting.*

*Years later when my sons were interested in sports I
decided to go back to the club and coach their football team.
I could have had them play in a suburban little league but
I realized that they had no contact with inner city kids.
There were no African American boys in our south town
neighborhoods. I wanted them to experience relationships
with kids who didn't have a lot of the things they might take
for granted. On our team we had kids from broken homes
and one whose dad was in prison. We also had a great mix
of city kids-Club kids. I still have memorable photos of our
team. They were a great bunch of kids who listened, tried
their best and enjoyed playing the game. We certainly weren't
the best team but I think, we all came away with something
special. I have my dad's original membership card from
when he was a kid. It wasn't the Boys Club of Buffalo then, it
was the Wasson House."*

Dan summed it up this way about his time at the Boys Club:

*"I think, if you talked to any of the members from the 50's
and 60's, they would all agree that some of the best times of
their lives were spent at The Club."*

I bumped into Danny at a gym in March of 2016 where he told me
a story about an accident he had a bit north of the Seneca-Babcock
area when he was about 12 years old.

*"I was riding my bike near the Larkin Building on the
right hand side when this man came too close and hit me
with the side of his car. I was lucky he didn't tear off my foot
as he hit me. The pedal got bent pretty bad. I was okay but
couldn't ride the bike with the pedal bent like that. He felt
so bad that he put the bike in his trunk and drove me all
the way up Seneca Street to Babe Boyce's shop at the corner
Indian Church Road. He got it fixed and paid for the repairs.
He put the bike back in his trunk and drove me back to my
neighborhood. I was amazed a stranger would do all that."*

That's the old fashioned way of taking care of small incidents.
Today, there might be a police summoned to the scene, the driver
of the car ticketed, a police report written up and perhaps, a lawyer
involved. Danny's story relates well to what Lynn Salomon said:

"People in our neighborhood took care of each other."

Some Boomers in the Seneca/Babcock Neighborhood

We talked about all the bars the Seneca Babcock area used to have, most of which are a memory, now. My three interviewees talked about a lady who owned one of those bars. She was more than over endowed. She had a fairly serious accident because of that physical trait. (Will call her "Jane Doe.") The way they told it to me,

She was feeding birds or something from a second floor porch and as she leaned over to throw the seeds to the birds, the weight of her large chesty proportion caused her to lose her balance and sent her over the railing to a nasty plunge to the ground."

She survived. They didn't know if she broke anything but said that they took her away in an ambulance wearing a neck brace. A fall from that height had to have caused some injury.

I got a few stories of individuals you might find amusing. Let's go with "Mr. Fix-it" or "Scrooge."

Lynn told me, *"There probably isn't a house in the Seneca Babcock neighborhood where he visited that he didn't fix something."*

Someone joked that he used a lot of duct tape.

She added, *"If he walked in your house and you said, 'this or that doesn't work.' He'd say, 'It's broke.' Then he'd fix whatever was broken."*

He went over to his sister's house one day and she complained that the washing machine didn't work. He took a quick look at it, smiled broadly and said:

"Did you ever think of plugging it in?"

Scrooge was a character. They told me that he once shaved only the right side of his mustache and only the left side of his beard just to get people's reactions. Every neighborhood has someone like him to make life interesting.

Then, there was the "pop bottle" lady who would go around the neighborhood picking up empty pop bottles. She cleaned up the neighborhood by getting rid of discarded bottles, and got plenty of exercise. It also put a few dollars in her pocket. God bless people like her.

A lady named Rita Harrington had a three wheel bike and would give little kids rides up and down the street.

According to my interviewees, there was another lady who they called the Cat Lady. Somebody said she had about a thousand cats. Another refuted that number and so they all settled on,

"Okay, an abundance of cats."

South Buffalo People
Connections to Other Areas

The Old First Ward, the Valley and Seneca Babcock families had connections with a lot of people who used to live there and moved. Many stayed right where their families originated though. With the migrations away from OFW, the Valley or the Seneca-Babcock areas, a lot of folks ended up in the areas of Seneca Street, Abbott Road, McKinley Parkway and South Park. But there's always that connection to the old neighborhoods. On my own street, there were at least a dozen families that had direct ties to the Old First Ward or the Valley.

Many families from Seneca Street had relatives who lived on, or off, Abbott, McKinley or South Park. Case in point: The Colern family from the South Park area have relatives in the Seneca Street area. Many Abbott, South Park and Seneca street families have relatives in the Valley or the Old First Ward. The South Buffalo Buckleys are direct relatives of the Old First Ward Guise family. There are numerous such cases.

South Park, Timon and Baker Victory are high schools where many students from all of the South Buffalo areas met and started friendships. This also includes students from Kaisertown and East Lovejoy. Joe Liberti from Tifft and Greg Vaughn from the Seneca-Babcock area (both South Park High students) have been close friends since high school.

Outside of school, students usually didn't venture into other sections of Buffalo unless they were invited there. Typically, a South Park guy would not go hang around Abbott, Seneca, Seneca/Babcock, Valley or Old First Ward areas unless he knew someone there. But keep in mind, because of family ties between all of the South Buffalo areas, relatives would end up visiting different neighborhoods for family gatherings and special occasions.

Areas where South Buffalo guys would not usually go to hang out were; the West Side, East Side, Kaisertown and East Lovejoy. It wasn't their turf. The Baby Boomers had all they needed right in their own neighborhoods and their lives pretty much revolved around it. I remember that going to downtown Buffalo gave me a feeling of being a bit out of place. It wasn't my turf. It wasn't home. It wasn't South Park Avenue. I am sure people from other neighborhoods like Abbott, McKinley or Seneca Street, had the same feelings. What we all enjoyed and felt comfortable with as Baby Boomers was our own neighborhood, neighbors, family, and lots of local friends. That's the way it was.

Chapter Seven
Seneca Street (South) The Other Downtown

Seneca Street was like another downtown to us. It had shoe stores, clothing and department stores, jewelry stores, pharmacies, churches and schools, butcher shops, a library, doctors, dentists, banks and who can forget the Seneca Theatre? Just about everyone in the South Buffalo area went there for the latest movies. It was a great old movie theatre. I believe the price of a ticket when I started going there was around 35 cents in the early 60's. You could do a movie with popcorn and a pop for a buck.

Caz Pool and Park

Before we get to the businesses, let's check out Cazenovia Park, Caz pool, people and activities. It is set between Seneca Street on the east side, Potter Road on the west side and on the north side, Cazenovia Street. Once upon a time, it was a great place. There was that little pool for the tykes, the huge pool for the bigger kids and the three level diving pool for the athletic types who would go and show off their ability to do dives like the jack-knife, the swan dive, back dive, front one and a half, a one and a half with a twist, and so on. One stunt was called the Hawaiian. A guy would jump off the highest board which was 10-12 feet high, grab one knee, lean back a little, and hit the water. There would be this huge plume of water that would shoot up maybe twenty or twenty five feet in the air. I tried it a couple of times and leaned back way too far, smacked my back on the water and came up cringing with pain. Needless to say, once was enough. I didn't care to try the Hawaiian again.

I certainly can't leave out everyone's favorite, the Cannon Ball. To get the best results and impress the most people, the highest board was where you'd launched from. It had two purposes. First, it was to create the biggest splash possible sending water in every direction and as far as possible, and second, to splash the guys and girls who laid out on the concrete near the pool to dry off. If you got the lifeguards wet, that might have been your ticket out for the day. Not that it wasn't refreshing, it's that the shock of a sudden rush of water hitting them was not the best feeling in the world.

The tale of Cazenovia Pool would not be complete if I didn't mention two unique individuals, Herb and Joey Keane. Herb was a slightly older gent who hung around inside and out of the pool. He did this thing where he would allow anyone to punch him in the stomach as hard as they could. I never saw a really burly type do it to him, but he'd let any young buck have a go at it. He'd stand there and say: "Okay, go." I never saw him buckle. Amazing! The second and most memorable person for sure was our beloved Mayor of Seneca Street, "Your Honor Joey Keane." His parents were Richard and Catherine Keane. Joey was one of 16 children. He had 7 sisters and 8 brothers. Joey's siblings are; Nancy, Richard, Mary Alice, Sally, Thomas, Michael, Cornelius, Catherine, Connie, Daniel, James, Margaret, Peter, Maureen and William.

Joey, who was a special needs individual, was a one of a kind; a lovable character who was befriended by everyone in Caz Park and all along Seneca Street. All the guys had his back in case any outsiders messed with him. His great personality and friendly manners earned him the righteous title, "Mayor of Seneca Street." As I was in the process of gathering material for this project, I was talking to Billy McEwen in April of 2007 at one of his singing gigs on Hertel Avenue. We were reminiscing about Cazenovia Park and Joey's name came up. Interestingly, about a week later, I saw in the newspaper that Joey passed away, April 13, 2007 at age 60. Later that day McEwen called me and said;

"Rog…., you won't believe who passed away…"

I said... *"Joey Keane. I know. I read it in this morning's paper."*

He said: *"Yeah... Can you believe that.....? We were talking about him last Sunday?"*

What Billy remembered about Joey was also what someone brought up during the eulogy at his funeral mass at Saint Teresa's Church. It was about a little game Joey would play with the ladies in the changing room at Caz Pool. He liked to run through there and freak out all the gals. He would either run in, then run right back out the door or run right through to the pool area and jump in. Billy asked him one day what he saw. Joey replied:

"I can't tell ya..."

Requiescat in pace, Joey. "Rest in Peace, Joey." You are missed.

Five Generations in the Hair Cutting Business

Tony Scaccia comes into play a little before the official Baby Boomer generation. Originally from Sicily, he was born July 16, 1938. I spoke to him the day before his 78th birthday. At his present location at 2083 Seneca Street, he had been cutting hair for 56 years, since 1961. His family has been in the barber shop business for five generations. His father Charles Scaccia passed the trade down to him and his brother Charles. He still cuts hair along with his daughter, Maria Scaccia Gawronski. Even his wife Yolanda became a barber, not a beautician.

Tony said: *"When I was sick for a while, my father told Yolanda that she should become a barber. And she did. She was one of the first women to obtain a New York State Barber's License. She trained under my father's tutelage as an apprentice."*

I asked Tony how he felt about being in South Buffalo. His reply,

"Coming from Sicily to South Buffalo and starting this business was the best thing that could have happened to me. Seneca Street was a prime location."

When I asked what era was most special to him. He said:

"The '50s." Seneca Street had so much in the way of stores and businesses. We had Sears, Penney's, Western Auto, four liquor stores, three jewelry stores, flower shops, a liquidation store, a Deco and Your Host restaurant and so much more. Fridays and Saturdays, the street was full of people. Besides the locals, we had people from Orchard Park, West Seneca and East Aurora who came to shop here."

Both Tony and Maria talked about their clientele. Maria said that even after some of their customers moved out of the Seneca Street area, they remained loyal. She told me:

"We have great clients. Many have moved away from here, but they still come to us for haircuts. It's about still belonging to this neighborhood. Even if they don't live here anymore, they won't totally disconnect themselves from the area."

Tony backed up the loyal customer phenomenon by stating that in his teens, Jimmy Keane, former Deputy County Executive, would come into his shop, sweep the floor and make coffee. He still does. Thanks Jimmy. (note: Jimmy passed away December 2016)

He had many friends in politics. He mentioned people like Jimmy Keane, Mickey Kearns, Brian Higgins, Stefan Iwan Mychajliw, Jimmy Griffin, and Mark Schroder. He said that several of the politicians who launched a run for office, did it from his barber shop.

Of Mychajliw, he said that when Stefan was a teen, he would walk all the way from the Seneca Babcock area for haircuts in his shop. Jimmy Griffin became a regular after his barber passed away, Tony became his permanent barber.

He said:

"Griffin was an early riser. He'd be the first one at my door, even before me!"

110

Maria jumped into the conversation and brought up the fact that a lot of the catholic school boys came to their shop for haircuts.

She said:

"There was a time, everyone was known by what parish they were from. A lot of boys came in and had to have their hair cut 'just right'. We would even get a sheet from some schools that gave us specific instructions as to how the haircuts should be."

Tony added: *"Our parochial schools lost so many kids between the 80s and 90s. In 1978 at Saint Teresa's school, there were 95 students who made their first communion. In 2016, only 5 students made it. Of course, today, Saint Teresa's School is closed. It's a shame."*

I asked Maria's thoughts about the neighborhood. She had this to say:

"Do I see changes in our neighborhood, of course? In view of the fact that so many places have closed, people ask us how we've made it here for 55 years. Well, that's easy. Our customers became our family and are very loyal to us. During all the years we've been open, our family has been privileged of being part of the lives of so many of our customers. Hey, I even took part in picking out a few engagement rings for some of my male customers' girlfriends. That's the kind of relationships we have with our clients.

Another interesting thing about our barber shop is that some family members (meaning clients) actually meet up here as a group, for haircuts. While one of them is getting a haircut, the others sit and catch up about what's been going on in their lives."

She continued: *"My dad knew everyone around here, and everyone knew him. That was good and sometimes, bad for me and my brothers if we did something we shouldn't have done. It meant that when we were out in the neighborhood, we needed to be on our best behavior. It was always expected of us growing up. You never wanted to disappoint your parents with a bad behavior report from one of the people in the community.*

A well-known fact is that barber shops are sometimes like confessionals. Many of our close and loyal clients share all

111

kinds of personal things about their family, their life or the neighborhood while sitting in our barber chairs.

Also, if we don't see a customer for a while, there's always a family member or friend who comes in and we can ask them about whoever hasn't been around. Then, the word usually gets out to those absentee clients via one of the regulars.

'Hey. Charley, they were asking about you at Tony's Barber Shop. You better stop in and say hi.'

You never lose that neighborly affection for South Buffalo and its people. When you want to know what's happening in the neighborhood, what happened to so and so, or who's running for office, you can always get an answer here at our shop. I think this is why our customers stay with us. We always ask about families, the neighborhood, or events in the lives of our people. Through the years customers have moved out into the suburbs, but always come back to reminisce about what used to be. A lot of happy and sad memories are shared.

Finally, Maria stated this about South Buffalo:

"What makes South Buffalo great is… our love and pride for the area, the memories we all hold onto and love to share. We were a strong community that helped each other. I am, and always will be, a South Buffalo kid."

Prior to interviewing Tony and Maria, I spoke to a customer named Kevin Nolan. I asked him how he felt about the area. He said:

"I wouldn't want to live anywhere else. I loved growing up here. When I was young, we were able to go home for lunch from school and had our moms there to prepare our meals. I remember going to Abbott Road to Jimmy the Greek's Texan Hots place for those great hot dogs. Also, I have old friends in the Old First Ward. We get together every Wednesday."

Former Seneca Street Resident Remembers

Baby boomer Gerald Regan, a retired teacher, spent his youth on Seneca Street and the Cazenovia Park area. He lived at 223 Seneca Street above his father's bar Regan's Bar & Grill and then moved to 2340 Seneca Street. At the elementary level he was taught by the Sisters of Mercy at St. John the Evangelist and then by the Franciscan Friars at Timon High School on McKinley Pkwy.

He said his front yard was Cazenovia Park. He remembers a chestnut grove in the park where he and his friends would gather chestnuts for chestnut wars and Caz Creek was where they'd fish and swim. Speaking of swimming, there was a water hole near the golf course. Gerry remembered that he and the other guys would dive for golf balls and sell them back to golfers for 25 cents each or 5 for a dollar.

Other activities that kept him and other Seneca Street boys busy were; climbing the Red Jacket Monument in Indian Park located between Indian Church Road and Buffum Street and hopping garages. Another dangerous pastime he and his buddies engaged in was to hop freight trains while they were going slow but then they would pick up speed and the boys had to wait till they slowed down again before getting off a few miles away. It was a long walk back home at times.

In the winter he and his friends would sled down Strickler's Hill behind School #70 on Buffum Street and skate on Caz Creek. They'd build fires by the banks of the creek, roast potatoes and warm their feet by the fire.

He remembers two neat parts of Cazenovia Park. One was "The Bowl." That's the part of the park where the baseball diamonds are. And the second, the swimming pools. He recalled that every warm summer day the place was packed with young people taking advantage of the facilities. He said: *"It's a shame that all of that is now gone."*

Besides sporting activities, families came from all over the area to have picnics and relax in Caz Park. Gerry and his crew would make rafts out all sorts of things that would float and sometimes they didn't float too far.

He said: *"There was always something going on in that park."*

He continued to reminisce:

*"There was an archery range near the Caz Golf Course.
We'd make and decorated our own bows and arrows. We also
built model airplanes from kits and equip them with motors.
It was great fun until they crashed or got caught up in some
tree. We also flew home made kites. I'd save the strings
from the linen supplies delivered to our tavern. I'd tie them
together until I had several yards of it to fly my kites."*

He remembered taking the Seneca Street bus number #14 heading
downtown to Shelton Square where he'd take the "Canadiana"
across Lake Erie to Crystal Beach, Canada. Once there, he'd ride
the Comet roller coaster and swim in the crystal clear waters of the
lake. His mom would pack a huge lunch for him which he hauled in
his Radio Flyer wagon.

He said that when he was at Timon High School, he and some of
the boys would hang out at Sullies on Abbott Road, drink cokes and
meet up with the Mount Mercy girls. He worked as an usher at the
Seneca Show which paid for his daily expenses.

For sure, he had to mention that the Friday night Timon dances
were a must and people from all over South Buffalo attended.
He remembers dancing to the music of Elvis Presley, the Everly
Brothers, Fats Domino, and Jerry Lee Lewis.

On weekends he'd grab a pizza at La Bella's on Abbott Road,
then go to listen to local bands at Michler's Bar while having a few
beers once he was old enough. Just a reminder,18 was the legal
drinking age in those days.

Bob Williams

Bob Williams was another Seneca Street area lad who lived
through the Baby Boomer years. He was from 64 Edson and like so
many of the guys and girls in South Buffalo, grew up a bit on the
poor side, not poor; it's just that it was time when there weren't any
frills or luxuries for most. That's the way life was for the majority
of the families all over South Buffalo. He said:

*"Most of the guys I knew and hung around with didn't have
much. No one had any spending money. Most families I knew lived
from paycheck to paycheck."*

He remembers one guy in his crew who didn't have a good shirt,
so he borrowed one of his sister's and hoped no one would notice
the buttons on the opposite side from those on a guy's shirt. He

also remembers that when some of the kids' shoes had holes at the bottom, they'd put a piece of cardboard on the inside to patch them up. He also said that he once saw a girl who wore plastic bags over her shoes one winter day because she had no boots. Times were very tough for a lot of the kids back then. How many of you had similar experiences?

Bob recalls when he was a kid and would go shopping with his mom, She'd put aside $1.25 so she could treat him at a soda bar after the shopping was done. They'd get a sandwich, a drink and dessert. The fact that his mom paid for all this with a budget of only $1.25 is pretty amazing. Today, you can't even get a cup of coffee for that price. By the way, a cup of coffee back then was a dime.

Activities experienced by many of the Seneca Street guys were about the same as those who lived in the surrounding areas of Abbott Road, McKinley or South Park. There were sports in the local playgrounds, Cazenovia pool in the summer, ice skating on Caz Creek in the winter, roller skating at Skateland on Orchard Park Road, bowling, and Timon dances. A lot of spare time was spent by Bob's crew hanging around in front of Joe's Delicatessen near the corner of Edson across Caz Park. According to Bob there was never a behavior problem hanging out there. He said that all the guys respected Joe and watched out for him. When elderly folks came down the sidewalks, they'd make way for them. They had a sense of respect and politeness. Today, I've seen older folks having to sidestep young people hording the sidewalk and having to walk in the street to get around them. That's just wrong.

Bob said that in the summer some young guys would raid gardens and fruit trees; not so much because they were hungry but just to have something to do. The plum, cherry and apple trees were the more desired targets. Well, at least they ate healthy. There were a few times when one garden owner came out and yelled, *"I've got a shotgun. You better get out of there or I'll shoot!"*

Nobody ever got shot but kids never knew if the man actually had a gun and would actually shoot?

Hopping garages was another fun thing to do, like the guys from other areas did. In his crew, one of the guys taking part in the garage hopping was a little on the heavy side. As Bob told it, their hefty friend broke through one of the garage roofs and landed on the car below. Now inside, in a little bit of pain and very panicky, he had to get out of there. The door was locked. He kicked the door open and fled the scene. That incident curtailed the garage hopping outings for a while.

Seneca Street Remembered

Bob remembers a lot about the neighborhood. In my conversation with him and his wife Jeannette (Sirolli) Williams, he recalled places starting from the "city line" where George's Hot Dog stand has been there since the mid 50s. He said that there were three hot dog places at one time, all near one another. Georges has been a family business since mid-fifties. It was also known as the "Slimeline" by the locals because it was at the city line. Texas style hot dogs were called slime dogs. The other hot dog places were a bit north

between Georges Texas Hots and Wildwood Street. Bob couldn't remember their names or exact locations. Speaking of Wildwood, he mentioned the bowling alleys that were there and Trautwein's Fish place near Daly's Bar at 2423 Seneca. He said that people used to form long lines outside of Trautwein's on Fridays to get a fish fry at a cost of around $1.25.

At the corner of Buffum and Seneca, Bob said there was Mohigan's Market and at Birch, a bowling alley that featured duck pin bowling. These were smaller pins knocked down with a smaller ball that didn't have finger holes. It was a bit larger than a softball but made of the same material as the regular bowling balls.

Across from Indian Church Road, there was Dr. Hanzley's office and directly across Indian Church Road was the original Full Gospel Taberbacle, now located in Orchard Park on Route #20 near Union Road. He also mentioned the Parkside Bar near where he lived and at Durstein Street, a bar called the "Zoo" by its patrons. He said:

"Two very different crowds made these their main hangouts. The Parkside Bar had people who just drank while at the bar we called the Zoo, there were those who drank and ingested 'recreational medications' and smoked other things than cigarettes."

There's a funny story about one of the guys who used to hang out at the Zoo.

"Joe" went in the Army for two years, did his stint and when he came out, he went back to reconnect with his old crowd at the Zoo, only to find out that some people didn't realize he was gone that long. He walked in, sat down, and one of the guys said to him:

"Hey Joe. Wow, man? I haven't seen you in here in quite a few days. We're you been, man?"

Anyway, he picked up from there and got back into whatever his old crew was doing.

He pointed out other businesses that are or used to be on Seneca Street. There still is Cannan's Funeral Home near Caz Park. There was a Twin Fair, Parkside Lounge at the corner of Edson Street and Berst Furniture on the corner of Indian Church Road. A bit further north was Kimaid and Matter men's clothing store where, even I came from South Park to shop for pants and shirts. A pair of good dress pants then cost between $10 and $18. They would take measurements and do alterations. It was a great store. I went to grade school with Mr. Kimaid's son Ronald who is a Timon grad.

A little further north was the well-known Seneca Theatre. It opened in 1930 with seating for 2,042. There was a wide staircase that led to the balcony where people could smoke. It closed in 1961 and reopened in 1965 with a reduced seating capacity of 1,330 seats. In its hay day they had double feature matinees with a cartoon or a newsreel between features. As a movie theatre, it was classy looking and a grand theatre that was certainly one of the best in Buffalo. The sad part is that in the mid-sixties, young people pretty much destroyed it. One source said that it came to a point where all the seats were either *"...sliced or torn by delinquents, both girls and guys."* What a shame to lose such a gem.

Williams remembered that the theatre became a night club called Club Helene and then was renamed Psychus. He said that top music groups performed there such as; The Buckinghams from England (Kind of a Drag), the Zombies, (She's Not There), Bob Seger (Rambling Man) and Country Joe and The Fish (Rock and Soul Music). Both clubs featured a ton of Buffalo's top bands.

Bob recalled bowling alleys upstairs from the theatre. One was known as Miller's Bowling Alleys, and another as, the Marx's Bowling Alley. He said that he and seven other guys would sometimes chip in $1 each and bowl for the pot. Hey, at 50 cents a draft, eight dollars in those days could provide a drinking guy beer for a few days. It depended on how much he drank, of course. There was a bigger bowling alley at Wildwood and another named Southside Lanes near Buffalo Creek. Eventually, the bowling lanes above the theatre were demolished and it became the Sky Room and then the Roof Top Bar. The theatre was demolished in 1970.

A Kind of Credit System

Another one of Bob's memories from his youth was moms and dads could go to the local butcher shop, markets, delicatessens and pharmacy and put their purchases on a tab. That's right, no papers needed to be signed. A person's word that the bill would be paid in a timely manner was enough. That was real community living. The store owners kept a book with names and amounts and when customers got paid at the end of the week the bill would be taken care of. Ulrich's Butcher Shop located between Edson and Durstein was one such place. The days of setting up tabs in any store are long gone.

Staying in the Seneca Theatre vicinity, there was Fishman's Five and Dime Store, complete with a lunch counter and soda bar. A couple of doors down, there was a clothing store, a shoe store, Your Host Restaurant, an auto parts store, doctors' offices, lawyers' offices, flower shops, delicatessens and several other businesses.

I can't forget to mention Saint Teresa's Church at the corner of Seneca and Hayden Street and one of Buffalo's 50 Deco restaurants located right near Buffalo Creek.

Some other businesses that have been there many years and are still there today are the Corner Florist at Yale, Bank of America and an M & T Bank near the corner of Cazenovia Street (names have changed). Further north, there is McCarthy's Funeral Home between Knoerl and Melrose, Artone's Pizza Subs & Wings place (once owned by Tony Augustine), and then Lomis, Offers and Lomis Memorial Chapel. Across Buffalo Creek on Seneca Street still stands the very well-known Len-Co Lumber.

Bob's Crew

Bob named some of the guys that made up his crew of red-blooded American South Buffalo lads.

Himself, from Edson Street, Bucky Kerns, Dan Smith, Bobby Fitzgibbons, Tommy "The King" Riley, Pat "Shiner" Shine, Pete "Pops" Geary, Dan Patschuk, Phil and Larry Williams, Pauly, Bobby, Billy and Ricky Bugman, Jeff and Jim Taylor, Chucky Held, and Tuffy O'Neil. It was rumored that Bucky Kerns was related to pitcher, the great Warren Spahn for which Cazenovia Parkway was renamed "Warren Spahn Way."

Bob and his crew played touch football against other teams in the South Buffalo area. According to him, the games turned into tackle football resulting in abrasions, lacerations and contusions along with a few broken bones and rattled brains. Speaking of rattled brains, a couple of those guys might have had the capacity of becoming nuclear physicists if their brains hadn't been so rattled. Only kidding folks.

Bob said:

"For the 8 or 10 years we played, we had 150 wins, 2 ties and 1 loss. Our best player, Pete 'Pops' Geary, was a bit older than the rest of us. He was our coach for these grueling, body damaging matches. It was fun. We had a great time."

I asked Bob and his wife when they got their driver's license. He told me that it wasn't until he got out of the Army in the mid-sixties. He didn't have to take a driver's test on Williams Street near the East Lovejoy area like everybody else because he had an Army driver's license that he could simply present to the folks at the auto bureau and obtain his New York State license. Jeannette didn't get her license until she was 18 years old and did have to make the trip to East Lovejoy to take the driver's test.

Noteworthy Cars and their Owners

Bob's first car was a 1967, 8 cylinder automatic Coronet 440 Magnum. Some other cars that were well-known on the Seneca Street strip were Phil Williams' Road Runner and Pauly Bugman's Mach I.

In the sixties and seventies, Baby Boomers who were fortunate enough to own a car got to go to drive-in theatres. Back then, the local drive-in theatres were the Park on Orchard Park Road, the Star on Lake Avenue in Blasdell, and the Sky Way on Saint Francis Drive in Hamburg. Bob talked about some of the car owners stuffing a few guys in the trunk to sneak them in. Cars back then had huge trunks. I think, back in the 60s, the ticket price was about 50 cents a head if you were an adult. Saving 50 cents back then could buy two gallons of gas, two packs of cigarettes or a quart of beer. Now can you see why those nice young lads snuck in the drive-in theatres? They had a better uses for the fifty cents they saved - cigarettes and beer.

Bob said that he knew a guy who took his fifteen year old girlfriend to a drive-in one night and the following ensued: (To protect the innocent, we'll call her, Suzy).

"After settling in, the guy lit up a joint with all the windows closed and smoked away. His girlfriend Suzy didn't smoke and became overwhelmed with the effects of the smoke. After a few minutes of exposure to the second-hand smoke, that was enough to give her a buzz. It put her out. Suzy fell asleep."

Some Seneca Street Bars

I heard tell that Daly's Bar is the oldest bar on Seneca Street. According to Tom Kelly, the building had been in the Daly family since the late 1800s and was opened as a Veteran's post by Bill Daly around 1923 during the time of Prohibition. He got a license to operate it as a soda bar. A customer I spoke to said that during Prohibition time, it also served as a Speak Easy and had a couple of bowling lanes in the back. In 1956, a second William (Bill) Daly, a South Park High grad, bought it from Uncle Bill Daly and ran it as a neighborhood gin mill and worked it to the age of 91.

Tom Kelley owns Daly's now as well as Kelly Expressions Photography which is a stone's throw from the inn. When you walk in to Daly's Bar, you sense that you are in a place that still has old time charm. It's been a popular watering hole for over 60 years for local retirees, politicians, firefighters, cops and area hard-working men and women who meet there to socialize. It's a great community tavern.

There once was a bar called O'Neil's at 2454 Seneca, which became the Shanahan House in 1959. Still going strong is the Blackthorn Restaurant and Pub at 2134 Seneca and Hopper's Rush Inn at 2104 Seneca. Beyond that, the next major bar was the Pomeroy House on the corner of Pomeroy Street close to Buffalo Creek. That bar eventually became the Bridge Inn. It caught fire and was never rebuilt. Only an empty lot remains.

Jerry Shea and Lou Dingledey

I stopped in the Blackthorn in the 2000 block of Seneca Street owned since about 1976 by Pat Lalley and Larry Adymy. I spoke to bartender, Jerry Shea and a patron named Lou Dingledey. Jerry was originally from Peabody Street. He said that the bar had a long history and that it changed names and owners a few times. From the Early Times Tavern in the fifties to present day Blackthorn it has had the following owners; Tom Gang, Tim Leary, Dan Nostrandt Kevin Gould, Pat Lalley and Larry Adymy. The Blackthorn Restaurant & Pub has had a colorful history.

Jerry flashed back a bit and mentioned some of the bars that are gone. He came up with the Golden Nugget near the city line, Parkside Grill across from Caz Park, the Southside Grill near Riverview and Seneca, the Shupper House that changed to Ireland's Own, the Thruway Inn at Harrison Street, Eddy & Wally's at Keppel Street, Charley O'Brian's at Elk and Seneca... which became Tobini's and then Luther's. There was also a Babcock Grill at the corner of Babcock and Seneca, at Morris Street, there was Old Sod. At Walter Street, there was Cigars, then Hank and Stelle's and yet another known as the Kentucky Tavern.

As you can see, there was never a lack of watering holes on the Seneca Street strip or anywhere else in all of South Buffalo. The structures for the bars were in many cases, modified homes that were turned into restaurant-bar establishments. Way back then, many housed the owners and their families who lived upstairs.

Going to work was real easy; a little trip down the stairs and into the bar they went. Most had family members who worked there bartending, or doing the cooking (if they served food). The job of cleaning up before opening time was done by one or two family members, wives, sons or daughters. Such was the case with Joe Lucenti's clan who owned a bar for years on Perry Street in the Valley.

Art McLaughlin Remembers

I got to sit down with Art McLaughlin, another Seneca Street area resident of days gone by, and gathered more information about how things were. Art lived at 136 Parkview and still remembered his old telephone number – 828-5131. He went to McKinley High School and knew a guy (I knew from South Park) by the name of Vinny Catanzaro. Vinny was from the Marilla Street area of South Park. Art used to take bus #15 downtown and get a transfer to get to McKinley High at 1500 Elmwood Ave in Buffalo.

He remembered a lot of what life was like growing up in that part of South Buffalo as a kid. Like Bob Williams, he remembers the many activities the young men used to do like playing football and baseball at Caz Park in the bowl, dances at Fazio's Hall on South Park and Timon High on McKinley, hopping garages, drinking at what they called "70 Fields" (behind PS #70), tobogganing down Strickler Hill and ice skating on the Caz Creek.

He brought up how Caz Creek used to rise high enough to flood surrounding areas with chunks of ice going as far as Potter Road and breaking through basement windows. They eventually did some flood control work in that area to prevent that from happening.

He recalls Lawn Fêtes at St. John the Evangelist Church at Seneca and Parkside. He said that since gambling was illegal, they worked in some other phrasing so the games of chance could take place. Wink. Wink.

One activity in particular that was somewhat dangerous was hitching on the back of cars in the winter. Art told me he did that too. It was fun until he got caught by his dad. He said that he was hooked onto a car one winter day... not knowing the car that was following behind him was driven by his dad. Oops! He didn't say if he got a lickin' for that or not. I wonder if his dad had done the same when he was a kid. He did say that Seneca Street was not a good place to hitch onto cars. It was usually cleared of snow and taking a tumble onto asphalt was not appealing to any of the guys.

He thought that swimming at the Caz pool in the summertime was one of the great pastimes. The older guys would go to the diving pool and show off what they could do. Art and his buddy Ernie Colern were normal teenagers who liked doing exciting and interesting things. One of them was, getting on the highest board at the diving pool, Art would get on Ernie's shoulders and they'd do whatever dive or trick they could come up with. Only one thing wrong with this, they got to do it only once. The lifeguard's duty was to tell them, *"Don't do that again."* or *"Get out."* The guys would always think:

"What's the big deal with doing a double man jump off the high board? What could possibly go wrong?"

Art's Crew

Here are some of the guys Art hung around with as well as some he only knew casually.

Ernie Colern, Bob and Ricky Chapman; Ricky became the mayor of some town in the Midwest. Mike Ciglia, Jimmy Stephens, Terry Collins, John, Paul and Fred Rich, John Denecke, Don and Ron Felchow, Jack Sherry, Al Gang, Billy "Weed," Gand and his brother Tom Gang (Blackthorn Tavern related) Jack Eustace, Ray Swartz, Mike Davis, Gary Canal and Dave Melisio. (I was in the same division at Fort Riley Kansas in 1966 with Jack Eustace (9th Infantry Division).

Terry Collins and Dennis Sears from Art's crew also served our country.

Small World

In my conversation with Art we discovered we both knew Greg Vaughn the photographer (Seneca-Babcock area son.) He did the photos for Art's wedding. I told him that I knew Greg years ago at South Park High.

I talked to Art about cars he and some of the guys he hung around had back then. His first car was a 2 door, 1962 Plymouth automatic 6 cylinder. He worked for the South Buffalo Railroad and made $2.30 an hour. With that he was able to make car payments of $28.88 a month. Some of his next cars were a 1966, four-speed, two door V8, Chevelle that he took on a trip to Florida for his honeymoon with Bev Williams May 25, 1968. After that, he had a '69 Chevy Sports Coupe and a '71 Olds Cutlass.

Bob Chapman, who Art hung with had a 1959 Chevy Impala convertible. It was a great looking car with huge fins. John Rich had a souped up 1952 Ford and Denny Sears had a 4 cylinder Triumph convertible and a '69 Olds 442 automatic.

We talked about some of the stores from back then. The stores won't be in order along Seneca Street and most have been mentioned but there are a few new ones.

A central point was the Seneca Theatre at Seneca and Cazenovia. Next came Dunn's Pharmacy, Fishman's 5 and 10 store, Penney's Store, Kimaid and Matter's Men's clothing store, Etore Photographer and Inglegerg's Jewelry. There was a Woolworth 5 and 10 store to the left of the theatre, Erie County and Buffalo Savings banks, Papa's Restaurant, a flower shop, Western Auto, Your Host Restaurant, Melrose Bar, a pizzeria next to Blackthorn's Tavern and a hobby shop. Berst Furniture at Indian Church Road used to be a Hens and Kelly's Department Store. Then, there was Babe Boyce's Auto and Bike Shop on the other corner, Coolie's Deli next to Parkside, the Southside Grill, Precinct 9 at Southside and the Julieta Ice House at Avondale and Seneca streets. Everyone remembers George's Texas Hots at city line. Art said:

> *"What a lot of people don't know is that George also had a hot dog stand near the Peace Bridge in Front Park. It once was another Ted's Hot Dogs. He bought it and served hot dogs for a while till it caught fire. He never re-opened the business."*

At this writing, Art is semi-retired and enjoys family and friends along with golfing and his 1946 Chevy Fleetline Aero Sedan that he rebuilt pretty much from scrap.

Ralph Batchelor Remembers

Ralph lived on Wildwood Avenue, right off Seneca. He remembers the soda fountain place on Seneca between Wildwood and the city bus loop. He stated:

> *"That was a fun place to hang out. There was the Greek hot dog stand right there at the bus loop. I used to go in there*

a lot, especially after partying; to munch up a bunch of those delicious Greek hot dogs with their secret sauce."

I asked him about memories he had of Caz Park.

"Cazanovia Park is where I played a lot of sports and enjoyed the pools in the summer. Besides the pools and the great ball diamonds, there were several gang fights from time to time; some small and some very big ones. They ranged anywhere from a few guys on to hundred or so. Most of the time the cops heard about it and arrested a bunch of us. There were a few times when some of the guys ended up in jail for a few days. I remember one guy who stood out from the rest of us. His name was Joe. We called him "Little Joe" because he was a bit on the short side, but boy was he tough. He originally came from Hungary and I remember him telling me that he and his father had to fight off invaders every once in a while."

One of the guys was more or less the leader of the South Park / Seneca Street gang. He hung around or associated with 40 to 60 guys. We'd get together on occasions hanging on street corners, swimming or playing baseball at the park, big parties or gang fights. The main group had about 10 guys who generally hung around together. The gang fights happened on rare occasions, not very often at all. Usually, each group pretty much stayed in their own territory. After a while, the confrontations faded and people got along okay, for the most part."

He mentioned that some of the boys from Seneca Street were the hoods (hard guys) with black leather jackets and motorcycle boots and used to fight with the Squeaks from Abbott Road. Abbott was closely linked to Seneca Street with some side streets connecting one to the other. Cazenovia Park and Cazenovia Creek separated those areas.

Ralph eventually moved away from street activities and taught himself to play the guitar. Within a year or so, he put a band together with friends who hung out together at a foster home he lived in. He taught some of the guys how to play. The drummer was a natural. They played at school talent shows, some dives and parties, but when they turned 18, they started playing in some of the best places around the Buffalo area like the Silhouette Club and Mel's on Broadway. Of the Seneca area, he said:

"Seneca Street will always be special to me. Lots of great times and many good memories."

Mr. Edward Miller

In closing the segment on the Seneca Street area, I want to share Mr. Edward Miller's memories of his younger days as a resident of South Buffalo and a teacher and swim coach at South Park High School. I was elated that I could reach someone who was up in age that would be a neat addition to the project. Thanks to his daughter Iva who put me in touch with her dad, I was able to gather interesting information about his past, the high school strike and his career as a teacher and swim coach.

Mr. Miller's life covered a lot of ground. He was born in 1927 and has lived in Lackawanna, the Old First Ward and on the following streets in Buffalo: Eden, Tifft, Mesmer, Columbus, Durstein, McKinley and Edson. He ultimately settled on Tindle Street on the edge of South Buffalo in West Seneca where he and his family have lived for many years. In his youth he attended PS #34 elementary in the Old First Ward at 108 Hamburg Street. That school was demolished around 1976. He then went on to Hutchison Technical High School on Elmwood. After high school, he obtained his teaching credentials from Canisius College.

For those of you who went to South Park High where he began teaching in 1958, you probably ran into Mr. Miller somewhere along the way. He was a Social Studies teacher and swim coach. Some of his best memories come from his time as swim coach in the sixties and seventies. He replaced Bill Sweeney and coached for twenty-three years until 1981. He said this about South Park High School: *"Once, South Park High was the elite school of Buffalo."*

His daughter Iva, named for her mom, remembers her father would often drive half the swim team home after practices and swim meets. Then, for a celebration after swimming season was over, he'd have the entire team over to his house for (you won't believe this) L.S.D. As his daughter Iva said this, I wasn't sure I heard correctly and quickly asked "L.S.D?" Relax folks. It's not what you're thinking. She proceeded to explain the acronym she used. It meant, **L**uscious **S**paghetti **D**inner. Mrs. Miller would whip up a huge pot of spaghetti with sauce, meatballs, bread and salad. Everyone would have a great time eating and talking about the season and reliving some of the great and not so great meets they had during their competitions. One of the swimmers was Abbott Road area's own, Kevin Caffery.

Iva also told me that the swim team felt close enough to her father that they took the liberty of throwing him in the pool. Mr. Miller had been wearing white pants and guess what appeared through those white pants? Valentine boxer shorts with hearts! She related another story about the boys on the team calling all night every ten minutes, and hanging up.

I don't know if he ever got back at the team for doing that or not. If it had been me, they all would have had to swim many extra laps in the pool. *"Keep me up all night? I'll show them."* But, I'm not Mr. Miller. He was a nice man.

Things Mr. Miller Remembers about South Buffalo

- Horse shoe pits at the Timon High School site before the school was built and the Seneca Show where he was an usher.

- He spoke about going to Mohigan's Market on Seneca Street where he loved to get their custard filled eclairs.

- Tommy Wright's Tavern on the corner of Zittle where he'd go and tip a few glasses.

- The building of the Caz Creek flood-control banks.

- As a teacher at South Park High- cookouts at in Taylor Park.

- The teacher's strike at South Park High in the early 70s.

- Teachers who crossed the picket line having their car tires flattened.

- Dock in pay for being on strike.

- Fined for being on strike with the money taken out of his paychecks. One paycheck he received was for a meager $5.00.

I asked Ed and his wife, who he met at the Seneca Show while he was an usher: *"What do you remember from the old days that you wished was still around?"*

Mrs. Miller responded right away:

"Quality Bakery in the Seneca/Babcock area and Sullivan's Ice Cream Parlor on Abbott Road where, in my time as a young girl, you could get a large hot fudge sundae for 10 cents. Also, Mum's Bowling Alleys above the Seneca Show." (That was before others took over and changed the name.)

Mr. Miller agreed. They often frequented those places.

Like most of my interviewees, I asked both Mr. and Mrs. Miller what they felt about having lived in South Buffalo area in the 40s, 50s, 60s and 70s.

Mrs. Miller: *"I wouldn't want to have lived anywhere else. So sad Seneca Street isn't what it was."*

Mr. Miller: *"It was great living here. I have many fond memories of this area."*

Chapter Eight
List of streets connected to Abbott Road

According to a local street map and an Atlas Road Map, Abbott Road doesn't have a route number tied to it. It starts at South Park and Bailey Avenue, goes to Bayview Road in Armor NY, does a quick left then a right turn where becomes South Abbott Road and ends at (old 219) Boston State Road, New York. Here are the local streets that are connected to it up to the Lackawanna City line.

Heussy
Alamo
Kimmel
Dash
Midland
Southside
Mumford
Robbins
Lakewood
Stephenson
Clio
Melrose
Hubbel
Ruthland
Kennefick
Milford
Como
Portland
Eaglewood

Tamarack
Strathmore
Athols
Columbus
(Timon H.S.)
Edgewood
Salem
Alsace
Meriden
Lorraine
Cazenovia
Red Jacket
Magnolia
Oakhurst
Peconic
Wheatfield
Coolidge
Woodside
Ramona

Minnetonka
Narragansett
Hollywood
Shenandoah
Dundee
Kimberly
Cushing
Eden
Densmore
Whitehall
Carlyle
Downing
Turner
Dorrance

Abbott Road The Triangle Area

Irish Center

Doc Sullivan's

Not many folks know that Abbott used to be known as Abbott's Corner Plank Road and South Park was White's Corner Plank Road. This junction of South Park and Abbott Road is also referred to as the Triangle. A bit to the south of that where Southside, McKinley and Abbott Road meet, there is a park known as Heacock Park.

Abbott Road isn't as long as South Park or Seneca Street, but it too, has a lot of great South Buffalo history. As in all other South Buffalo communities, Catholic parishes played a central role in educating so many of its young people and offered many other functions that brought its parishioners together. The churches along with their elementary schools on Abbott were:

- Saint Agatha's near the Triangle

- Saint Thomas of Aquinas between Athol and Tamarack Streets

- Saint Martin of Tours between Downing and Dorrance

- Saint Martin of Tours School later became Notre Dame Academy on July of 2006.

The Leahy family remembered the priests who served at Saint Thomas in the 60s and 70s: Fathers O'Loughlin, McNichols, Masser, Beichler and Swich.

The nuns they remember at Saint Tommy's were:

Sisters Marie-Bernard, John-Elizabeth, Dionisha, William-Marie and Mary Austin

Abbott Road has its own unique place in the hearts its people. Not only for those from that area, but also for others who spent time there and have various connections; it may be friendships, relatives, businesses, night clubs that had great bands or restaurants that were special to them. One restaurant that comes to mind right away is Smitty's (now, Doc Sullivan's) located not far from Mercy Hospital. They had some of the best chicken wings in the area when chicken wings first became the rage. The YMCA became the Irish Center. Michler's Tavern was also close by. I remember going to Michler's many times, mostly to hear bands that provided cover tunes of the latest pop groups. Abbott Road was as business packed as South Park or Seneca Street. One of its biggest residents is Mercy Hospital.

Larry Murtha and Chestnut Wars

A former resident, Larry Murtha, along with his seven brothers lived in the area of the Triangle and hung out in Heacock Park. He spoke of an event he and his compadres used to do every chestnut season. He and his friends took part in the yearly ritual of chestnut battles. Many, if not most of you (yous guys) know how that went. You'd gather chestnuts (the bigger the better), drill a hole in the middle, slip a string through the hole (usually old shoe laces), tie a knot at the bottom of the string and go to war. Larry shared how his crowd decided who would go first.

"After a quick two-out-of-three rock, paper scissors preface, the winner would select whether or not to attack or to defer.

The object was taking turns, back and forth, hitting the opponent's chestnut and breaking it apart. One guy would strike, and if he failed to break it, it was the other guy's turn. Larry, being one of the combatants, tells how one of those battles unfolded between him and a challenger named Toby. Here's his story of that battle.

"We took turns, back and forth, back and forth, until the outer shells were decimated and nothing remained but the cream-colored fruit exposed to enfilading fire. I let go a fierce and final fling and sent Toby's chestnut sailing over the crowd in a spray of splintered slivers."

After such battles, Larry described how the boys kept track of their wins.

"Like the notches in a gunfighter's handle the contestants would garrulously display with bellicose bravado, the long chain of victories represented by chestnuts necklaced onto a different shoelace; usually tied to his waist belt."

I believe this game was played all over the Buffalo area. Heck, when I lived in Welland, Ontario in the 50's, my friends and I did the very same thing. I usually didn't do too well. There were always guys who had given their chestnuts some special treatment to make the shells and inside pulp harder. They would easily destroy the average virgin chestnut and there was always some guy who would show up with a monster chestnut. Right way you knew you were doomed. It was fun, simple good fun.

The Leahy Family Remembers Abbott Road, the Way It Was

Eileen Leahy Stack, an early 70's Mount Mercy Academy girl, grew up in the Abbott Road area. It was her family of Baby Boomers' main stomping ground. She sat down one day with her clan; brothers Pat, Bill and Dan, sister Susan and her parents, Tom and Peg; and came up with all sorts memories of people, events, activities, and places of business from the Triangle to the Lackawanna City line. Everyone there had a blast reminiscing. They came up with a ton of names of people they knew; way too many to list, but here are several:

The Byrnes family on Red-Jacket, the Asteks and Comerfords from Strathmore, the Carrs from Whitfield, the Cronins from Edgewood, the Dickman's from Alsace, the Fitzgerald from Ruthland,

133

the Freedenburgs from Oakhurst, the Klines from Cumberland, the Leahys from Abbott, the Myers from Eaglewood, the Quivilands from Tamarack, the Quinns from Como, the Reddingtons from Abbott/Magnolia, the Sullivans from Ruthland/Egdewood/Belvedere, the Sutto's from Tuscarora, and the Waltons from Lorraine.

The Leahys' talked about growing up in the area of Abbott, Whitfield and Red Jacket. The kids had a church parking lot to play in that belonged to the Salem Lutheran Church. They named it Stone Lot Stadium because it wasn't paved; it was gravel. The local kids played baseball, relievio or hung out to pass time. There were two empty lots on Whitfield where some would gather. They were named First Field and Second Field. Some of the kids made forts in those fields.

Eileen remembers a beloved pine tree that graced McLellan Circle at Red Jacket, Choate and McKinley Parkway. It was decorated every Christmas until somebody cut it down.

She stated: *"It looked so beautiful when it was decorated. We were very upset when it was cut down! We really missed it."*

Area folks were upset for a long time with whoever did it. This was their neighborhood and someone came and messed with it. It is still a mystery to this day as to who done it.

Eileen mentioned other activities that kept them busy. Such games as; You're it, Pies, Mother may I, Tag and PIG. Basketball was played in every playground and even at St. Tommy's during the summer. They would open the gym for basketball from 6 PM to 9 PM under the direction of Mike Breen, Vic LaDiscio and Mike Dickman. There were also various grammar schools from South Buffalo that would compete in track races on Saturdays at Cazenovia Park under the supervision of Mr. Head.

The Leahys came up with as many stores as they could remember that operated on Abbott Road including; the L.B. Smith Plaza at 1234 Abbott Road. I found it interesting that the address number was: one, two, tree, four (1234) Abbott Road. It's unique. Hard to forget.

They sat around and began reminiscing about the numerous businesses that existed in the 50s, 60's and 70's. For those of you weren't around in those days, the list will at least give you a glimpse of what was there.

The stores will all be on Abbott Road and will not necessarily follow in order down the street. Sorry for any of the stores missed or any misspellings.

Bete's Tire Service, Howland's Esso Service, Mister Doughnut at Abbott and McKinley, Quinn-Amigone Funeral Home, Heat Moffett Heating Service, The South Buffalo Branch YMCA which became the Irish Center at Lakewood, a laundromat, Micheler's Bar, M & T Bank at Melrose and Stevenson, Liquor store at Como, Jimmy's Meat Market, Park Edge Candy at Hubbell, Shanley's Dry Cleaner at Salem, Fred Walter Jewelers, Haft's Fresh Cut Meats, Downer & Till Automotive, Bob Rigby's Sport Store at Edgewood

Trophy Shop between Alsace and Edgewood, Pete Snajack's Sporting Goods between Meridan and Salem, Parson & Judd Pharmacy (est. 1923), Lawanda's Linoleum, Kulp's Hardware at Eden, Frank's Shoe Repair at Portland, Kennedy Mortuary, Hoff's Paint and Wallpaper, Kelly Photography and Bridal Shop at Potter Rd.

Cecile's Dress Shop at Robbins St., LeTeste Red Goose Shoes at Ruthland, McKay's Work Clothes at Ramona, Runner's Roost, Brooke's Drug Store at Portland, Thompson's Bridal Shop at Potter, Coniglio's Drugs Store, Hortman's Music at Woodside, Trend Furniture at Woodside, Lamps Pharmacy at Densmore, Rexall at Stevenson.

Karn's Flower Shop at Mumford, Joseph's Flowers at Shenandoah, Louie's Cleaners (run by Louis Pacifico), Henry's Hamburgers (Maybe the last Henry's in Buffalo which became Dino's Bocce Club and then Imperial Pizza), across the street was Bachelor's II bar, Dairy Queen at Downing before coming to Dorrance Avenue, Prudential Insurance Office.

South of Dorrance Avenue, somewhat considered part of South Buffalo, one would find Robert Hall Men's Store across the L.B. Smith Plaza (1234 Abbott), Lucky Strikes Bowling Alleys, Crean's Restaurant, the Abbott (Town) Theatre, O'Daniel's Bar-Restaurant, a Texas Red Hots (Used to be the Knotty Pine Restaurant in the mid-fifties with operators Nick and John. In 1989 it became Abbott Texas Hots.) Lastly, Laurel and Hardy's Nightclub near Ridge Road.

Old First Ward born Tim Fitzgerald and wife, Ann Kenefick Fitzgerald came up with a few that were missed by the Leahys.

Coffey's Deli, Harry's Deli, Ko-Ed Candies, Doc Sullivan's, Campanili's Barber Shop, Roots Collision, and Pinarpo's Market. (Spelling could be off, sorry.)

The L.B. Smith Plaza

Before the Seneca Mall existed, a lot of people from South Buffalo came to the L.B. Smith Plaza on Abbott Road near Ridge Road to take advantage of a variety of stores not found in their neighborhoods. As you see the list below, you'll understand why.

When the Leahy family came to what was called the L.B. Smith Plaza at 1234 Abbott, in their reminiscing, they pretty much got all the names of the stores that made up that plaza in the 50s, 60s, and 70s and a few into the 80s.

AM & A's, Brand Names, L.B's Men Shop, Bell's Quality Market, Century then Naum's Catalogue Wholesale, Columbia Market, Hen's & Kelly's (gave Green Stamps), Kresges, Marine Midland, Liberty Shoes, Scott Del Children's Clothes, Zawaki Jewelers, Zilliox Optical.

Again, Tim and Ann Fitzgerald came up with a few more in the Plaza: Loblaw's Market, Page's Restaurant and the ACME Market.

According to sources who worked in the trade, the following car dealers that were at Abbott and Dorrance: L.B. Smith Ford in the 50s, next, Sherwood Sheehan Ford which later became Anderson Ford, then Atkins, and one of the last - Basil in 2000, which lasted 5 years.

Past and Present Bars on Abbott Road

Griffin's Irish Pub at 81 Abbott, Conlon's Bar & Grill, Molly McGuire's, Michler's, Smitty's Bar, (once owned by Dennis Dargavel and Jim Morrissey), Doc Sullivan's (once owned by George Hermann), the Ounce and a Half at Abbott and Hollywood (once owned by John Curran and Charlie Smith and then, Jim Pongo and Terry Brown), Bachelor's II near Carlyle Street.

More Memories - Abbott Career People

I've included three men from the Abbott Road area I had the pleasure of interviewing. They spoke to me about their times in the old neighborhood and their ongoing love and ties of where they came from. They spoke warmly about friends, schools, activities and the neighborhood itself. All three spoke of their accomplishments. I wanted to feature Kevin Caffery, Tom Best and Dennis Dargavel as examples of what some of the Abbott Road lads ended up doing.

Kevin Caffery, "The Legend"

Photo courtesy of Kevin Caffery

Captain Kevin Caffery's family was originally from the Valley before moving to Pries Street. His father worked for Nickel City Railroad. Kevin went to Holy Family and then to Saint Thomas Elementary School on Abbott when the family moved to Milford Street.

In his teens, he hung out at the South Buffalo YMCA (now the Irish Center). He was a member of the swim team there for many years under coach, Bob Mullens. He praised Mr. Mullens for being a "nice guy and great coach." In good weather, he spent a lot of time at Caz Park playing baseball. His grandmother Margaret worked at the Caz's shelter building during active seasons.

Throughout his high school years at South Park High, Kevin was on the swim team with Mr. Ed Miller as the team coach. His skills as a swimmer earned him the honor of making All High.

137

After high school, he joined the Erie County Sheriff's Department in 1969. After twenty-three years of regular duties, he headed the Erie County Sheriff's Department's Aviation Unit as their prime helicopter pilot. Twenty-two of his forty-five years of service were spent in the air. He retired in 2014.

He, along with Flight Officer Art Litzinger, was often seen on newscasts as part of the helicopter crew that took part in risky rescues of Lake Erie boaters who capsized, or ice fishermen who found themselves stranded after the ice had cracked and separated. When I spoke to him in June of 2016, he told me:

"I took part of literally hundreds of such rescues during my career, of men stranded on ice flows. I remember that in one day my crew and I retrieved over 20 stranded fishermen. One of the guys we rescued wanted to be pulled up with all his fishing gear. We told him no!

We brought him up and put him in the co-pilot's seat. As we flew away from the rescue site, I noticed out of the corner of my eye that a fish was flopping on the floor of the helicopter near the guy's right foot. Can you believe it? This guy had slipped a string of fish down his snowmobile suit."

"Well that was it! My partner and I had enough of this character and at about 1,000 feet, we dropped him out of the helicopter. We kept the fish, of course!"

Only kidding folks! Kevin and his crewman didn't do that. They saved this very imprudent angler's life and let him keep his fish. What a nice rescue team.

Kevin said that in his helicopter, there were usually two men; himself and one other crewman for the easier emergency calls. At other times, there could be as many as three or four crewmen aboard to take care of more complicated airlift needs and rescues.

One of the duties called for Kevin and his crew to do flyby sweeps over rural areas where possible marijuana growers were known to try their hand at farming. He and his partner would scout out fields for any signs of marijuana plants and report back to area law officials. Local law enforcement and State Troopers would in turn move in, make arrests and destroy the plants.

He's was also called on to fly over areas where there were reports of people shining laser lights at air aircrafts. One such case led to three men from Kaisertown being arrested.

He and his crewmen even joined Canadian authorities from time to time by flying across the lake to join them chasing down criminals.

On occasions, Kevin and his crew in the helicopter used infrared cameras to track suspects. He would coordinate operations from the air as officers on the ground pursued bad guys who were on foot. *"The infrared equipment was a tremendous tool,"* he said.

Another incident he was involved in was when he chased two guys in a stolen SUV. He stated:

"I took part in a number of car chases, but this was the longest one I was ever involved in. We were running out of fuel and had to turn back. It was very disappointing that we couldn't continue the pursuit."

He also shared the heartbreak of having to pull out of rescue missions. There were times he had to abort situations that were deemed too dangerous to the victims and/or the helicopter crew. Other means had to be used to finish certain rescues he and his crew were forced to abandon.

He told me that he nearly abandoned a rescue once when a man contemplating suicide had waded into the Niagara River near the falls. He said:

"It was a very scary situation. This was one of those rescues where I was afraid I might have to pull back and not attempt an air rescue. I was hovering over a man who had waded into the river. My crew was getting ready to snag him out of the water, and I could see that the blades of my helicopter were creating a situation that made him very unsteady on his feet. My heart was pounding. I thought the turbulence would surely knock him over and the river would carry him over the falls. I could literally see him mouth to me 'Help me!!!' This guy didn't really want to die. Thank God we were able to get him out of there. I came very close to pulling away from that one.

That rescue and many more, were often lead news stories featured on TV, not only in the Buffalo/Erie County area but also on TV stations in neighboring states and Canada. Having made a name for himself as an "Ace" helicopter pilot who constantly risked his life to save others, Kevin and Deputy Chet Krupszyk were guests on the Oprah Winfrey Show in 1999 to talk about their rescue of nine year Anthony Trigilio who fell into freezing water while his seven year old friend Rich Burst held on to his hand.

Sheriff Timothy Howard, head of the Erie County Sheriff's Department said of Caffery:

"He's a legend. Kevin is a very humble man, but he's got to be one of Erie County's greatest heroes. He's an asset to the whole region, not only Erie County. His reputation is nationwide. I've gone to many police events all over the country, and had other Sheriffs walk up to me and ask about our helicopter pilot." (Source: Dan Herbeck, Buffalo News)

If you spoke to Kevin, he would have hundreds of stories to tell you; some funny and some very sad. I asked Captain Caffery to give me his thoughts about the South Buffalo he remembers from the 60s and 70s.

"It was a great life. I established long friendships. It was a time and place of close knit families and safe neighborhoods to grow up in. Our local police and firemen were wonderful models. I knew I wanted to be a cop at the age of five. And, I can't forget the guys I could count on in those days; the Operating Engineers, iron workers, and scoopers. If you ever needed anything as a young kid, you only had to ask those guys."

Photo: Courtesy of Kevin Caffery

Kevin's father, Frank, served as a New York State Assemblyman. He has two brothers, Mike and Fran.

Captain Caffery, thank you for the many, many lives you and your crew helped save, and for the many critically injured you got to the hospital on time. You will indeed be remembered as a hero and as your boss called you, a "legend."

Tom Best

Tom and his six siblings first came from the Abbott/Choate area and then moved to 18 Densmore Avenue in Saint Martin Parish. When I spoke to him about his days in South Buffalo and what he felt about the area, he said:

"If I could, I'd go back and live in the Abbott Road area in a heartbeat. I loved the camaraderie we had."

I asked if he could provide names of some of his neighborhood comrades of the past, he gave me the following names:

Joe Denecke, Buffalo police officer, John Pavlovic, John Hamilton, Ray Jerge, Mark McNichol, Paul Fabian, Jim Quinn and Bobby Russell (Timon guys) also, Michael Caffery (lawyer and brother of Kevin Caffery, Erie Co. Sherriff helicopter pilot)

I asked him for names of some of the girls who hung with them during his teen years on Abbott. His statement rang true for most of the Baby Boomer guys who hung out at their favorite gathering spots.

"Oh, there were no girls in our group. It wasn't like today where girls and guys all hang out together and guys treat the girls as their equals. It's wrong. It was pretty much taboo for any girl in my day as a teenager to hang around with us guys. If she did, she was looked upon in a negative way. It wasn't the proper thing to do. The girls had their own places to hang out, it wasn't on the streets in front of some store or pizzeria. That's the way it was. As the guys got older and had girlfriends, they'd date them but never brought them to hang with the guys."

Tom was in law enforcement for 34 years. He spent his first two years from 1967 to 1969 with the Blasdell Police Department then the rest of his career, with the Town of Hamburg Police Department from 1969 until his retirement in 2001. During his stint with Hamburg, he started off as patrolman, went on to become a detective and then, Detective Chief. After his retirement, he entered politics and was elected Hamburg Councilman from 2007-2008. In 2009, he ran for and won the post for Superintendent of the Hamburg Highway Department.

Dennis Dargavel

Dennis lived on McKinley and attended Holy Family until he moved to Edgewood and subsequently, to Turner Street where he attended St. Martin's. After grade school, like a ton of South Buffalonians, he attended South Park High. I asked Dennis who were some of his close friends and where they hung out back in the 60s. One of the main hang outs was Papa's Pizzeria near Mercy Hospital on Abbott Road. As for a close circle of friends, he mentioned:

Jack Reville, Mike and Paul Grys, Mike Griffin and Buddy Harbicheck.

After graduating high school, Dennis went to the Buffalo Police Academy. He made it all the way through training and was ready to be sworn in as patrolman when a more appealing opportunity presented itself in Real Estate. He's been in that field since 1971. His longstanding success in realty has earned him the prestigious recognition of Realtor Emeritus. That means he's been a member of the National Association of Realtors for 40 years or more.

Jim and Diane Mahoney and Memories of the Abbott Road Area

Jim, like so many people who lived in South Buffalo has very fond memories of the area. As I spoke on the phone with him and his wife Diane, they both expressed great disappointment about the way the whole area has changed, all the stores that have closed, the lack of real community feel that existed, and the fast-changing demographics. Jim and Diane said:

"It's really sad to see how much of what we had, is now gone. It was great growing up there."

Jim remembers some of the guys he hung out with. Here's list he gave me. (Forgive any misspellings):

"Biff" Fabe, John Schreier, Bill Fisher, Dan McNaughton, Dan Honan, Jim "Moose" Kelly, Steve Nelson, Mike Grogan, Jim Stillwell, Gary Matteson, Mike Walton, Paul Culligan, Jim and Dave Comerford, Vince Lonergan, Pat Stanton, Pete Carr, Fred Ode, Tom Gang, Pat Hurley, Paul Fitzpatrick, Rick Mozdzier, Billy Botten, Jack Smith, Fred Pannozzo, Steve Munson.

I'm sure he could have come up with a ton of other names of people he knew, but these were the guys who made up his main group.

He mentioned that he went to Saint Martin's for grade school, Timon High, then on to Lemoyne College in Syracuse.

As he got older, a couple of his main watering holes were Ounce and a Half and Early Times. Also, he remembers the Irish Center where so many events took place that related to Irish heritage and culture. Like all of the others mentioned so far in this project, he remembers the activities he and his friends took part in at Caz Park, baseball, the pools and ice skating. He was very fond of the Tosh Collins Recreation Center at 626 Abbott Road where he played basketball with many of the guys in the area. At first, the center only had a gymnasium and some exercise equipment. Later on, they added the enclosed ice rink where Black Hawks star Patrick Kane of South Buffalo honed his skills.

Chapter Nine

McKinley Parkway

Here are the streets tied to McKinley Parkway- starting at Bailey Ave and moving south. It ends at South Park where it comes to the Buffalo Botanical Gardens near the Lackawanna border.

Kimmell

Midland

Almont

Lakewood

Mesmer/Cleo

Hubbell

Kenefick

Como

Eaglewood

Olcott

Strathmore

Columbus

Tifft/Edgewood

Richfield/Alsace

Loraine

Bloomfield

Belvedere

Choate (McClellan Circle)

Red Jacket (McClellan Circle)

Whitfield

Sheffield/Coolidge

Woodside

Mariemont/Ramona

Harding

Culver

Ridgewood

Okell

Arbour Lane

Eden

Cantwell

Downing

Latona Court

Aldrich

Dorrance (McKinley Circle)

McKinley Parkway

McKinley Parkway has always been an awesome street to me. I call it the Queen Street of South Buffalo. It has remained relatively unchanged. Ninety-nine percent of it is residential with some of the grandest houses in Buffalo. The only non-family dwellings on the Parkway are podiatrist, Dr. Barry Fitzgerald at 843 McKinley, the South Park Presbyterian Church at 519 McKinley, Timon-Saint Jude High School at 601 McKinley, the Salem Evangelical Lutheran Church at 10 McClellan Circle, and yet another at 231 McKinley called Our Lady of the Rosary RC Church at Kimberly where they have a 10 AM mass on Sundays in Latin.

One of the greatest houses on the Parkway is a white three story house at 60 McClellan Circle. I call it the White House of South Buffalo. It is majestic and has these great, tall pillars at the front. It's been my favorite South Buffalo house since I was a kid. While I was taking pictures of it for the book, a man in his early forties who was walking his dog said to me: *"I've lived here since I was little and have always loved this house. It's fantastic."*

Ed and Lori Cudney

I wanted to speak to the present owners, Ed and Lori Cudney in May of 2016 but got no answer when I knocked. I went across Choate to Jack Heitzhaus' house at 54 McClellan. He wasn't home either but his daughter Mary Heitzhaus-Lombardo was there visiting her dad. Unfortunately, he had stepped out to go to the store. When I asked Mary about the white house, she pointed to a young mom with her daughter sitting in a chair across from her.

"You can ask her. That's the owners' daughter, Alexa."

Alexa Cudney Zippier wasn't able to give me details about the history of the house and said that I would need to speak to her parents. I came back the following week and spotted Mr. Heitzhaus sitting on his porch and figured I'd talk to him before going to the white house. He didn't have a lot of facts about it and directed me to Margaret Nash Richards' house around the corner on Choate. He told me:

"She's related to the people who used to live in that house. She would know a lot about it."

I went there and found Margaret and Lori Mortellaro Cudney sitting on the front steps. Between Lori and Margaret, I was able to find out that the deed dates back to 1913 for a Jeanette Baron. It then went to Thomas and Anna Crotty until, at least 1921. In 1921, it wound up in the hands of Doctor James and Mary Nash. (Margaret Nash Richard's grandfather) from 1921 until the 1940s. The next owners were Elizabeth (Nash) and husband John Gormley. It has remained in the Nash family until, 2005. From 2005 to the present, Ed and Lori Cudney have been the proud owners. I thought the house might be a historical landmark but found out from Lori Cudney that it wasn't. She stated:

"I wish it had that distinction, but it doesn't. However, McKinley Parkway is part of the Olmstead Park Conservancy, and that Park/Parkway system is on the National Register of Historic Places."

She added: *"The Conservancy has Design Guidelines for the Parkway but they won't interfere with the home owners' properties with regards to remodeling or upgrades."*

Lori continued:

"They (Conservancy people) stated that there is no need for approval from them to make changes, but that our front porch was under their guidelines, meaning that if my husband and I want to make any changes that are visible from McKinley, they have to be approved by the Conservancy."

In short, Ed and Lori are to a certain degree, under the Conservancy ruling with regards to changes to their fantastic home. I asked Lori what she and her and husband Ed felt about living in South Buffalo. She said:

"There is no other place we would rather live than right here in South Buffalo. It's a wonderful place; close to theatres, green space, and our awesome waterfront. We even like the winters."

Talking to Cudney's Neighbor

Looking to get more information about McKinley Parkway, I went back to see neighbor Jack Heitzhaus. He's actually pre-Baby Boomer, but close enough. He was very interested in talking about the area. We laughed at the confusion of the intersecting streets that make up McClellan Circle. Mostly everyone figures that all of the houses have McKinley addresses, but that's not the case.

The houses that face McClellan Circle have addresses that are not McKinley Parkway addresses. The white house is 60 McClellan Circle, not 60 McKinley Parkway. Jack's house is 54 McClellan Circle, not 54 McKinley Parkway. Interestingly, the house to his left has a McKinley Parkway address. Weird huh? I found out that McClellan Circle was once known as Woodside Circle. Jack Heitzhaus, his wife Patricia and their eight kids originally came from Pries Street and have lived on McClellan Circle for the past 29 years. When I asked him what he felt about living in South Buffalo, he said:

"It's the most wonderful place you can live in. The people here are magnificent. I wish that it would stay the great place that it is...but, things are changing. Right now, it's still good but I worry about our children and what they may have to put up with in the future."

Sitting on the porch with Jack felt very comfortable, we were looking out toward McClellan Circle. It was quiet and peaceful. As I left, I could see that he looked relaxed and totally enjoyed sitting on his porch taking in the comfortable 75 degree day and watching people and traffic go by.

Our Lady of the Rosary Chapel

I spoke to a lady named Angela who lives near Our Lady of the Rosary Chapel, 231 McKinley Parkway which was established in 1993. She told me:

"It used to be a Methodist Church. They've been doing masses in Latin on Sundays for several years now. A priest comes in from Rochester or Syracuse to say mass. They do things the old traditional way. For example, some ladies cover their head with veils. The mass usually lasts about forty-five minutes."
I asked what the attendance was like. She replied: *"It's usually packed most Sundays."*

This church has traditional Latin masses on Sundays at 10 AM. It is headed by Father Adam Purdy. I was told by parishioner, Maryjean Kraengle that Father Purdy comes in from Syracuse for the services. One half hour prior to the mass, those who congregate say the rosary and there is also confession during that period of time. There are two altar boys for the mass dressed in their cassocks and surplices (altar boys' robe and top garment) with their hands folded. The priest faces away from the people as in the old days.

Maryjean was very gracious in providing me with information about the church. I asked her about head covering for the women and girls. She said,

"Head covering is required to attend mass. Some women wear hats but most girls and ladies wear chapel veils.

She pointed to two signs with the rules of the church affixed to the doors as you enter the sanctuary. One states the dress code:

"Men and women need to dress modestly. All women need to cover their head as is the code for Apostolic Custom and Church Law. No slacks, shorts, sleeveless dresses and low cut dresses are allowed that do not meet the norm of Christian modesty. Dress that is too casual is inappropriate. Proper dress is done to honor the Lord.

I noticed all the women and young ladies were appropriately dressed with hats or chapel veils.

The second sign explains the rules for taking communion:

"Fasting is recommended three hours before communion, but one hour is presently binding under the church law of Apostolic Custom and Church Law."

You older Baby Boomers who were altar boys and had to respond in Latin might find it interesting to attend a mass at that church, for old time's sake. It brought back a lot of memories of - the way it was.

Chapter Ten
Roman Catholic Memories

Since I just covered a bit about a church and Latin masses, the fact that South Buffalo was predominantly Catholic at one point, I thought it would be a good idea to look back and see the way the Church functioned in the 40s, 50's and 60's. Those of you who are Catholic and lived through those years, might find it interesting to look back and reminisce. Here we go.

Sign of the Cross

Remember having been taught that when you walked or rode by a Catholic Church in a car, you would make the sign of the cross? And, being a good Catholic meant that you went to church every Sunday and holy days of obligation. On various holy days of obligation, if parochial schools were in session, it was very common to see the entire student body march from the classroom building, escorted by the full habit clad nuns, or teachers. It was always in two lines; with the girls going ahead of the boys "in silence, please!" After mass the students marched right back to the classroom.

Back then, people put on their Sunday best to go to church or at the very least, wore neat-looking clothes. And the churches were packed. I mean packed. In fact, ushers would have to go up and down the aisles on Sundays and special mass days to see if there were seats available for people standing at the back who had not found an open seat. Today, in some large churches, you can have a whole pew since services are not well-attended anymore. So many have closed due to poor attendance and low contributions to support them.

Christmas and Easter were the two most attended days, as I remember. Midnight masses on Christmas Eve were always standing room only in several churches I attended. Yes, it was good seeing people do their religious duty, but it was sad to see a few people in attendance who had too many drinks before coming. Some folks would start celebrating Christmas Eve a few hours before midnight mass. When standing or kneeling, you'd see half a dozen or more tipsy people sway a bit, and as mass went on some seated parishioners nodded off to sleep. I remember on a couple occasions when ushers had to escort out men who were talking too loud during the liturgy. Apparently, they were too drunk to realize that sound travels. Other than that, midnight masses ran smoothly. After mass, a lot of the adults went home to celebrate with relatives; eat moms' famous special Christmas dishes, have a few drinks and open presents. The general rule for the little ones was to be in bed.

Entering Church

In the past, there was a certain way you needed to do things before you got to your seat. The procedure for entering the church, being at mass and exiting the church used to follow certain guidelines. First thing, females had to have their head covered with a hat or chapel veil. As we well know, a lot of the rules have been changed and women do not have to cover their heads any more. You'll also see many young females in dresses with plunging necklines, wearing shorts, halter tops, tube tops and ripped jeans. It seems anything goes.

Reverence for what should be considered sacred ground as well as showing self-respect does not seem to be a concern for some. In the past, there was an understood dress code that went with going to church. Some things should not have changed. A lot of guys also miss the mark with regard to proper dress when going to spend time in the House of the Lord. By the way, this goes on in non-Catholic churches as well.

As one entered a Catholic Church back then, silence was one of the first things observed. Then, one would bless themselves by dipping their right fingers into the holy water bowl and making the sign of the cross. This relates to the Bible (Deut. 12:6) *"Blessed shall you be when you come in, and blessed shall you be when you go out."*

Once people found their seat, they genuflected in the aisle and again made the sign of the cross. When mass started everyone stood when the priest entered. After that, there was that series of sitting, standing and kneeling as well as responses at certain times during the mass, and making little signs of the cross on one's forehead, mouth and heart at a point in the mass. After the mass was over, exiting your pew was also done with reverence and in silence; again genuflecting and making a sign of the cross. On the way out, attendees again dipped their right fingers in the holy water and made the sign of the cross.

The Mass

There used to be daily masses; 6:45, 7:15 and 8 AM at Holy Family. For a long time on Sundays there were at least six masses. Eileen Leahy from Abbott Road said that Holy Family used to have a 7 AM, 8 AM, 9 AM, 10 AM, 11 AM and noon High Mass with the 6 highest candles lit on the altar. Steve Banko added that there was a choir and organ player filling the church with music and songs. There was also, a 5:30 PM mass. The latter was for people who worked weekend day shifts at the plants. Eventually, churches began having a Saturday afternoon mass that would count for Sunday observance. Steve reminded me that Holy Family students were required to attend the 9 AM mass on Sundays during the school year. One of the staff nuns would be there to oversee them. They were expected to sit in a designated area with the boys separated from the girls.

In the 40s, 50's and 60's, Baby Boomers heard all masses in Latin with the altar boys responding in Latin. I was one of those altar boys.

After the Second Vatican Council of 1962-1965 it was decided people should hear the mass in their native language and have the priests facing the people. Today, the masses are said in all different languages. Not all Catholics agreed to the change. The Society of St. Pius X still says mass in Latin.

Communion

Up until the 60s, people had to follow very strict guidelines in order to receive communion in Catholic churches. Fasting from midnight until after communion the next day used to be expected until the rules changed in 1964 to fasting three hours before taking communion. Now, one must abstain one hour, consuming no food or drinks with the exception of water. The elderly and the sick can have something to eat even if it is within the hour time frame before communion.

Before taking communion, remember the right fist action of lightly striking your chest three times and saying, *Mea culpa, mea culpa, mea maxima culpa.* *"By my fault, by my fault, by my most grievous fault."* It was a moment to get right with God before receiving communion; reflecting on one's sins and asking forgiveness.

Remember when everyone came to the communion rail and knelt? Yes, knelt. You'd wait with hands folded for the priest and the altar boy with the communion plate to approach and serve you the wafer (the communion plate was to catch fallen wafers). There was no such thing as receiving the host in your hands at one time. Only priests were allowed to touch the hosts and gently put them on the parishioner's tongue. The priest would say in Latin: Corpus Christi "Body of Christ" and you'd respond "Amen", open your mouth, and receive communion.

You were not supposed to chew the host or even have it touch your teeth. You were expected to let it soften on your tongue until you could swallow it. Lots of changes, eh? Today, the priest either places the communion wafer in your hands or if you'd like it done the old fashioned way, you can still have it placed on your tongue, and you may chew it.

Lent and Fasting

According to (Canon Laws 1251 & 1252), refraining from eating meat on Fridays was once a church law for all Fridays until 1966. In 1983, the Code of Canon Law was revised and stated that eating meat would be prohibited for Catholics on Ash Wednesdays, Good Fridays and all Fridays throughout Lent, but the Catholic Church still recommends not eating meat on Fridays. During Lent, people were urged but not required to fast and to do one's best to give up something. For young people it was giving up candy or TV programs, going to the movies, dances, or some other things they enjoyed having. Adults might give up a meal, not see a movie or eat out, give up cigarettes, drink fewer beers or deny themselves some other things that was meaningful to them on a daily basis. Would you believe a guy once actually said to me?

"I'm gonna try giving up swearing for Lent?"

What? Like that was really something that belonged in the category of things to give up for Lent.

A Bit of Culture Stuff

Easter was a very revered day in the Church. People took their outfits up a notch on Easter Sunday. You'd see adults decked out more than usual. How many of you remember men in suits, shirts, ties and buffed shoes; ladies wearing colorful dresses and coats with fancy hats? Then, there were the little girls wearing pretty dresses, patent leather shoes, bonnets and colorful jackets with white gloves. Little boys wore their neat suits, white shirts and ties and spiffy shoes. It was a time for celebration and family time. At the house after church, men were to stay out of the kitchen. It was time for moms and grandmas to shine.

For the Irish

"Beannachtaíz na Cásca." *Happy Easter*

"Barr an maidin go dtí duit. *Top o' the mornin' to you.*

"Slainte" *Cheers.*

"Erin go bragh" *Ireland forever.*

Irish moms' and grandmas' menu included their famous Irish stew, corned beef with unsliced bacon, boiled with cabbage and potatoes, farl (a bread), maybe, boxty (Irish potato pancake).

Desserts were perhaps, Irish tea cake, Irish apple cake, plain or with custard, Irish whiskey cake, or maybe Bailey's Irish Cream cheesecake.

For the Italians

"Buona Pasqua." Happy Easter

"Mangia bene, ridi spesso, ama molto." Eat well, laugh often, love much.

"Mangia e statti zitto." Eat and shut up.

My Sicilian wife has that one on the kitchen wall.

Italian moms' and grandmas' menus included huge pots of spaghetti sauce with plenty of garlic (I love garlic.), meat balls, mushrooms and sausage, beef braciole, lasagna, manicotti or chicken cacciatore. They'd fit twenty or twenty-five people at tables put together.

Desserts would be pizzelles (of course.), cucidatis, anisette cookies, anise biscottis, cheese cake, maybe a ricotta pie and for sure, cannolis. Mmmm, quello è buono. "Mmmm, that's good."

For the Polish

Wesolych Swiat Wielkanocnych *"Happy Easter"*

Na zdrowie (pronounced - Na sdrovieh) *"Cheers"*

Smacznego (pronounced – smachnego.) *"Enjoy your meal"*

Polish moms' and grandmas' menus always had tons of pierogis, golumbki (stuffed cabbage) potatoes, cabbage, kielbasa (sausage), klopsikis (meatballs).

Desserts were paczkis (doughnut), piernikis (spice cookie), babka cakes, karpetka cakes, faworkis, szarlotka cakes.

Mmmm   to jest dobre. "Mmmm, that's good."

Chapter Eleven
Common Life in South Buffalo Neighborhoods

Safe Neighborhoods

One of the unique things I remember about living in my neighborhood was that it was safe. Many people kept their doors unlocked. No one in our family had a key to the house except our parents; I never saw them use it. The house was always unlocked, day or night. It seemed that it was that way in most of the homes all over South Buffalo, especially, houses with large families. There was no need to lock up since somebody was always home. People knew each other up and down the street. For the most part everyone got along, even with so many different nationalities on every street. That's the way it was in most of the neighborhoods throughout our area. It was great!

Nationalities

Our family was French Canadian. In the duplex we lived in, the next door family was Polish. A Hungarian family moved in after they moved out. To our right, we had a Puerto Ricans, on our left, an Irish family and across the street, Italians and Mexicans. Down the street, on either side, we had several Irish and Italian families. Joe Nigrelli, an Italian man, down the street from us helped me out when I got my United States citizenship in 1968. He was a Buffalo Detective with 39 years on the force. Joe and wife Margaret (McCarthy) had four sons; Stephen and Michael who became State

Troopers. Their son Peter served on the Buffalo Police Force and another son, Joe Jr. went to work at the Police Dispatch Center in Indianapolis. Their only daughter, Susan, married State Trooper Joseph Denahy.

Families and Mothers

The neighborhood was also a place where a lot of moms fed other kids along with their own. Some kids were sent out and told: *"Go out and play and don't come home till it's time to eat."* Some families with so many kids in the house had to shoo them out so they could get housework done or entertain a guest without having interruptions from their four, five, six or more kids. Neighborhood parents had each other's backs concerning raising kids. There was a sense of real community and was very family oriented. Moms watched over their children and neighbors' children as well. If children were playing at someone's house that was somewhat far from their own at lunch time, it was a given that the host moms would feed their children's friends too.

If a neighbor saw a problem, he did not hesitate to straighten out a kid who was out of line. You might say neighborhoods were self-policing. Neighbors got involved and respect for adults was expected. A kid who disrespected an adult neighbor would usually result in the neighbor and parents resolving it quickly. The outcome was never good for the child. Moms and dads got things resolved pretty quickly by loud chastising or the sting of the belt. The child would get straightened out and apologies followed. That's the way it was.

Hardly any family was above the other status-wise. Most of the dads were blue-collar, hard-working men with a lot of stay-at-home wives. Many of the men worked the local grain mills, the docks, sanitation department, mail delivery, Bethlehem Steel along Route 5, (I worked at Gate 6 myself – '66) or Republic Steel on South Park near Allied Chemical on the other side of Buffalo Creek. Then there was the Donner Hanna Coke Plant, the Trico Plants, Buffalo Tank Division in Blasdell, the Woodlawn Ford Stamping Plant, the Chevy Plant on River Road, Buffalo Railroad, Buffalo China on Seneca Street, the Westinghouse Electric, Worthington Pump near Clinton and Bailey and a number other plants throughout the area.

156

Discipline

Stay-at-home moms would watch the roost and if she had trouble with one of her own, there was always that threat,

"Do you want to go to Father Baker's?" (home for defiant children and teens) or *"Wait till your father gets home."*

In those days it meant something. You would be in trouble. I know a lot of kids were dealt with harshly by parents for having done something wrong. In many families punishment was, *"No supper for you tonight. Go to your room,"* Or... losing one's allowance, not having friends over, being grounded or no going out on the weekend. Sometimes kids got a double dose', a lickin' and they couldn't go out for the night or weekend. It depended on the infraction. In really bad situations, a kid got all of the above, but that didn't happen very often. There was usually order in the neighborhood homes.

I lived next door to a large family and hung out with their sons George (Jorge) and Joe (José). More than once I saw their dad George Sr. come out the door chasing Joe or George with his belt in one hand and holding his pants up with the other.

Bleeding hearts who think this was brutal, relax. They were never vicious beatings; just enough to get the boys' attention and adjust their attitudes. Not only did dad take care of business with the leather belt, ma too, would often be seen coming out that same door wielding the menacing piece of leather. Apparently, the boys thought that running outside would offer some form of safety, but they always had to go back in. They had to eat, sleep and bathe. If they ran too fast and too far, mom and dad knew they'd catch up with them later. That's the way it was.

If you still think that was bad, you should've seen the action when their grandfather or grandmother would come after them with the belt.

Margie Weber from Altruria told me:

"I remember a family near my house where one of their dad's belts was kept on a hook in the kitchen by the stove. It belonged there as much as the pot holders next to it and served its purpose for any of the kids who got out of line or mouthy, as we used to call it."

In our own family when we were younger, our dad, Leo, would sting the defiance or attitudes out of us when it needed to be done.

For the most part, we minded. Mom and Dad were the bosses, not us. It was that way for our neighbors, our family, and a ton of other South Buffalo Baby Boomers. We didn't think much of it. We didn't like getting a lickin' but we knew that if we broke the laws of the house, it was very likely there would be consequences. None of us became so traumatically damaged that we couldn't handle life. If anything, as José told me"

"It taught us about respect for parents and consequences for bad actions. I believe I was successful in life because I had parents who taught me discipline and respect."

Respect and Manners

For most of us, there was no talking back or arguing with our parents. In my house, none of us ever talked back or argued with our parents. Today, a lot of the kids lack respect for parents big time. Many simply have little or no idea what it is to have values, manners and respect. There was another code of conduct among most of the kids I grew up with. It was always Mr. or Mrs. so and so when we addressed older folks. Today, kids think they are at par with everybody, of any age. Using an older neighbor's first name was not an option for us as kids. Even as we became adults, we still used Mr. or Mrs. It was all about respect.

If company came over, children were expected to show respect for the guests and use proper manners. They were expected to greet them and communicate with them when spoken too. If a child were sitting in an armchair or sofa, it was understood that he or she would give up the seat for the adult.

If you were at your own house, a relative's house or even at a friend's house back then, it was considered very rude and improper to put your feet on the couch, armchair or coffee table. As kids, we were taught that feet belonged on the floor not on the furniture. Even today, on my own couch, I'm very conscious about not doing that. Therefore, I certainly wouldn't do it anywhere else.

Oh, and if you went into a house where the mom had custom-fit plastic covers on the living room furniture, that room was out of bounds for children and their friends. Only adults could sit there and only on special occasions. It was weird, but that's the way it was.

Large Families

Most family men and their wives focused on living as good a life as possible by making a living and raising a family. It was very common for a couple to have 10 or more children. In the Seneca –Babcock area, the McCabes had 16 kids, the Sitarskis had 12 kids, the Greens, 12 kids. The Caz and Seneca area Keanes had 16 kids, the Murthas from the Triangle area had 8 boys, the Halls on Whitfield had 13 kids. There were ten in the Gannon family on Woodside, as well as in my own. The Bankos had eight kids, the Cloudens on South Park Avenue, eight or more kids, the Pughs down the street had six, the Smiths next door to us had five children and the Colerns on Lockwood Avenue had at least seven kids. The Rodriguezs to the right of us ended up with at least ten kids. To each of those families, add moms and dads. Many of the homes were three bedroom homes

It was so common that it became a way of life. You got married, had children and didn't worry too much about how you'd feed them all. It would all work out and, work out it did. What's interesting, back in the 50's and early 60's, the average yearly income was $3,500 to $5,000. This put anyone with a big family in a low to very low income bracket. When it came time to fill out the tax forms though, large families had deductions. Between 1917 and 1920, the tax deduction was $200 per dependent. In 2016 it is up to $1,000 per child under the age of 17.

Special Cudos to the Baby Boomer Moms!

God bless the Baby Boomer moms. I mean that very sincerely. If you could ask the moms of the Seneca/Babcock McCabe family with 16 kids, or the Hall family on Whitfield with 13 kids what they went through to maintain the household and their sanity, they'd have stories to tell you that would make you cry. Think about it. In those huge families, moms probably had at least three little ones at a time in cloth diapers. There were no disposable diapers then.

With three in diapers at time, you have to figure they needed five or maybe six cloth diapers for the day and night. That's at least 15 diapers in a 24 hour period for the three babies. At the end of the week, 15 a day times 7 days, gives you a whopping 105 dirty diapers. Moms needed to rinse them out in a pail or the toilet, wash them in an old style washing machine, put them through the wringer, hang them up on a clothes line outside and finally, go get them when they were dry. The job still wasn't done. The easiest part was to fold them and put them in a drawer or cupboard. The cycle would go on and on; day after day, after day and didn't stop until all their kids were potty trained. Imagine adding the rest of the family's laundry.

Doesn't it get you tired just reading this? I needed a nap after thinking about those moms' daily routines. It was an unending, exhausting job. Enough about diapers. Let's see what else those incredible moms from the Greatest Generation had to do to manage their family. Dads, I'm not leaving you out, but I'm sure you'd agree that your wives had the harder job.

Food Handouts

Back in the day, a lot of large families got one kind of handout or another. I can remember families drinking powdered milk and getting butter, margarine, peanut butter & jelly and cheese from the Federal Food Distribution Centers. In the 60s, moms (mine included) would buy day old bread for ten cents a loaf from the Wonder Bread Bakery on Clinton and Adams Streets. It was fine. We ate it and survived. When you think of the many families with dads who went to work, and kids who went to school, all needing lunches, a whole lot of bread was needed. If you factor in bread, lunch meats or peanut butter/jelly and lunch bags; it took quite a chunk of a family's budget. For the most part, it was the moms who put lunches together at night or got up early to do that task. Those of you who were from very large families, do you remember mom writing your name on the lunch bags and lining them up in the fridge? This too, was done day in and day out.

School Lunches

If they even had cafeterias in their schools, a lot of kids from large families couldn't afford to buy lunches. Let's look at the McCabe or Keane family with 16 kids. Hypothetically, if only 7 of the 16 kids and dad needed a lunch, at two sandwiches each, it meant 4 slices of bread per person per day. It comes to 32 slices of bread a day for lunches. Multiply that, times 5 days a week. It comes to 160 slices a week. Based on an average of 22 slices per loaf they probably needed over 7 loaves of bread a week just for lunches. Oh yeah, don't forget toast for breakfast. Maybe 10 loaves or more was needed a week to keep the Keane, McCabe or Hall families in bread. And, the budget said ouch! I can remember my own mom buying seven to ten loaves at a time for the week for 10 kids and dad. Very often, it didn't even last to the end of the week.

Chapter Twelve
Education for Baby Boomers - Elementary and high schools

Writing Cursive

Ours is not to reason why, ours is but to do (and die).

How many of you remember having to perfect the grownup way of writing around the second grade level? In Québec in 1952, no kindergarten. I started in 1st grade and went directly into writing cursive. As a matter of fact, I didn't learn how to print until I went to college. As I taught languages at Medaille College in 2012, I wrote something in cursive on the board and a student actually asked me, *"What does that mean?"* Folks, I'm talking college level, here. That student along with many others were never exposed to cursive. What happens when someone says to them:

"We need your signature to finalize these very important documents. Please print your name on this line and sign your name, on the line below."

If all they know how to do is print, isn't it a problem for non-cursive writers when it comes to signing checks, credit card receipts and documents. Grade schools need to bring back teaching cursive to the classroom, don't you think? I asked a friend of mine, Ray Colpoys who is in his 70s, if he still wrote cursive. He told me:

I don't mean to brag, but my penmanship is excellent. The reason for that is because when I was a kid, my mom made me go to Mount Mercy every Saturday morning for a year, where her sister (a nun), had me practice pages and pages of me writing cursive. I'd even have to go home and practice all week and the following Saturday bring back the sheets. I got really good at it. Even to this day, my wife comments on how good my handwriting is."

Lots of Baby Boomers have the special ability to write excellently in cursive. My sister-in-law Diane and my daughter-in-law's aunt Donna, write incredibly well. *(See sample of Donna's cursive writing on the previous page)*

Writing Tools

Many Baby Boomers didn't have ballpoint pens when they started school. It was either pencils or pen and ink with pens that had steel tip nibs that were inserted into pen tip holders, then, dipped into little bottles of ink that were located at the right hand top corners of students' desks. I believe all those desks were designed for right handers.

Right-handedness was the norm, while left-handedness was very often discouraged by nuns and secular teachers. This was partly due to the Latin word for left, sinsitra. The Latin word also means evil. Then, there is dextro and sinistro, meaning right and wrong. Also, there is the Bible passage of Matthew 25:31-46, referring to Christ putting the righteous people at His right and the unrighteous at His left. A lot of Baby Boomer students were forced to change hands, but I was not. I'm still a lefty.

Back to Writing

There were two big problems for the Baby Boomers with the pen and ink system. First, people could only write a few words at a time before having to dip the tip of the pen into the ink bottle, again. They had to be careful not to load too much ink in the tip. If they did that and started writing, they could end up with a blob of ink on their paper and smear their work. If they had a blob of ink, there were blotters to soak up the excess. Lefties had the worst of times with pen and ink and couldn't avoid lots of smears. I'm a lefty. I know. I used the pen and ink system for a couple of years back in the 50's.

If you had a couple of dollars, you could buy a fountain pen that had a self-contained bladder that you'd fill by moving a small lever to deflate the bladder, dip the tip of the pen into an ink bottle, release the lever and the ink was sucked into the bladder. This allowed for uninterrupted writing of many words. How many of you used those?

A modification of the fountain pen was the cartridge pen. Those pens were even easier to use than fountain pens. You'd buy a pack of ink cartridges, unscrew the tip portion of the pen, slip in a cartridge into the hollow part of the pen, screw back the tip and the cartridge would automatically get punctured by an inside tip orifice, and away you went. By the way, cartridge pens are still in use today. Cartridges came in black, blue or red ink. The down side is they too, could smudge up your writing if you were a lefty.

The ballpoint pen came into common use in the late 50's and early 60's. We are all familiar with those, so I won't go into any details. Not too long after ballpoint pens came to be, felt tip pens came along. They were good writing implements. From there, all different kinds of ball point and felt tip pens flooded the market.

Parochial and Public Schools

People in South Buffalo and throughout the City of Buffalo were very much connected to a parish as a way of establishing what part of Buffalo they were from regardless if the children went to a public or parochial school. The parishes covered certain areas and that became what people were associated with. If someone said "I belong to Our Lady of Perpetual Help," you knew right away that they lived in the Old First Ward, ...OR, if someone said: "I belong to Saint Teresa's," that would mean he or she was from the Seneca Street area between South Side and Mineral Springs.

Parishes with Schools

Saint Brigid on Louisiana Street

Saint Valentine on South Park (OFW)

Our Lady of Perpetual Help (corner of O'Connell and Alabama, OFW)

Saint Monica's on Orlando streets in the Seneca/Babcock area - Dan Neaverth's elementary School. It was demolished.

Saint Agatha/All Souls near the Triangle Abbott Road

Holy Family - South Park & Tifft - Tim Russert's school

Mount Mercy on Red Jacket Parkway

Saint Ambrose on Ridgewood

Saint Thomas on Abbott Road)

Saint Teresa on Seneca Street

Saint Martin became Notre Dame Academy on Abbott Road

Saint John and Saint Bonaventure both on Seneca Street- Tim Russert.

High Schools

Mount Mercy Academy on Red Jacket Parkway (all girls' school)

Timon High School on McKinley Parkway (an all boys' school).

Quite a few of the local guys and gals went to Baker Victory.

Catholic School

Being predominantly Catholic communities throughout South Buffalo, it was the Sisters of Mercy who taught kindergarteners to eighth graders in the parochial schools. Learning the three "R's" was one part of their agenda. The students learned values, discipline and morals. Their objective was to guide their students to become educated, respectful, virtuous adults. Being realistic and understanding the nature of boys and girls, I know that a lot of the teachings of these good sisters didn't always stick in the minds and souls of their pupils. Many a former parochially-educated individual either disregarded or discarded the good teachings of those ladies. Overall though, the sisters did do a good job and planted good seeds in order to set their students on the right path to become well-educated, productive individuals. For the most part, their efforts were not in vain. That is to their credit, and I for one, salute them. They affected a lot of lives in many good ways.

Public Schools List

The other side of the coin here is the public school system. Not very far from where the parochial schools were located there where public elementary schools. Starting from the same general area as the parochial schools, some of those schools were/are:

P.S. #4 in the Old First Ward on South Park

PS #34 elementary at 108 Hamburg Street in the Old First Ward (The school was demolished around 1976.)

P.S. #33 on Elk Street in the Valley

P.S. #26 on Harrison Street in the Seneca/Babcock area

P.S. #28 (South Park and Abbott)

P.S. #29 (South Park and Okell)

P.S. 67 (Abbott Rd and Naragansett.)

P.S. #72 (on Belvedere St. behind Mercy Hospital)

Although religion was not part of their curriculum back then, public school teachers instilled the same code of conduct and moral convictions in their Baby Boomer students as did their Catholic counterparts. If you were a Catholic student attending a public school, you attended Religious Instruction Classes once a week. It wasn't mandatory, but parents made the call on that. Most of the Roman Catholic students attended the classes.

Discipline and Corporal Punishment

Anyone from that era remembers full well the practice of corporal punishment. It was all about teaching consequences for bad actions. There were rules and regulations. Anyone guilty of not following the rules were well aware of the possible meting out of some sort of punishment by the administrators. All in all, most schools ran well with few incidents of applying the dreaded ruler to the knuckles or the yardstick on the behind. Parochial schools had the kneeling down in a corner remedy on a nice, cold, marble floor for a half hour or so, as one of the ways of curing a defiant child.

For severe infractions, a young lad or lass needed to go to the principal's office. Some of those sessions were the worst. Many students entering a principal's office for a major offense never left. No one knows what happened to them. Only kidding! But... in such cases, the parents were often consulted and that's when the rebellious child might have gotten a double dose of corporal punishment. The school administrators dealt out their punishment and the parents got a shot at their kid as well when he or she got home. God only knows what some of the kids got when they got there.

Parents trusted and backed the school administrators and accepted the discipline their children got. As a matter of fact, when students got in trouble and were punished for it, they didn't want mom or dad to know about it. Parents knew it meant their sons broke a rule and probably got what they deserved. Since the school already took care of the discipline, they didn't want mom or dad to dish out their own brand of punishment. I won't say that the punishment students got was right in every case, but most of the time, it was. Rules were in place and were expected to be followed. It was that simple.

School administrators and teachers were in control back then. Today, a lot of schools have discipline problems. Some schools are even chaotic at times. Many of today's schools are in shambles because of students' rights. There is no fear of repercussions for bad behavior. It's a shame. Today, corporal punishment does not exist. If a principal or teacher should put a ruler to the knuckles of a student or a paddle or yardstick to their backside, they would tell their parents and all hell could break loose. Cops and lawyers would be called and heads would roll. The principal or teacher would most likely lose their job. In some schools, teachers are afraid for their safety because of student threats. There's really something wrong with that picture. It boils down to, disregard for authority.

Public School 29 and Holy Family

I remember only a few guys with whom I became friends and still talk to from PS #29. Bob Regan is one I mentioned before. To this day, I can still see him in my mind's eyes. He was playing handball behind the school and seemed to me to be a tough hombre. He wasn't big, but I could see that he was packed tight like a stick of dynamite and could blow up big. I noticed the guys in the yard paid attention to him when he spoke. Apparently, he was one of the guys you minded. He was tough and direct, but he loved to laugh and had a great sense of humor.

Bob recalls that they would often station one of the spectators of the handball matches on top of the roof connected to the handball playing area. Rather than having people climb up every time the ball ended up on the roof, they thought it was a good idea to plant someone up there for the duration of the match. Poor guy.

There, I also became friends with Mickey Guzda from Lockwood Avenue and Eddy Dacey from West Woodside when I first moved from Orchard Park. As a matter of fact, Eddy from West Woodside saved me from some guy who wanted to thump me. I was walking home from School 29 and passed a young lad and his buddies. For some reason, I don't know why, either I said something or he said something, I responded in a manner that bushed his button, and it lead to the threat of me being roughed up. Eddy Dacey happened by and said:

"He's okay," leave him alone."

I was a runt at thirteen. The guy who gave me trouble was a bit taller and stouter. Thank you Eddy. Years later, that ruffian and I became great friends.

Holy Family School (est. 1902)

After PS #29, I attended Holy Family School at the corner of South Park and Tifft streets from September of 1960 to June of 1962 for 7th and 8th grade. It was a great school for the Catholic kids who attended there, as were all of the other Catholic grade schools in the area. Tim Russert, nationally known political analyst, was our most famous student. He attended Holy Family for a few years then transferred to Saint Bonaventure on Seneca Street after moving away from Woodside Avenue. In his book Big Russ and I, he speaks very fondly of his experience and mentioned that many of the people with whom he had made friends with, continued their friendship for many years, and some remained his friends until his passing.

One of the things I still remember about the school was that there was no mixing of the genders in the school yard. Girls had to stay on one side and the boys on the other. That's the way it was for most grade schools back then. When the bell rang for class, we formed two lines. The command was given to march, and in we marched. The girls entered first, then the boys. There was no talking in line. Violation of this rule meant an immediate tongue-lashing or perhaps some sort of corporal punishment.

The girls were under a bit more scrutiny than the boys. They had to wear skirts, at or below the knees, with a white blouse, socks and shoes. The nuns were very aware that some of the girls would try to wear their skirts a bit too high. If and when one of the young ladies would dare break the rule, you can be sure Sister would attend to the problem, post haste. The boys on the other hand didn't have a problem. We had to make sure we had on a dress shirt and tie, dress pants, and shoes. The neat thing about the ties was that they could be string ties like the cowboys wear.

All of the classes were taught by the Sisters of Mercy in the upper grades. Some of the students would dispute the word mercy in their title. Several of the nuns put the fear of God in many a young man or woman who wanted to test their patience. One of the nuns there was Sister Mary Clementia, an elderly lady. She seemed to us to be about seventy years old but could be as mean as a cornered wildcat if you didn't do things her way or crossed her.

True Story

After I had graduated 8th grade from Holy Family and attended South Park High, I had a school break for some reason. Joe Predergast and I were shooting baskets at Mulroy playground right behind Holy Family School. From one of the windows, we heard this elderly voice telling us to leave the playground; that the basketball bouncing was distracting her students. Well, being in high school and no longer under the authority of the good sisters, we decided we weren't going to leave. We kept playing. Suddenly, we saw this little lady in her habit, with a sweet look on her face coming towards us.

As she got near Joe and me, she said with a smile in a very sweet voice, *"Could I see your basketball for a second?"* Not thinking, Joe handed it over. She tucked it under her arm, promptly turned and walked away. My reaction was *"Get the ball back."* I followed her and asked for it but there was no way she would not give it back. Brash as I was I tried to grab it. She quickly twisted away so I wouldn't get it. I can't believe I did this (forgive me Sister) I made a quick move and popped the ball out of her hands as though I was doing a steal during a game. Got it! She put her hands on her hips and stared at me with one eye shut tight and her teeth clenched.

It's been over fifty years and I can still see that stare. We shot a few more baskets and left. Maybe it was fear, I'm not sure but we left.

Sister Jeanne Marie was my eight grade teacher. Maybe my memory does not serve me quite right, but it seems to me that she hardly ever got out of her seat to teach. Everything was done from her desk. She was pretty stern and didn't put up with any nonsense. I may have seen her smile twice the whole year I had her for 8th grade. She did smile when I graduated. Draw your own conclusions.

I can remember vividly one guy I used to trip on a regular basis when he came down the aisle. His name was John "Jack" Lafferty. I don't know why I did it; maybe to break the monotony. I wasn't a bad student. I guess, I just wasn't focused enough.

Another memory is how one of our classmates would pass out from time to time. He would intentionally hold his breath until he passed out and of course, got a free ticket out the door to go home to convalesce.

There was another guy who came in one day beet red. He looked like he had been to Florida. The only problem it was the middle of winter and he hadn't been to any warm climate to get the sunburn. He had fallen asleep under a sunlamp. Ouch!

Then there was the boy who had no winter boots. His father ruled that he wasn't going to walk to school through the snow and ruin his shoes. He was made to wear his mother's brown, zippered rubber boots with the fur piece around the top. Baby Boomers know the kind. Well he thought that if he flipped the fur pieces up on each boot, no one would notice. They did and of course, laughed. He didn't. Poor guy. He didn't wear them for the walk back home after school. He tucked them under his arm hiding them as best he could. That poor schnook was.......... me.

Holy Family Gym

Anyone who went to Holy Family remembers the Gym which was not even close to a regular size gym. It had a very low ceiling and pillars. You had to be sharp when playing basketball there. A few of the players came to an abrupt stop because of those pillars. They weren't padded either. I remember once when we played a game against another Catholic school, we won. It wasn't so much because we were better than they were, but because we were used to practicing in that gym. Going in for a long shot, we knew how low to aim while the opposing team would arch their shots more and hit the ceiling. Of course they complained that it wasn't fair. We laughed. We basically didn't care how we won that game as long as we won. Needless to say, there were no more contests played in our gym. We always had to go to a school with a real gym for our games.

Lunch Break

I remember going home for lunch each day. There were no cafeterias in most grade schools when I attended. You had to wait until you got to high school for that. It was interesting seeing all the South Buffalo Catholic and public school Baby Boomers filling the streets at noon. I'm talking about hundreds of kids.

It was good for students who lived relatively close to their school but for the kids who had a long walk, you have to wonder if they had much time to finish their meals. My walk to and from school was only four blocks. Some of my friends had to walk nearly a mile, one way. In good weather, it wasn't bad, but in foul weather, it was down right, miserable. I do remember that they made some accommodations for kids who live really far or who had no adults home to prepare food for them. They'd have a long table in or near the gym area where those students ate lunch. Some of the kids didn't have stay-at-home moms and still went home had to fend for themselves. Who knows what some of those poor kids ate or if they had much to eat at all.

Today, with so few stay-at-home moms and bussing, most all grade school students pack a lunch or buy from their school cafeteria. Someone brought up setting up neighborhood schools again and having children go to those schools instead of being bussed across town. I'd be for that but it's a different time with different family dynamics. It wouldn't work well. But, wouldn't it be nice to go back to neighborhood schools, stay-at-home moms and children being able to go home for lunch with moms and siblings like in the old days? Oh, the good old days.

Timon High School, est. 1949

The original Timon High School was located on the 3rd floor of Our Lady of Perpetual Help in the Old First Ward. The new location is on McKinley Parkway between Columbus and Strathmore where they've educated young men for many years and many areas. The freshmen attended class in an annex known as Nash Hall, housed in an old telephone company building on Como Street for a while. The McKinley school building was a huge center of activities that included Friday night dances, bingo games, lawn fêtes, special performances and karate tournaments in the 70's. About everyone in South Buffalo attended many events held there.

I read something about one of the dances held at Timon in the 50s where Paul Anka made an appearance. Of course he sang *"Diana"* a hit at the time.

Timon prided itself in providing a well-balanced education, complete with great book knowledge and spiritual exercises as well as sports and clubs to allow students outlets for their talents, be it on the basketball court, track and field, baseball, or football. One of their alums, Joe Kempkes, set a record in track when he ran the mile in 4:53 minutes in 1962. One of the well-known clubs was the Radio Club where Danny Neaverth was a member and became one of the top Buffalo DJs heard for miles via WKBW Radio. By the way, he started his professional radio career in Coudersport, PA.

Religious Instructions for South Park High Boys

Any of the Baby Boomers who attended Timon came in contact with Father Tim. He seemed to be ten feet tall. He would have made a great drill sergeant. I remember once when we South Park High School boys attended religious instructions and some of the guys acted up, he kept us after and made us sit and stare at the clock for a half hour. Do you know how slowly time passes when you're staring at a clock?

South Park High, est. 1915

South Park High School on South Side Parkway was known for having teachers and administrators who were highly dedicated, with strong values and no-nonsense attitudes. A former teacher, Edward Miller, said this about the school:

"Once, South Park High was the elite school of Buffalo."

South Park High was a fairly big school with lots of students. When I attended, the principal was Dr. Norman Hayes with Mr. Raymond J. Schanzer as assistant principal. It was filled with young men and women from many neighborhoods of South Buffalo. As with all of the Catholic and public high schools back then, we had a dress code. All the guys showed up every day wearing a shirt, neck tie, dress pants, socks and dress shoes. No male student was allowed to roll up his shirt sleeves during school hours. If Dr. Hayes passed a student with sleeves rolled up, he was known to get a grip on one of the sleeves and rip it off at the cuff. Now, that meant the student had to go home and explain to mom and dad why his shirt had one sleeve shorter than the other. It was understood; *you will come to school in proper attire and breaking behavior or dress code rules will not be tolerated.*

The girls were expected to dress like ladies. Their dress code was simple enough. They wore neat blouses, skirts of an appropriate length, socks or stockings and shoes. Most didn't wear much makeup. Only a few would put on lipstick and maybe some rouge. There certainly were a lot of puffed up hairdos back then. You would see a whole lot of the girls with teased hair, always kept in place with hair spray.

Assistant principal Schanzer was one man you didn't want to toy with. He was the school's sergeant-at-arms in charge of discipline. From time to time, there were guys who got to have a bit of special time in his office for one infraction or another. Some came out a bit sore but had a better understanding of the policies, rules and expectations of the school. No one wanted a return visit to his office for misbehaving.

It was a good school, but not perfect. There were occasional incidents of lack of respect for a teacher, too much clowning around in class, harsh words between students, bullying, shoving matches or even a fight now and then. Any misbehavior happening in the school was dealt with post haste.

Class Incident

One day, Assistant Principal Schanzer received a list of names of about nine young scholars from Mrs. Lewis' math class who needed an attitude adjustment. It all started one winter day in 1963 when Greg Vaughn, one of our fine young men discovered that he could do a rapid-fire tapping with his foot that he could keep up indefinitely. Mrs. Lewis, who was a bit hard of hearing, heard the racket at a lower tone. She stopped teaching and yelled:

"What is that noise?"

The young tapper pointed toward the windows and said that it was the radiators knocking. He even kept the tapping going as he gave her this information. She sort of believed him. He continued the tapping on and off during the class and we'd laugh. Again, Mrs. Lewis stopped teaching; looked toward the radiators, turned to see us laughing, frowned at the class and continued the math lesson. I'm sure she figured it out after our class left because the noise stopped. I suppose we weren't smart guys just wise-guys.

Learning the Hard Way

As students, we knew if we messed up, there would be some sort of consequence. Here's the account of the group session we had with our beloved assistant principal for misbehaving in Mrs. Lewis' class. In our group was Mike Catanzaro, Greg Vaughan, Clyde Leto, George Amplement, four other guys and myself. I'm glad I wasn't one who got one of Mr. Schanzer's best shots. Clyde Leto was his first target. Schanzer walked up behind him with the list of names and comments to address the conduct unbecoming of young South Park High School scholars. Bang! He got hit from behind. George Ampleman was next. Our dear assistant principal twisted his ear pretty hard. He then said a few words to Mike Catanzaro followed by a back hand to the side of his face. Mike didn't say a word. He took it like the tough Old First Ward boy he was. He didn't move. I believe Greg got a few hard hits on the head with his knuckles.

I must've had a kind face or the list had me down as a lesser culprit; he only flicked his finger at my left ear a few times and began reading us the proverbial riot act.

At any rate there were no more problems in Mrs. Lewis' class for the rest of the year. There's probably something to be said here about the effects of corporal punishment. I know that with the kind of discipline we received at South Park, things ran fairly well for the size school it was. We didn't have the problems we see in some of the high schools today. We all knew who was in control at South Park and it wasn't the students. The teachers and administrators ran a tight ship.

A True Story

Lunchtime at South Park was uneventful for the most part but a few things stick out in my mind. One is that the boys and the girls did not sit together. It was probably a good thing. You know, hormones and all.

The great "Smokey" (Dennis Wojciechowski) never brought a lunch to school. He would come to our table, wait till all the boys were settled in to eat, then he would go out and see who had what in their lunch. He'd simply ask guys for something they could spare. He'd come back to the table with sandwiches, cupcakes, drinks and even, ice cream!

Another True Story

Daniel Arthur Shea was a great guy and a cut-up who loved to laugh and joke around. One day, dressed in his shirt, tie, sports coat and glasses, he passed Mr. Curry, our lunch monitor and cordially greeted him, "Good afternoon Mr. Curry" then walked away past a point where he could not be seen. He took off his glasses and sports coat, and a few minutes later walked past Curry and asked:

"Mr. Curry, did you see my twin brother Arty Shea? He's wearing a sports coat and glasses."

"No, I haven't," was the response.

Danny went back, put the glasses and sports coat back on, returned and asked:

"Mr. Curry, I heard my twin brother Danny Shea is looking for me. Have you seen him?"

At this point, Mr. Curry had enough, gave Danny an earful and threatened detention. The twins never re-appeared from that day on. Good one Dan!

Recycling is Not New

Recycling of lunch bags was part of the norm for many who took lunches to school, offices or plants. Many of them brought back their empty lunch bags. Tim Fitzgerald who went to Timon High remembers that a lot of students would regularly re-used their lunch bags. He said:

"Sometimes, we'd use the same bag all week long."

When I was in school in the 60s I would fold the bag and bring it back home for reuse as long as it held up. I found that I was able to reuse each bag at least three to four times. With five of the older children in our family needing lunch bags, one bag a day for each person would require 25 bags a week. Multiply that 40 weeks of school and by the end of the year we would use up about 950 lunch bags. That would have been a lot of wasted paper, had we not recycled. We didn't waste things back then. If it could be reused, we would. It was like the jelly jars that became drinking glasses or old orange crates and the empty cigar boxes that were used for storing things. We even saved the strings the butcher shop used to tie meat packages with.

How many of you Baby Boomers remember saving every brown paper grocery bag mom would get from doing the weekly groceries? That was before plastic grocery bags. The bags were all neatly folded and put in a pile or stacked in a certain place to be used in the kitchen trash can. Once full, someone took it to the trash cans out back. If you remember, by the end of the week, you'd throw out five or six grocery bags full of trash, maybe more, depending on the

176

size of your family. Most families had two galvanized trash cans out back. With twelve people in our family, we had three cans.

How many of you remember that when you took out the garbage, you often didn't quite make it to the trash cans? The bottom often fell out dumping the contents on mom's clean kitchen floor because someone placed a liquid or slimy substance near the bottom of the paper trash bag? Sometimes, some of you in that situation would make it outside your back door and almost make it to the trash cans. If a neighbor happened to be watching and saw the trash blow right through the bottom of the bag onto the front of your pants, your shoes and the yard; he'd laugh, and laugh. But, not you. You'd find yourself using several expletives, right? All of the above scenarios happened to me.

Great Book Covers

Remember using those saved grocery bags to cover your text books. I'd get a bag and cut it large enough to have folds that went inside the hard-bound front and back covers. Those folds would act as slots to slide about an inch and a half to two inches on the insides of both covers. They were rugged enough to withstand almost a year's worth of use. People would write and draw on them. Of course, the names of the subjects were written on the front and the spines, and the student's name was usually on the bottom. People would draw all sorts of things on the fronts and backs. The girls would write their boyfriend's name or initials somewhere on the cover with hearts and an arrow through it. You know, the common puppy love kinds of things.

No Backpacks

Speaking of books and school, remember not having backpacks back then? The boys carried their books under their arm and the girls held them in front with one or both arms. School supplies were very few. We were only required to have pencils, pens, rulers and erasers. That was about it. No calculators back in the 40's, 50's, or 60's, folks. That's when we used our brains to do basic math in our heads or on paper.

Demographics

The great thing about the school was that people from all over South Buffalo and beyond went there. Our knowledge of other people doubled, tripled, and even quadrupled. One of the things that happened for the first time to a lot of students was that they would be integrated with African-Americans. Most of us from the South Buffalo neighborhoods had not attended grade schools that had black students. But, at South Park, that all changed. For the most part, people from the various neighborhoods got along. Some good and lasting friendships even came out of that experience.

I remember one of the black students I came to know and befriend; his name was James Thomas. The homeroom teacher kept mixing up his name when taking attendance and called him Thomas James. He would tell the teacher:

"The name is not Thomas James, it's, James Thomas."

Guess what? He still messed it up from time to time. When it happened, James Thomas would look at me and smile as if to say: *"He did it again."*

Culture Experience

In October 1962 I met a very pretty girl at South Park named Carol Gardon, who I liked a lot. She lived on Clinton near Bailey in the area known as Kaisertown. I went to a dance with her at a school on Clinton. When the music started playing, it was a moment of instant culture shock! They were playing Polka music and Carol wanted me to dance. "Wait a minute!" A French Canadian boy from South Park did not dance the polka. Why? Because it's the Polka! It wasn't what we did in our neighborhood at Timon or Fazio's Hall. But in that neighborhood there was great pride for their Polish heritage. I found it interesting that the young people were into it. That's what they did – polka music and polka dancing. In South Buffalo, we were into the music of Elvis, Bobbie Vinton, The Drifters, Dion, Ray Charles, the Four Seasons, the Everly Brothers and Chubby Checker. The dances we were into were what you'd see on American Bandstand; not polka music or polka dancing. I wasn't a good dancer anyway. I was lucky I could slow dance, let alone do the polka! I did manage to get in a few slow dances with her though.

Chapter Thirteen
Let's go Shopping Downtown

In 1940, Buffalo's population was ranked 14th in the United States; in 2016 it fell to around 26th. It certainly has seen better days. There were a lot of stores in South Buffalo during the Baby Boomer era, but downtown Buffalo had many more and different ones.

Getting to Main Street in downtown Buffalo was easy from all three main South Buffalo streets. You took the #15 bus from Seneca Street, the #14 bus from Abbott Road or the #16 from South Park at a cost of 15 cents a ride in the 60s.

Going downtown back then was like any big city in the United States. There were all sorts of department stores, specialty boutiques, lots of theatres, restaurants, bars, the Hippodrome poolroom, great nightclubs with great bands and very well-known performers.

Just about everyone from any of the seven main South Buffalo areas went downtown, either regularly or occasionally. You could do serious shopping there or have a choice of over half a dozen movie houses: Shea's-Loew's Tech, Hippodrome, Center, Shea's Buffalo, the Century, the Lafayette, Broadway or the Palace.

Before the malls existed the big attractions were department stores like AM&A's, Hengerer's, Berger's, Hens & Kelly's, Kresges, Kleinhan's, Woolworth's and of course, Sears and Roebuck. During Christmas time these stores were packed with shoppers. Main Street was full of cars, busses and cabs. Sidewalks were jammed with pedestrians. The great choice of stores provided excellent competitive prices. You could shop cheaper or go high class if you could afford it. By the way, those were the days most of the purchases were done in cash.

A Bit of Credit Card History

Credit cards first came into play in 1946 but it wasn't until 1959 that American Express introduced the first plastic credit card. There were other cards prior to the plastic American Express card but they were made of cardboard or celluloid. In 1959, we had Master Card followed in 1966 by Bank of America. Visa and Discover followed. With all those credit cards available, they came to be known as plastic money. It was very convenient to make purchases but created a very slippery path to bankruptcy." Many are in deep debt today because of credit card use. Some people have multiple cards and use them all. I have one but I still prefer paying in cash

The Blue Law

It's very nice that we can shop seven days a week, but once upon a time, shopping on Sundays was not possible. How many of you can remember the Blue Law (also known as the Sunday Law) which dates back to 1781. If you remember, all stores used to be closed on Sunday. Even the milkman and the iceman didn't provide deliveries on Saturdays and Sundays. If there was a local deli on your block and the owner lived in the back of the store, you would knock on his door and ask if he would go into the store to get you a couple of quarts of milk to see you through Monday's milk delivery.

Businesses eventually saw that a lot of people who worked on Saturdays couldn't get to the stores; especially after many women who once stayed home joined the work force. That was money lost for the businesses. So, the Blue Law was relaxed and stores opened on Sundays around noon. Many closed between 5 PM and 6 PM. The law prohibiting the sale of alcoholic beverages on Sunday lasted longer but again, what about people who worked on Saturday and were only off on Sunday? That changed, but liquor stores could not open until noon.

Ice and Milk Delivery

Going back to the fifties in Québec, I remember home delivery of milk and ice Monday through Friday. We had an icebox rather than a refrigerator. The iceman would bring in a large 40 or 50 pound cube of ice and set in the icebox. Keeping ice cream in one

of those was not an option. As a matter of fact, what we call junk food today was not known to us. Ice cream was a once in a while treat for special occasions only that we could buy at the corner delicatessen for a nickel. Also in the fifties in Welland, Ontario, we still had a milkman delivering milk in a horse-drawn wagon. When we moved to South Buffalo in 1960, we had one of those little milk compartments at the back of the house where we left our empty quart glass bottles and the milkman would replace them with a fresh supply

No Cash

How many of you Baby Boomers remember neighbors borrowing bread, milk, sugar, butter, cream, coffee, money or cigarettes? We called it borrowing, but it was really a handout, except for money, that is. Most of the time, moms would replace a bottle of milk or loaf of bread, they borrowed. Your mom might have said to you:

"Hey, Shamus or Katherine, go over and ask Mrs. Milligan next door if I can borrow a cup of sugar and a couple of dollars? Tell her I'll pay her back when dad gets paid from the plant on Friday. Oh, and tell her I'd like a couple of cigarettes if she can spare them."

In our neighborhoods we were pretty much equals financially. So many folks were broke by the time payday rolled around. Dads worked steady jobs and a few moms too, but not many. They didn't over spend, and learned to stretch the dollar. Our parents went through the Depression years (1930s) when they had to do with a whole lot less than we ever did. Many of them knew about soup kitchens and soup lines. We never experienced that, thank God. When it came to budgeting money most moms were experts.

What Money to Spend?

Money was tight. I don't remember any kids having any steady pocket money back then. Some of us had a couple of coins, but it was an exception to see anyone with a few dollar bills in their wallet. In some households, there was the special treat of an allowance. Those of us whose parents didn't make this one of the benefits of being part of the family corporation were a bit jealous of those fortunate individuals who did get it. If a teen got a two, three or maybe five dollar allowance a week, they were fortunate. If we figure conservatively, $3.00 a week allowance came to $150.00 for the year. In those days, that was a lot of money for any teen. A lot of us were lucky to have a quarter in our pocket. Most kids asked their parents for enough money to cover a ten cent ice cream cone, a bottle of Coca Cola, the price of a movie ticket, fifty cents to skate at Skate Haven on Orchard Park Road or attend dances on Friday nights at Timon or Baker Victory High.

Admission to dances was fifty cents and a movie at the Capitol or Seneca show was around thirty-five cents in the late fifties and early sixties. You'd often hear from parents:

"Okay, you can go to the dance. Here's the money, but don't ask for any more this week. We've got bills to pay. Money don't grow on trees, you know."

Very often the answer would be, *"Sorry, I don't have anything to spare this week."*

The families I knew lived from paycheck to paycheck. Things were tight for a lot of folks. Many people didn't have a dollar left by the time Thursdays rolled around. Those families had to run tabs at local stores for a quart of milk, bread or baby food. There weren't many snacks around the house either. The cupboards had staple foods, not snacks. The meals we had were usually very basic. I remember my mom opening up a huge can of pork and beans for supper. We'd have that, a couple slices of bread and a glass of milk. "What's for dessert?" was not a question we asked. And forget having a snack before going to bed. That luxury wasn't part of Baby Boomer perks. Times were hard.

Hard Times

When Lackawanna Bethlehem Steel, employing over 20,000 men went on strike in June 10, 1959, many South Buffalo family men who worked there were in dire financial straits. Paychecks stopped. It was a very bad time. It was called *The Big Fight*. The strike lasted 116 days and people suffered greatly. One such family were the Smiths next door to us with seven mouths to feed. The Lackawanna plant produced steel from 1922 until 1983. Little by little, all 20,000 lost their job when it closed. The Buffalo area lost a great number of people who move elsewhere to find work.

Youths Earning Money

When we were pre to early teens, we could make $1 or $2 shoveling snow in the winter. Nobody, and I mean, nobody, had snow blowers then. We'd grab whatever shovel the family had and go knock on doors to see if people wanted their sidewalk and driveway shoveled. For the girls, the primary way of making a few bucks was babysitting.

As teens, many of us had a paper route. It was always good for a bit of spending money. I delivered the Courier Express seven days a week (1961-62) to houses on South Park between Choate and Bloomfield and I also had all of Bloomfield and Richfield streets. I had maybe fifty or sixty customers.

Other guys I knew who delivered the Courier Express were Joe Prendergast from Sheffield who he delivered on his street. Tony Pacella from Columbus delivered on his street and Tifft from South Park to McKinley Parkway. Joe Liberti from Tifft Street had about a hundred-sixty customers. He handled part of Tifft from South Park to Hopkins, Folger, Payne, Garvey and some of Hopkins Street. John Carney from Crystal delivered the Buffalo Evening News. We Courier Express delivery boys were up very early every single morning.

Prendergast said he was up around the time the Courier truck dropped off his bundle of paper around 4 AM or so. I was a bit lazier. I'd get up at five or five-thirty. I didn't like it at all but like I said, it was a bit of pocket money. The better paper route was delivering the Buffalo Evening News because it was an after school thing. There was no getting up in the wee hours of the morning. Not only that, the Buffalo Evening News didn't have a Sunday paper, only Monday through Saturday. Those carriers didn't have to deal with inserts or a super heavy load. A daily paper back then cost only 7 cents and the Sunday paper with all the advertising inserts, comics and special magazine sections was 20 cents. By 1963, the Sunday paper had gone up to 25 cents.

Price Check

It seems to me that the price of items were more reasonable back in the day. Here are prices of items in the 50s. Fresh bread cost about 12 cents a loaf, a quart of milk 20 cents, a pound of coffee 37 cents and a cup of coffee, a nickel. A phone call from a telephone booth could be made for 5 cents and a newspaper was also 5 cents. In the fifties and sixties a good size candy bar was a dime, a pack of Juicy Fruit gum, a nickel; large pretzel sticks, a penny each and a bottle of pop cost 12 cents. It was 10 cents for the liquid and 2 cents bottle deposit. There were no cans or plastic bottles then, only glass. Speaking of pop, I may be wrong, but I could swear Coca Cola tasted different in the fifties and sixties than it does today. There was a rumor going around that you could remove rust from chromed bumpers with Coke Cola. I never tried it myself but heard the rumor more than once.

Back in my teens, things were made in America. I don't remember reading the labels on my shirts or pants and seeing *Hecho en México* "Made in Mexico". Nor did I have anything made in Pakistan, China or some Central American country. Pretty much, everything we had was made in the States. A decent pair of shoes cost about $12 to $20. A pair of US Keds high top sneakers could be had for as low as $2.50 and basic girls' sneakers could be bought for $1.00. A good white, dress shirt cost $2.50 to $5.00 and pleated dress pants, $8 to $12.

Gasoline was around 23 to 26 cents a gallon and the average car cost between, $1,500 and $1,600. A new house at the end of my street went for $15,000 in the early sixties. That same house now is between $70,000 and $90,000; maybe more. The cost of a regular postage stamp is quite high compared to the five cent stamp of the sixties. When I was in the Army in 1966, I used to send a lot of letters back home. A regular stamp was five cents and airmail was seven cents.

Treats

Pizzas were one of the major takeout treats in the 50's and 60's at a fairly low price. Today, for some families it has become a scheduled meal of the week and not so cheap. I remember working for the Bocce Club Pizzeria in the early 60's on Clinton and Adam Street. A large 18 inch cheese pizza cost $1.80. If you wanted pepperoni the cost was $2.10. Today, that same size cheese and pepperoni pizza is around $20. Bocce's was very popular back then and people would come from all over for a Bocce Pizza.

South Buffalo and most neighborhoods had hot dog restaurants. The price for these tasty treats was around 20 cents each back in the late 50s and early 60s. Today, at Louie's Texas Red hots, they are $2.39 each. Comparing prices to today's makes Baby Boomers cringe. A regular cup of coffee which once cost a dime is now $1.50 or more.

Great Trash Pick Up Service

Talking about money, we got a lot for the taxes we paid to the city in sanitation service back in the day. We had curb service for trash day. Tim Fitzgerald who, in his younger days, worked for the sanitation department said:

"We had what we called Rollers. These were the guys who went into your yard starting at 4 AM, take the metal garbage cans from the back of the house and bring them to the curb for pickup. A lot of them used hand carts with wheels to roll out the heavy cans. Hence, the name, Rollers. After the trash pickups were made, the same guys or a different crew would come around and return the cans to the sides or backs of the houses."

I remember one of our own, Jack Pugh from Altruria Street who was big and very strong. He could pick up six full cans at a time and take them to the street. He'd put one under each arm, then grab two cans by the handles, two in each hand and off he'd go to the curb. That was a great service.

According to Jack, that lasted from around the fifties to the early eighties. He remembers that for a long time the city of Buffalo had over 600,000 residents. It whittled down to less than 300,000 as the city and surrounding areas lost a lot of manufacturing plants and people headed elsewhere to make a living. That is an immense drop. He also remembers that when he started out in with the sanitation department in the 1960's there were around 400 men working there. By the time he retired in the mid-eighties there were only about 85 men needed to take care of garbage pickup. The reason for that was the department got mechanized garbage trucks and didn't need so many men. The new trucks were equipped with a hydraulic compressing mechanism to cram as much trash into the truck container as possible. Only two men per truck were needed, same as today.

Hey Baby Boomers, remember in the old days, they only had open-bed dump trucks for our trash pickup? There were usually two guys on the ground and two guys in the dump-truck. Those on the ground would toss the cans onto the truck and the guys in the truck bed dumped them and threw the empties back down to the men on the ground. On and on it went, up and down each street.

185

Now, that was work. I always respected what they did. Those men really earned their money. There was a running joke among them with reference to their pay:

"We don't make a lot of money, but we have all we can eat."

Bad joke. God bless them."

NOTE: John J. "Jackie" Pugh left us much too soon at 65 years of age on January 27, 2012.

Chapter Fourteen
Activities and Hangouts

As with all of the South Buffalo areas, the South Park area had a ton of Baby Boomers on every street. The young people didn't have a lot but managed to stay busy doing one thing or another.

Baby Boomer, Margie Weber remembers:

"Who can forget Mr. Softee and his jack-in-the-box music? Ninety percent of the time he came at dinner time. And the carnival rides-remember the bumper cars on the back of a flatbed that went from street to street? Who needed Darien Lake or Fantasy Island? We had our own amusement park and refreshments out front. Talk about curb service. Then, there was the man who drove down periodically in the summer with comic books in his trunk for free. And, the man who hollered out of his truck window on hot summer days: 'Rags, rags for sale.' They were used as dust cloths and our Moms who would run out to get them. With the red smoke dust from the Coke Ovens blowing around, all windowsills had to be wiped down daily in summer. There were many times the sheets and other laundry had to be pulled off the line while drying outside and rewashed when Bethlehem Steel spewed out its red soot."

Friends

All the kids made many friends and knew a slew of the neighborhood people. A lot of the young folks formed their own little groups which was natural. Despite the groups that existed, just about everyone interacted and would play sports in Mulroy park behind Holy Family School, go to Timon dances on McKinley Parkway or at Fazio's Hall (also known as the Peppermint Lounge for a short while) at the corner of South Park and Southside. I went to school at Holy Family with Mr. Fazio's son. There was a soda shop across from Fazio's where we'd spend time drinking a malt and talking. In the winter, there was always the Cazenovia ice rink for outside open skate. The rink drew a lot of people from Seneca, Abbott McKinley and South Park.

Things to do in the Neighborhood

A lot of the kids from different streets met at someone's house with their circle of friends and played all sorts of games or hung out and talked about anything and everything imaginable. Some would play catch or baseball on some lot, wrestle, hop garages or play basketball if they were lucky enough to have a basketball net in their yard. My neighbor, Brian McDonald had a basketball net on his garage and I played there for a while till I moved into another group of friends as did Brian.

A couple friends of mine and I would meet up at the Cazenovia ice rink with a few of the girls from our school, Margie Morrison, Anne Schneeberger and Karen Lobuglio. We would also go to CYO group skate nights at Skate Haven on Abbott Road in Lackawanna. Skate Haven became Lucarelli's Banquet Hall. Skates were the old style four-wheel roller skates with two wheels in back, two in front and a rubber stopper at the toe. It was always funny watching people who couldn't skate well, crashing into the walls to stop.

Some of the guys and girls we mixed with were:

Sam and Joe Parisi, Bill Nicholson, John Lafferty, Brian Moran, Joe Prendergast, John Tevington, Bill Graber, Jim McDonald, Nick Vertalino, Lenny Weber, Joe Calabrese and Marilyn (Sue) Lafko, and Rosemary Stebbins, Marjorie Weber, Adele Petrilli, Mary Bussman, Carmela and Danny Giganti, Susan Padolic, Margie Morrison, Ann Schneeberger, Barbara Buckley, Kathy Pugh, Diane Macri, Maureen Masterson, Patricia Nigro, and Margaret Tomasello.

The Playgrounds

A lot of the guys went to schoolyards or playgrounds to meet up with friends and pass hours chatting and playing. Those who went to local parks played sports like softball, baseball and basketball and football. Most games were pick-up games. They weren't organized by adults. Guys got together, picked sides and played – for the sake of playing. That was nice. Lots of good times.

There were several parks in South Buffalo that kept the youth occupied: Mungovan Park on South Side Parkway/Bailey Avenue near the present site of Southside Elementary School. Hillery Park on Mineral Springs Road, Mulroy Park behind Holy Family on Tifft Street and the Okell Playground behind School #29. They were busy from morning till night in the summer time. Some baseball, softball and basketball games were often organized by park athletic directors all over the area. Caz Park had great baseball diamonds in the bowl.

Mulroy Playground, Activities and Crap Games

As parks go, Caz Park was the gem of parks for South Buffalo. The biggest draw for sure were the pools and its casino for the kids, and a golf course for adults. Tons of kids and teens from all over spent hours there. But Mulroy playground was also very special. In the summer, George Hermann was in charge of the park building that had bathrooms and a section for sports equipment. He would hand out the equipment. The park had horse shoe pits, a half and full basketball court, swings, slides, teeter-totters, a small pool for the kids, and baseball diamonds. I can't forget the picnic tables under the tree near the equipment building where guys would congregate and play cards, mostly pinochle. I watched them play and tried to catch on but I was too dumb I guess. I could never follow what they were doing. I heard terms like:

Aces or Kings around, Bare run, Bid up, Meld bid, Runs and Marriage, Common marriage, Royal marriage, Lead back, Round house, Trump, Trick, Jack of Diamonds and Queen of Spades. I just couldn't process all that.

Crap Games

Shooting craps was much easier to follow. The games went on everywhere in Buffalo. In our own area, breaking up crap games was one of the activities that kept the local police busy. Some played at Mulroy Park and other crews would go behind PS #29. The games usually took place in the summer months after the parks closed and all the little kids were gone or on Sunday afternoon. The bets weren't usually very large. Normally they were 25 or 50 cents or dollar bets. No one had very much money to gamble with. At Mulroy, if someone yelled "cops", everyone would scramble to pick up their money and run like hell. As you can imagine, some of the guys weren't very choosy as to what part of the pot they picked up in their rush to pick up and run. The games would go on all summer long. A few guys were scooped up by the police, interrogated a bit then, let go. I don't remember anyone having to go to court for this. It was one of those things that was harmless, but still, against the

189

law. Guys as young as twelve to grown men played. I remember Pat L, an Italian teen guy the cops had in a lineup in the park. When the police asked his name, he said with a Spanish accent: *"My name...José Jimenez."* He was imitating a Hispanic comedian that was popular at the time. The group got yelled at and released.

One dice player I remember had a short scruffy beard - wore a baseball cap and metatarsal shoes from the steel plant. He was only known as "Pops." He spoke very little, and when he did, he was soft-spoken, saying only what needed to be said to place his bets. Now, Mulroy Park is a shadow of what it was. Too bad. It once was a great place to meet up with friends, hang out and play sports.

Some kids stayed beyond the park's closing time. The police would come by and shag them out as it got dark. Of course, kids would be obedient to the law officers - until they left. Then, some would go back in. For the most part, it was to sit around, chat and smoke cigarettes.

Speaking of the police, COPS (Constables on Patrol) rode in cars, usually in pairs. I also remember policemen walking a beat back then. Many of the officers walked up and down South Park, Abbott and Seneca. A lot of them got to know the locals personally. I can't deny that a few of our young men got to visit their local Precinct on occasion where they were detained for inappropriate behavior and had a time out inside a jail cell.

More Police Involvement in the Neighborhood

For the most part, the neighborhoods were safe and peaceful. There were very few incidents that would be deemed as criminal or posing a danger to the general public. Most of the problems came from too many young people hanging out on street corners during the warm weather with nothing to do. Remember, the Baby Boomers were numerous and hanging around the house with siblings wasn't fun. Hanging around with people their own age, usually on street corners, provided them with a way of passing time, have a few laughs and talk about whatever was on their mind. Guys shared a lot of useful information among themselves, as well as bad. It was the same for the girls wherever they congregated. Let's be honest, that's probably where most teens learned about the bird and the bees.

Now and then, since there were so many bars on all the main strips, there were times a drunk would be confronted by law officers and maybe taken home in the squad car or sent home in a cab. On street corner hangouts, police would sometime come by and break up groups when they got too large or boisterous. Some even got hauled off to local precincts when the requests to move along or disperse weren't obeyed.

Group Arrested

One such incident happened when a group of older teens got arrested in front of PS #29 back in 1963 for loitering and rowdy behavior. They were put into three squad cars, hauled off to Precinct 15 and put in their cells. Then, the lads got a ride downtown in the Paddy Wagon to the Holding Center for the night. The next day all nine stood before the judge. It was one of those cases that should not have gone that far. I believe the Cops were a bit frustrated with so many young guys loitering on so many corners that they figured it was time to make an example of this crew. The case was dismissed with a strong warning from the judge to *"Stay off the street corners."*

The law officers proved their point and the boys now had to deal with mom and dad. By the way, all nine made the Buffalo Evening News with names, ages and streets they lived on. How embarrassing. From then on, they made better choices as to where they hung out.

Hopping Garages

Not all of the kids read books, belonged to groups who did creative things or spent their time constructively. A lot of the Baby Boomers did not have much direction, or goals they were working towards at that age. One of the activities some of the young men used to take part in was hopping garages. If you're not familiar with this activity, you're in for an eye-opener. There were only select individuals who took part in this activity. It wasn't a sport or a game. It wasn't even logical. It was a dare thing. I remember one of the streets where they would hop garages was Whitfield Street. The first dumb thing was they started on the roof of the firehouse that was right behind the Precinct #15 Police Station. The second dumb thing was that the first garage was a ten-foot drop from the roof of the firehouse. They could have broken a leg, twisted an ankle or worse, gone right through the roof and landed on who knows what inside the garage.

The game plan here was to go from one garage to the other as they alternated left, right, left, right. Most were close enough that it would take only a short jump to get from one to the other. They could go to a certain point then have to go back because the next garage was not close enough to jump onto. Once though, they went as far as they could and all sat on the roof of the last garage and pondered whether or not they could make it to the next one and continue down the street. The only problem was that it was at least a twelve foot leap to grab the edge of the flat-roof. Then, they'd have to do a pull-up to get on top of the roof. No one bit on that idea except one guy. He chewed on the idea for a few minutes, then, took a run, leapt and slammed his entire body against the side of the garage as he tried to grab onto the ledge. It didn't end there. Down on the ground with his knees killing him from the crash, he was stuck. The only two ways out were the driveway where a lady was screaming at him, *"Get out of my yard"* alongside her barking, growling German shepherd or take route number two; escape over the neighbor's fence where there were thorny rose bushes. You have to ask yourself the question at this point in the story; which option would you have chosen. Which one do you think our flying ace chose?

Choice number #1 - the driveway where the dog was, that could have chewed him up a bit? OR

Choice number #2 - go for the fence with the rose bushes and receive cuts, lacerations and abrasions?

The sanest thing to do in the minds of the guys atop the roof counseling him was for him to take the bushes. He struggled for a few seconds in the middle of his confusion and pain with the dog barking, the lady yelling and the guys telling him to go for the fence; he finally took the advice of his loving buddies and over the fence and through the bushes he went. Yes, he got some nasty scratches and cuts but was spared dog bites. We kind of wondered what would have happened to him if he had taken the driveway toward the lady and the dog.

Dumb Fun Winter Activity,

About the only readily available winter activities we had were: ice skating, sledding, tobogganing and skiing. Well, don't you know, for the guys, there was one more fun thing to do when the snow fell. Those of you who lived during that time must remember hitching a ride on the back bumpers of cars, trucks or busses when there was snow on the streets. You'd hook onto a bumper, do boot-skiing, and go as far as you dared. If the car was going fairly fast when you let go, your legs couldn't keep up with the momentum and you'd end up rolling around like a desert tumbleweed; and the guys watching you would laugh and laugh at you. It was really funny to watch. It was the same for the poor schnooks who would be seen hitting dry pavement during their joy ride. They would end up with road rash. Again, the guys watching this would have a good laugh - but the bashed up victims didn't find it funny.

Chapter Fifteen
People around the Neighborhood

Just about everybody in these neighborhoods could relate to a ton of people from their respective area. Bob Greene sent me a list of 75 names of people he either hung around with or was familiar with. Eileen Leahy, along with her brothers and parents came up with over 72 friends and acquaintances from their immediate area from the old days.

One of the guys who moved from Lackawanna to South Buffalo was Chuck Aldridge. His brother Bobby was a Golden Gloves Champ boxer and New York State champ. We called Chuck "Elvis." He lived on my street (Altruria) and was known to walk right down the middle of the street when he left his house. We all knew that. From a distance, even at night in the dark we'd see a figure walking towards us and we knew... here comes Elvis. We came to call him that because he looked a little like Elvis and had a certain swagger when he walked. To us, he was cool. He wasn't arrogant and didn't play the tough guy although he had some size to him. He was soft-spoken and friendly but we knew not to say anything stupid or mess with him. He'd walk by and we'd say "Hi Chuck." He'd come back with something like: "How yous doin'?"

We got along fine. He was one of us, an Altruria guy; a South Buffalo, South Park guy. I'm sure that in all the other sections of South Buffalo it was the same. Kids had older popular guys and girls they looked up to for one reason or other.

Several guys from our neighborhoods passed way too soon. One was Roger Brennan. He lived right next to Ullenbruch's Delicatessen. He was a real nice guy, quiet, always pleasant and probably one of the few guys I ever met that didn't have a mean bone in his body. He passed in his early twenties maybe. Another guy from the neighborhood who passed was Mike Knezevich who lived on Richfield and died in a car crash. Ted Pasiecznik from Aldrich Street also died in one on McKinley Pkwy around 1971 when he hit a tree near the Erie County Fairground. Ted married a girl name Brenda, served in the armed forces as a paratrooper, trained in Panama and went to Viet Nam.

Speaking of Vietnam, I must mention Tim Nightingale, a marine from Altruria Street. He died in one of the Viet Nam fields on 4/6/68, five months shy of his 19th birthday. His mother Peg was given Tim's Purple Heart. There were several more South Buffalo area soldiers who died in Nam, I'm sure. Whoever they are, I salute and commend them also.

Another guy from the neighborhood who passed away was Richie Yox. He is well remembered by an awful lot of guys. If you mentioned Richie on the South Park strip, most guys would know who you were talking about. He lived near the Harding Street area. He had trouble processing information. I remember that he had to carry a pad and pen to keep track of things. His short-term memory wasn't good. One of the neat things about Rich was that he could play the guitar. He often brought it out on the strip, sat down on a store front stoop and began playing and singing. Eventually, that playing paid off. He hooked up with Chuck Carr (Crystal Ave), one of South Buffalo's many talented musicians. They formed a group and had gigs all over the Buffalo area. One of the bands Chuck formed was "Flashback." In his youth, before music, he was a top basketball player. There weren't many in the area who could match his court skills. Chuck passed away in December of 2016.

Other Neighborhood Groups

There were frat groups. The Esquires consisted of older guys like Johnny and Tony Orsini. The Little Esquires wanted to emulate the older guys and tagged on little in front of Esquires. They consisted of Pat and Joe Liberti, Andy Collura, Tony and Mario Pacella, Sam Parisi, Bobby Domzolski and Tom Willard. They had frat jackets with Greek lettering for the Latin version of Veni, Vidi, Vici "I Came, I Saw, I Conquered". There were a few other such organized groups. It was all done as a way of belonging to a group, doing things together and having fun; much like Sam Accordino's group near Taylor Park.

Right across from our house were a couple of cousins, Frank Morabito who lived downstairs and Frank Mariano who lived upstairs and were friends with my brother Jacques. They had their own crew that hung out. Some of the names connected to them are Mike and Corky Hess, Neil Curtin, Bob Ulrich, Ray Colpoys, Tom Tighe, Tommy Ford, Dick Kemp, Paul, Owen and Gail Roland, Tommy and Jimmy Lasker and Dick Brown.

They would gather at the Deco at the corner of Harding and South Park. From there, they'd go wherever there was an event or a place to meet up with others for car races, boxing matches, and billiard games downtown, parties or bars where bands were playing.

A few of the guys who come to mind as some of the first to ride motorcycles down South Park Avenue were Mike Hess, Joe McGir and Bobby Fulmer. Joe once came down the strip a la Evel Knievel at about thirty miles an hour, jumped up on the seat, stood up, arms up to the side and coasted for a while doing what was called a Flying Eagle. A couple of the guys were connected to Buffalo motorcycle clubs, the Leathermen and the Road Vultures. That lifestyle lasted only a short time.

Joe was a fairly good golfer. One of the ways he kept a supply of golf balls was to dive into South Park Lake and scoop up all the balls he could find that the less talented golfers either hooked or sliced into the lake. He made a few dollars selling dozen to golfers who frequented the South Park Golf Course.

A list that Dennis Wojciechowski "Smokey" gave me of guys who hung out together between the Deco, the pool room and a few bars were Danny Shea, Jimmy "Stanley Stingray" Wilczak, Earl "The Duke" Thompson, Danny Jordon, Bill Nicholson Mickey Guzda, Mike Colern, Paul Aquisto, Carmen Nappo, Frank Daliusio, Carl and Dave Villalobos, Jimmy "Shy" Shine, Angelo "Sonny" Ferrari from Hayden Ave (off Seneca Street), Jim Buckley, Dan Manley, Rick Gianoni, Bill Clancey, Paul and Denny McDonald, Eddy Dacey, Billy McKuen, Harry Everly and Smokey, himself.

Very often, individuals from different groups would mix in with others for a while then reconnect with their original crew, while remaining friends with past acquaintances. The whole phenomenon was great.

On summer nights in the early sixties, a group of fourteen to sixteen year olds hung out at the Hartman's house on Lockwood Avenue. This bunch included Sharon Pieczynski her twin sisters, Jeanne and Joan Hartman, Jerry Bonafede, Pat and Joe Liberti, Sam Parisi, John Carney, Tony Pacella, John Harmon, Tom Willard, Bob Domzalski, Paul Williams and Mike Banko.

Another group who hung out near Tifft and South Park included Roger Pasquerella, Sam Bambrick, Lou Sprague, Bob Duke, Jimmy Miller from Pries Street, Jim Patterson and Sam Parisi.

Chapter Sixteen

South Buffalo area individuals whose names became well-known

Pitcher Warren Spahn

Spahn was born in April of 1921 and spent his formative years in Buffalo's Kaisertown. He played ball for South Park School. That led to him signing with the Boston Braves in 1940. He was a southpaw, the best left-handed pitcher, ever.

One of his trade-marks was his high kick as he got ready to pitch the ball. The famous sports writer Al Silverman wrote:

"Watching Spahn for the first time go into his delivery was an esthetic experience. The Spahn windup was the most picturesque, most graceful, the most beautiful windup I had ever seen." (Source: Buffalo News Feb. 29, 2016)

Buffalo honored him by changing the name of Cazenovia Parkway at Seneca to Warren Spahn Way. Former Mayor Jimmy Griffin was very instrumental in changing the street name. Spahn was one of Griffin's heroes. Spahn died in November 2003 at the age of 82 in Oklahoma.

Steve Banko Highly Decorated Viet Nam Vet

Steve Banko III, born in 1946 is another South Buffalo son. His father Steve Banko II was of Czechoslovakian descent, and his mother Pauline (Post) Banko was from Texas. The family first settled in the Valley on Elk Street and moved to Koester Street when he was five. He is second in line of eight children. The list goes like this: Jim, Steve, Mike, Paula, Margaret, Mary, Tom and Danny. He attended Holy Family School, Timon High, Saint Bonaventure College and then to UB to earn his BA degree in 1973. He also took journalism courses at Buffalo State College in 1976.

Pre-war and pre-college, Steve had friends from South Park, Abbott, McKinley Pkwy, Seneca Street and a few other close neighborhoods. Some of the memories of his younger days in South Buffalo include hooking up with his crowd of friends at Holy Family Parochial School such as: Jim Bausch, Joe Leary, Bob Domzolski,

Jerry Bonafede, Bob Duke, Judy Conrad, Janice McGrath, Mary Zucarelli, and Jane Ward

Friends from Timon High years include Mike Kull, Mike Grys, Paul Fitzpatrick, Greg Calveric, John Collins, Suzie Bradley and Sue Gallagher.

Some of his favorite hangouts during grade school were Mulroy Park, Parsons Judd, Friday night Timon dances and during high school years, it was LaBella's Pizzeria on Abbott. When he hit legal drinking age, he could be found at Michler's Bar on Abbott Road. By the way, he readily admitted that during the time of the Squeaks and the Rocks, he was a Squeak.

Playing basketball was one of his passions. He played a lot B-ball at Mulroy Playground under the watchful eye of playground supervisor, George Hermann. Here's what he had to say about Mr. Hermann:

> *"The role of George Hermann in the lives of many young men in the South Buffalo area can't be overstated. He was equal parts; coach, teacher, mentor and surrogate father. So many of our own fathers were working in back-breaking, mind-numbing jobs like those in plants and mills. They rarely had time to see us play, to help us get to games, or guide us. They were too busy earning a living and keeping us food, clothing and shelter. So, men like George at Mulroy, which is now George Hermann Playground, and Paul Head at Hillery Playground on Mineral Springs, went way beyond the call of their profession and really impacted our lives."*

So many of the guys around Steve's age spent hours playing ball on the playground courts. He related in an article that he witnessed one of the best games ever played at Mulroy Park. Some of the players were: Billy Roberts, Louis McManus, Duke Forsythe, Tony Bevillaqua, Whitey Martin, Mike Marley, Bob Duke and Kevin Milligan.

In 1967 he was drafted and went to Fort Benning, Georgia for basic training and then Fort Dix for advance training. On January 20, 1968 he went to Viet Nam for his first tour of duty. He saw a lot of action. One of the most terrifying and heart wrenching things he experienced was his entire company being wiped out. Many close Army buddies died on the battle field. Having made it out alive, he's had to live with that... not an easy thing to do. Time may heal all wounds, but scars remain. He was seriously wounded in December of 1968 when he sustained a shattered leg being hit by shrapnel. He also suffered burns to his hands. From the Viet Nam fields he was sent to Yokota, Japan for his medical care. He did a second tour starting on October 1, 1969 to January 28, 1970. In all, he was wounded six times during battles.

For his wounds and service to our country Steve was awarded Four Purple Hearts, two Bronze Stars for valor, two Bronze Stars for service and a Silver Star, our nation's 3rd highest award for valor. Although he was highly decorated as a soldier, here's what he had to say concerning those medals:

"I had the misfortune of being in a lot of action that resulted in a lot of wounds and a few medals. The wounds are more of a reminder of my service than the medals."

He listed some other guys he knew who served our country; not all went to Nam.

John Ranne, Jimmy Riley, and Gerry Nostrant from his class of '65 at Timon who were "grunts" along with Mike Kapture and Tom Glavey. He said that Joe Duffy O'Connor from Baker High was a decorated MP. Joe Duffy was another grunt from St. Ambrose and Timon (class '65.) Other guys Steve knew that went to Nam were Dave Fennessey from St. Theresa's. He was in the 101st Airborne and was killed in action during his second tour on May 20, 1967. Then, there was Bobby Smith from Seneca Street, also killed in action as was Jimmy Cummings from Good Avenue and Tim Nightingale from Altruria Street. Others guys who served were: Paul Schaeffer from the Seneca-Babcock area, one of the Fitzgibbons boys and retired Buffalo firefighter Phil Ryan from Seneca Street.

He mentioned that he served with another South Buffalo man, Jim "Mo" Maloney and that he knew his brother Dan and his mother Annie who worked at Michler's Tavern. He also remembered another guy who was a Marine, Terry Cannan who went to St. Tommy's and Baker Victory High. Steve said: *"Terry took a bunch of shrapnel in his legs."*

After Nam, Steve went through some rough times as did many of the men who returned after having experienced the hell war brings. He saw a lot of gore and death all around him during battles, especially when his company got wiped out. Here's what he had to say about that:

"I survived because of a lot of guys and a lot of heroism. That in itself creates other psychological issues, including 'survivor guilt'; feeling bad about living when so many of your friends died."

In Nam, he battled the Viet Congs and when he came back, drinking became his enemy. After several years in that battle, he won the war. To date, he's been clean for the past 37 years.

He attended the University of Buffalo and St. Bonaventure. He was in government for three decades. His first position was as advisor to former Mayor Anthony Masiello. He then held a position with New York State's HUD Department as Field Supervisor. He oversaw 48 of New York's 62 HUD operations.

He hosted the Viet Nam War Memorial Moving Wall when it came to the Buffalo area. It was first displayed at Chestnut Ridge in 1989 and again in 1995 at the waterfront's Naval Park.

In 2009 he delivered a speech to a Veterans' Expo in Utica, New York. It was judged as "The Best Speech of the Year" by the Cicero Foundation. In 2009 he spoke again at the Purple Heart Memorial on the Memorial Walk of Buffalo's waterfront. That speech was published on Memorial Day and Vice President Joe Biden quoted Steve by name at the National Address at Arlington Cemetery. He has spoken to audiences in more than twenty cities across America.

"Thank you Steve for your heroic actions and faithful service to America. Those who went know firsthand how it was; and what horrible memories they carried back home with them. A special thought to the many who may still be tormented by it all. God's best to you. We salute you." -RRR

Tim Russert

I must include Tim Russert in the lineup of South Buffalo-connected achievers. He was the most notable individual from our neighborhood. The son of Timothy "Big Russ" and Elizabeth Seeley Russert, he grew up on Woodside Avenue near McKinley. Tim was honored by Woodside being given a second name, *Tim Russert Way*. He too walked the very same streets many of us walked. He frequented the pharmacies,  delicatessens, soda shops, library, movie theatres, parks and eateries that most of us did. He went to the same elementary school I went to, Holy Family. He then went to Saint Bonaventure on Seneca Street after his family moved from Woodside. His high school stint was at Canisius.

Like most of us from the area, he came from a blue collar family, holding the same values, faith, ideals and convictions as most folks who live near him and his family. The one exception about Tim Russert was that he looked way beyond what any of us did. No one I knew from the neighborhood had any notion of becoming a nationally known celebrity. I'm sure Tim didn't know this as a teen or young man in South Buffalo, but he took steps that led him on to achieve celebrity status. He established himself as one of the nation's top TV commentator, reporter and show host. He became a political analyst/commentator and hosted the very well- known show *Meet the Press*, for NBC.

He visited Buffalo on a regular basis and expressed his great love for South Buffalo on many occasions. In his book written in the early part of 2000 called *"Big Russ and Me,"* he mentioned some of the very same places I've already mentioned. It was apparent in his story that he felt very much at home in the neighborhood and had a great time being raised there. He left us suddenly when he suffered a heart attack in Washington on June 13, 2008. The ceremonies and memorials that took place to honor him were simply amazing. His wake was attended by numerous notables such as President Bush, former President Clinton, a great number of TV colleagues, senators, singers, actors and other prestigious people. One of the state politicians proposed a bill to name part of Route 20A near the Bills' Stadium, after him. For a South Buffalo boy who did extremely well, that was a fitting and honorable tribute. He was one of the Buffalo Bills biggest fans. At the end of his Meet the Press shows, when the Bills were scheduled to play, you'd hear him say, *"Go Bills!"*

Dave Caruso

photo courtesy of Det. Mark R. Stamback

David was born and raised in the South Park-Hopkins area of Saint Agatha's Parish. He lived on Lilac Street with parents, Vincent and Jennie; brothers, James and Michael and a sister, Connie. He went to elementary PS #28 and Hutch Tech High where he graduated from in 1964. During his teen years there were a few people he hung around with who were close friends. He stated that he probably associated with at least a couple of hundred people his age back then but couldn't possibly remember them all. That's the way it was with most of the guys and young ladies in South Buffalo. Everyone knew a slew of people outside their immediate circle of friends. Some of the people he hung out with were:

Joe Morganti, Dan Podgorny, Greg Collins, Barry Russell, Bill McCoey, Jim Parks, Rick Jones, Karen Maroone, Sue Jindra, Jeanne Grosjean, and Bonnie Eich.,

Places his crew hung out as teens were The Villa Pizzeria, Timon dances, Capitol Theatre and Caz Park.

He did what all of the South Buffalo guys did, swimming and baseball at Caz Park and football at Mungovan Playground. Cazenovia Park was one common thread among all of the South Buffalo guys I interviewed. Everybody went there mainly for swimming and baseball no matter what area of South Buffalo they were from.

In 1964, Dave went to Buffalo State Teacher's College where he majored in English. After a short stint as a college student, he changed his mind and pursued a career in law enforcement.

He began as a Police Cadet in 1966 and worked out of City Hall's Police Athletic League (PAL) Office. In 1967 he started his police duties as a patrolman out of the Old First Ward's 7th Precinct. For several years he also supervised PAL leagues at the Summer Street Youth Center in the Walden and Bailey area.

In 1980 he was promoted to Lieutenant and was stationed at Precinct 15 on South Park. In 1983, he became a Captain and worked out of Precinct 3, the downtown station that was located in the old Grey Hound bus station on Main Street near Tupper. In 1990, he was again promoted to the rank of inspector. Until his retirement in 1996 he was then stationed at the old Precinct 15 which was South District Headquarters on South Park. I asked him if he thought cops should still be walking a beat in the neighborhoods like in the old days. He said:

"Walking the beat is one of the elements of community policing the Department still uses to some degree."

I asked him for names of some of the men on the force that were close colleagues or served with him. Here's a short list:

Bob Carey, George "Hobie" Amplement, Norm Appleford, Pat O'Brian (Abbott Road lad) Bill Vivian, Joe O'Shei, John Montondo of the Old First Ward, Joe and Lenny Weber from Crystal Street, John Brill of the Old First Ward and the Harmons, Kevin Sr., Kevin Jr, and John from Crystal Street.

The topic of precincts came up. I asked Dave what he thought about the closing of precinct houses the Baby Boomers were used to having in their neighborhoods. Was it a good or bad idea to do that? He said:

"The time was right. With the population shrinking and the fact that most of the precinct houses were old and in poor condition, I believe the decision to go to larger district headquarter facilities to accommodate a modern police force was a right decision."

The five main district headquarters that resulted were: District A,B,C,D, and E. Focusing on the South Buffalo area; District A presently covers what once was Precinct 7 in the Old First Ward and Valley areas, Precinct 9 is the Seneca Street and the Seneca-

Babcock areas, and Precinct 15 handles the South Park, McKinley and Abbott areas.

I asked David to give me an example of something that made him wonder about his career choice. He said:

"During my rookie year on the Department, UB along with many other college campuses was experiencing some unrest due to the Viet Nam conflict. One evening, several patrol units were dispatched to the campus. Lines were formed with police and demonstrators facing each other. The atmosphere was very tense and unfriendly. I noticed some acquaintances were on the other side and I wondered whether or not I had I picked the right career. That thought hit me even harder as the order was given to move in to disperse the crowd. As we did this, we passed a demonstrator with crutches sitting on the ground. As we moved along, he got up and hit an officer with one of his crutches."

As with most of my interviewees, I asked Dave what his feelings were about the South Buffalo he knew as a Baby Boomer

"South Buffalo was a great community with strong family values and family ties. It was a place where everyone had numerous friends from diverse nationalities."

Daniel Shea

Dan hailed from Evanston Street, off Downing. He went to PS #29 and South Park High. Like so many of the Baby Boomers, he too hung out with a crew of guys on several of the street corners, mixing it up with people he knew from other crews or areas of South Buffalo. He mentioned that he hung out at Harry's pool hall between Choate and Bloomfield and that he spent a lot of time there with many of the guys from his area and others from up and down the South Park Avenue strip.

He felt that most of the guys from South Buffalo had an advantage over guys from the suburbs in the way of moxie, meaning: cleverness, having skills or street sense to deal with the kind of life people experienced in South Buffalo. This was not so much the case during elementary school age but was more as he got into high school and encountered people from numerous areas of Buffalo. He learned about different ethnic group mentalities, different crowd

203

mentality, drinking, drug problems, and respecting turfs. He, along with everybody else, learned early on about boundaries.

Part of his crew were Jimmy Reidy, Vinny Catanzaro (Seneca-Babcock), Mike Catanzaro (OFW), Earl (St. John) Thompson, Jim "Stanley Stingray" Wilzak, Pete Chmura, Gary Williams and a few older guys, Tom "Bull" Kate; at one time considered the toughest guy in South Buffalo.

Then, there was Bill Held and Butch Wilson who he hung with once in a while. He remembered that a lot these guys and others would gather behind School #29 to play craps.

As for growing up in South Buffalo, here's what he had to say:

"I was always proud to say I was born and raised in South Buffalo. We had deep roots and a sense of pride in the neighborhood. Good old South Buffalo. It was sacred."

As Dan got into police work, his street knowledge came in handy when he had to deal with all sorts of behavioral and criminal cases. He made his mark in law enforcement on the Hamburg Police Department. He began as patrolman and moved up the ladder to Detective, Lieutenant and finally retired as a Captain.

Billy McEwen - Music Man

Billy McEwen lived on West Woodside Street and went to Public School #29 with a lot of the other South Buffalo boys. He too, hung out with his own crew of guys but mixed it up with numerous other crews. By the age of sixteen, Eddy Dacey prompted Billy to start a band. That's when his singing career in the Buffalo area started. He remembers playing in the Stix and Stones Band in 1965 at Michler's Lounge, 410 Abbott Road and Portland as the house band. He said:

"We'd play Friday and Saturday nights and got $12 a night."

The very first time I saw Billy singing, barefoot no less, was in 1965 at one of the bars out at the lake called the Grand View Casino on Old Lakeshore Road. The place was packed. This was a time of the *music revolution.* We were into The Beatles, The Rolling Stones, Sly and the Family Stones, The Animals, CCR, The Monkeys, The Young Rascals, Jimmy Hendrix, Paul Revere and The Raiders, Donovan, Bob Dylan, Neil Diamond, The Who, The Guess Who, The Beach Boys, Crosby, Stills, Nash and Young, Peter, Paul and Mary and so on. New bands were springing up all over the country. Billy did great cover tunes and some originals. He quickly developed a following that stayed with him for years.

Checking proof at the door back then was slacker and there were many under-aged individuals who slipped through. There were hordes of full of energy young people looking to drink, have a good time in nightclubs and find good music groups to dance to. Billy's bands were of that caliber.

Billy said he used to play the Grand View Casino five or six nights a week and made $75. He was paid in single dollar bills that came from the dollar a head cover charge. The owner was a man by the name of Eddy Monin who also owned a couple of other bars in the area where Billy and his bands got to play also. Monin told Billy that his gigs had earned him $250,000 in the summer of '65 at the Grand

205

View alone. Billy wondered why he didn't get a bigger share of the take. Oh well, as they said in the Godfather movie:

"It's not personal. It's business."

He also became the lead singer in the bands Bo Diddly, Posse and, Billy McEwen and the Soul Invaders. The bands were some of the best known in the Buffalo band circuit. His soulful singing and great harmonica playing became well known throughout the Western New York area. He's also pretty good on conga drums.

Besides singing engagements all over Western New York and beyond, he was the voice in a number of radio and television commercials. You may have heard him in commercials for; AM&A's, Tops Market, City Mattress, Holiday Valley Ski Resort, Buffalo Raceway, Delta Bingo, Keyser Cadillac, Auto Place, Dick's Sporting Goods, Skill Buick, Heritage Stove Shop and several more.

To his credit, he is in the Buffalo Music Hall of Fame along with Seneca Street son, Joe Head. Billy and Joe did a lot of gigs together with another great Buffalo Music Hall of Famer and one of the best base players around, Jim Brucato. One of the places they often graced their listening audiences was Talty's Bar.

Ask most people of the 60's generation in the Buffalo area who regularly went out to listen to local bands if they ever heard of Billy McEwen, and 90% of the time you will get the answer:

"Oh sure I know him. My friends and I went to hear him sing many times."

Billy Held

Bill Held, another notable from South Buffalo, along with brothers Larry and Dwayne, came from Cantwell Street. As crews go, he was part of one with such individuals as:

Doug Kroll, Doug Alessandra, Butch Wilson, John Ranne, Billy West, Bob Regan, Vinnie Catanzaro, Lloyd Hogan and Bob Fulmer and Ted and Mike Pascieznik.

He was a colorful character with a great personality. One of the things I remember about him is that he was a bull. I mean that in a flattering way. He was built. He was one of the guys that if there was trouble, you'd want Billy by your side.

Besides those qualities, he loved to sing. He took some guitar lessons at the Park Ridge Music Store on Ridge Road until he got good enough to form a band. I remember him bringing out his guitar at Deco 22 one night and showing us what he could do. He and his band played in such places as Ann's Inn on the corner of Bloomfield and South Park, the Astro Lite on Ridge Road in Lackawanna and the Ground Round at the Seneca Mall. I believe I also saw him play at Michler's Bar. He had many other gigs in other establishments in the Buffalo area.

Like so many in South Buffalo, Bill worked at the Bethlehem Steel plant as did his father. As a matter of fact, his dad died there in a most unfortunate accident. He went on to drive tractor trailers for Sealtest Dairy Products and became their top salesman. His next driving job was for Riverside Trucking which is where his driving career ended. As he drove his truck one day, the transmission blew up and parts of it tore through the floor of the cab, causing major damage to his leg. After he healed, rather than going back to driving, he started his own business, Held's Janitorial Service. He eventually had contracts in Buffalo, Rochester, Syracuse and Naples, Florida. The Florida business was called King of Clean. It was the largest janitorial service in Florida. He sold that part of his business interests but maintains services in Buffalo, Rochester and Syracuse. His sons Bill Jr. and Mike now run the family businesses. Billy's son Bill Jr. is in charge of running the janitorial services part of the Held Corporation and his other son Mike, is in charge of the Gulf Club Protector business. (see video on youtube.com https://youtu.be/sLfav94kw6Y)

The Gulf Protector business was born when Billy Sr. became interested in golf and eventually joined the Orchard Park Country Club. An idea struck him as he played the game and got caught in a few downpours. He saw golfers throw coats, towels, blankets or some sort of tarp over their golf clubs or hold a large golf umbrellas over their expensive clubs. That idea proved to be extremely rewarding. In 1982, he invented the Golf Club Protector which is a golf cart enclosure. His invention sold very well and sales are still going strong nationwide. He even established a maintenance service for Golf Club Protectors and provides services to all country clubs. Sales and service keeps Bill's son, Mike very busy. They have a West Seneca office.

Roger Pasquerella

Roger was born in 1946 and lived through all of those glorious years this book is featuring. He lived in Orchard Park as a kid in the area they called The Hill, located across from Sacred Heart Church and Capriotto Auto Parts on Abbott Road. He was raised there by his grandparents until he went to 7th grade and then they moved to 109 Amber Street.

He finished elementary school at PS #29 and attended South Park High where he graduated in 1964. That's where he met his wife, Donna Williams, from the Seneca Street area. It was a two mile walk for her and many others to South Park High. Roger was not a mean guy, but he told me that he locked his girlfriend, Donna, now his wife, in a locker at South Park High.

He said jokingly:

"I paid for that little stunt with 49 years of marriage."

They're doing fine. They have a boy, Jayson, who is the owner of *Lucia's Restaurant on The Lake* across from Hoak's Restaurant along Route 5.

During his preteens and teen years, Roger hung out at Mulroy Playground, Chat and Nibble's Soda Shop, Harry's Pool room, the Deco Restaurant, Capitol Theatre which became Fazio's Hall and on a rail (for sitting on) in front of an electric building near Tifft and South Park. His crew comprised of guys like:

Jimmy (Pries Street) Miller, who was best man at his wedding later on. Then, there was Jim Mahoney, Fran Manzella, Jerry Bonafede, Tim Regan, Billy Heilich, Pat and Joe Liberti, Sam Parisi, Steve Banko, Mike Grys, Bobby Duke, Danny Shea, Jack Carney, Lou Sprague Tom Willard and, Norm Appleford

He said that when he and the other guys hung out on South Park that they were always respectful to older folks who needed to walk by their group.

"We were brought up to do that, respect our elders." and added

"But sometimes, we would tease and mock certain individuals our own age as they passed by, doing what teenagers do for the fun of it; not necessarily being malicious."

He also remembers gravitating to other groups for a short while, to check out other people he knew, then hook back up with some of the same guys from his former crew.

In his mid to later teens, Roger remembers some of the boys were into sipping a bit of wine. Yes, they were all under age. People in all the other crews on the strip and the other neighborhoods were doing the same thing. Anyway, he reminded me of the close to rot-gut wines the guys would drink such as Wild Irish Rose, Ripple and Thunder Bird. Colt 45 was the beverage of choice for the beer drinkers in the group. After high school, he went to UB for Social Studies, then enrolled at Buffalo State College for his master's degree in Exceptional Education. He taught school for a short while before getting into the transmission business. He started out with Cottman's Transmission and later –became the owner of a franchise of six Continental Transmission shops. He also owned the Macaroni Company on Pearl Street and Garcia's Irish Pub near the Buffalo Convention Center, which is now the Pearl Street Brewery.

I asked him how he felt about having lived in South Buffalo:

"It was one of the best neighborhoods because of friends, locally and from other neighborhoods, and other schools. There was a strong camaraderie..

Section 3
Life and Times of Baby Boomers

Chapter Seventeen
Simple Technology of the Baby Boomers

The early Baby Boomer days was a time when life was technologically simpler. There were no calculators, boom boxes, Walkman radios, computers, cell phones or I-pods. Heck, only accountants, businesses and banks had adding machines as far as I know. We knew how to do basic math in our head. When you were a cashier it was all manual. You needed to know how to make change. Today, if an item cost $5.87, and you give the cashier a ten dollar bill and 7 cents, he or she might freak out. Computing giving back $4.20 in their head would be a small nightmare for a lot of them who are used to letting computerized cash registers do the work for them. We've gone from using our brains to letting machines do the work. Not that it's all bad, but it goes to show that we're not using our brains as much as we used to. The song, *In the Year 2525* from the 70's Zager & Evans' song is scary. It talks about future times when machines would be doing everything for us, it's happening more and more.

Back in the 40s, 50s and early 60s, I'm sure all of you from that time remember the rotary dial telephone, party lines and the way phone numbers were given out. I still remember my old phone number from the 60's as TA5-8527 or 825-8527. Also, those were the days you could actually speak to an operator right away by dialing "0." It was great.

How about those old phone booths with a door, a seat and 5 cents a call? It kind of bummed us out when they hiked the price to 10 cents. The good thing about the calls back then was you could talk as long as you wanted to. Several years later, the phone companies found a way to make more money by raising the price of a basic call and charging by the minute after three minutes. Back then people had private conversations by using a phone booth with the door shut. Today with everyone using cell phones, you can hear everybody's conversation. I find it very annoying. Oh, to go back to the good old days with private phone conversations when in public, using phone booths. Now, here's an idea. Cities and restaurants should set up old style booths with doors and a seat for people who want to be private when out in public. Hey, if it ever happens, remember it was my idea.

Phone History

The rotary dialing system was introduced in 1904 and came into common use in 1919. It was phased out and replaced with push button dialing after it was introduced at the 1962 Seattle's World's Fair by the Bell Telephone company. For those of you who used the rotary dial phones, do you remember when you miss dialed, and had to do it all over again? What a drag that was, huh? I still have three in my house that actually work and are connected. Now and then I'll phone people on one of them. My grandsons asked: *"What is that, Papa?"* It's become one of those items that the very young can't relate to at all. The touch tone dialing system was indeed a great and welcomed innovation. Thank you Ma Bell.

Music Contraptions

You couldn't go any more basic than a crystal set as a means of listening to the radio. I latched onto one around 1962. You could only get one AM radio station on it. For me, it was WKBW radio. It had no speaker. There was a single ear piece and the sound was not very loud. It was cool at night when I went to bed. I could listen to KB without disturbing my other four brothers in the bedroom. KB had a very powerful output from its towers located in a field off of Big Tree Road in Hamburg. It put out a 50,000 watt signal that covered the greater Buffalo area, ran down the east coast as far as Florida and was received as far as Europe. Can you imagine that? WKBW was regarded as one of the top AM radio stations in the country.

If you were a normal teen or young adult of the fifties and sixties, you listened to some kind of (pop) music. For most of the younger generation *rock* was the choice. It was new, different and somewhat of a phenomenon compared to what our parents listened to. In the fifties, there were only AM radio stations. FM stations came in a bit later. For a lot of us WKBW 1520 AM radio was the most listened to radio station. DJ's such as Joey Reynolds, Tommy Shannon who attended Bishop Ryan High on Clinton St., Danny Nevearth, Jeff Kay from Baltimore, Stan Roberts from New Jersey, Sandy Beach and several others were popular voices on the AM airwaves at the time. The theme song for the Tommy Shannon Show on KB was done by the Rebels with Kipler Brothers, Mickey and Jimmy from Aldrich Place in South Buffalo. The theme song did so well that it was recorded as *"Wild Weekend"*. It was heard throughout the nation and is still played today. No one from that era can forget George the "Hound" Lorenz who attended South Park High. He joined WKBW Radio in 1955. I remember the howling sound that became a trade mark for the Hound as the show got started and ended.

What's interesting is what people are using today to listen to their favorite tunes. Forget the Hi-Fi stereo system which was an expensive and bulky piece of furniture that sat in your living room. Many were combination radio-record players. It was larger than most TV's in a lot of cases. It only played the radio and records; no tapes, eight track cartridges or CDs. In case you were too rough with the needle you needed to have a spare on hand. When it went, the music was over.

78 Records

The 78 RPM speed record I listened to in the 50's first came out in 1925. It was close to a foot across and only had one song on each side. There was the A side which played the popular hit and the B side which played a less popular song. They were made of various brittle materials and coated with shellac. If you dropped one it could easily shatter and if you scratched it, it would skip and repeat the line before or skip forward to another line in the song. The needle would follow whatever groove it caught. I first heard Elvis Presley around 1956 on one of those 78's. I can remember resetting the play arm on the record player over and over again to listen to *"Don't Be Cruel"* which I memorized and loved singing along.

Reel to reel tape players

Reel to reel tape players were available for our music listening pleasure since the 1930s. One could buy pre-recorded music of various artists from music companies. They were usually 7 inch reels, containing several hundred feet of acetate magnetic tape usually played at 30ips (inches per second). Later, the units offered various play speeds: 7½, 3¾ and 1⅞. One could have several hours of uninterrupted music. Reel to reel was somewhat popular in the late 60s and early 70s. Some of you readers had one of these, right?

The 45 Records

Baby Boomers also had a smaller and flexible vinyl record. It was nearly seven inches across and like the 78 record, it too had only one song on each side. It was called the 45 RPM record complete with a large hole in the middle where you needed to insert a plastic disc in the middle of the record to fit onto the spindle of the record player or the Hi Fi. Hi Fi stands for high fidelity as in high quality sound. I remember buying the Beatles' *Hey Jude* 45 record around 1969 and playing it over and over till I wore it out.

As with the 78, you could stack several 45 records on top of each other on your stereo system where there was an automatic gadget that would release the next record when the previous one finished. It repeated that process till the stack was all played out. It was a nice invention. To listen to the flip side of the records, you needed to take that entire stack and flip it over for another half hour to forty-five minutes of songs

The LPs

Around the same time the 45 came out the LP was introduced. People would buy stereo Hi Fi players with stereophonic sound. They had big, bold sounds that could fill a room with never before heard separation of sound. If your sound system was a good one with the right speakers or headsets, you could hear horns on the left, drums and vocals in the middle and guitar and bass on the right. It was like you were right there at the concert. The LP was over a foot across and very flexible. If you scratched it, it too would get to skipping and repeating lines. You had about five to eight songs on each side of the LP album, depending on the length of each song.

"In-a-gadda-da-vida" by a group called Iron Butterfly Evolution came out in 1968. I heard the title was derived from the phrase *"In the Garden of Eden."* The long version of the song runs something like seventeen minutes fourteen seconds. The featured drum part alone is around three minutes long. That sort of song length wasn't done by many other groups. The movements were repetitious but moved well from one movement to the other for a more or less psychedelic song. One thing that rings true, the musicians could actually play their instruments well. Much of the rock music after the mid 80's and the 90's became muddy and not much in the way of distinctive sound for any of the new and upcoming bands.

The LP format lasted a good while but then two other ways of listening to music became popular the tape cassette and the eight track tape cartridge. Both formats existed along with the 45s and LPs. They became the preferred means for listening to music by most young people. Cassettes could also be played in your battery powered boom boxes also known as a Ghetto Blasters. Boom boxes were a hit in the sixties and seventies. Some were quite large and put out very loud sounds. Hence the moniker, boom boxes. Some people would carry them around on their shoulders with the speaker right next to their ear. It wasn't very good for the hearing. In a study on sound pollution I did while attending Buffalo State College in '72, I came across a report that stated:

"By the time a person realizes he or she has a hearing problem, he or she could have as much as a forty percent hearing loss."

216

The auto manufacturers quickly incorporated both the eight track and tape cassette players along with the AM and FM radio into their cars. You may know someone who still has a functioning eight track player at home and even plays it regularly.

The tape cassette marketed in 1962 is a 2½ by 4 inch format that held the same amount of songs as any album. Blank cassettes were available in 30, 60, 90 and 120 minute formats. All sorts of cassette players with combination AM/FM radio were made. They played continuously till it hit the end. Then, flip over to get another side's worth of tunes. Eventually, manufacturers made tape players that would hit the end of one side, then click over to start playing the other side automatically.

The idea behind Eight Track Cartridges was to offer better sound, much like the LP's did with separation of sound. The eight track endless loop cartridge became popular and you didn't have to flip it over. It would simply go to the beginning again. One of the nice things about it was that if you had a good player, you could pick out certain song selections by pushing a button. With cassettes, you had to search to find a favorite song. Eventually a cassette tape player was made that allowed going back to previous selections with the push of a button.

Television in the 50's and 60's

The very first TV I ever saw was in 1952. Only one man in my neighborhood had one. That was Monsieur Lemay in Waterloo, Québec. He brought it outside so the neighbors could get a look at this newfangled thing. People gathered around it in awe. At 6 years old, I thought it was magical.

Black and white TV

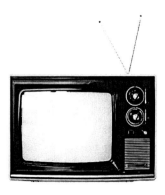

I spoke to a few people who remembered what watching TV was like back in the 50's and 60's. A TV back then was in black and white. It was a real treat in the mid-sixties when color television came in. Although color television was a great improvement, we still had either rabbit ears or an antenna on the roof to bring in the local stations and maybe Hamilton or Toronto. The rabbit ears were part of your TV set, but the antenna was attached to your chimney or anchored somewhere on the roof. Unfortunately, antennas didn't always stay put during some of Buffalo's nasty weather conditions. Quite a few ended up lying down horizontally on the roof. People who were fortunate enough to afford a bit of technology could get a rotary antenna that was connected to a control unit on or near the TV set. This item would actually turn the antenna on the roof to bring in better reception. Non-rotary antenna owners were envious.

Back in the 50s and early 60s in Buffalo, the clearest stations via antennas were channels 2, 4 and 7. Later, we had channel 17, an educational station.

For changing channels and volume control, we had dials on our TV sets; no remote controls. That meant having to get up, walk over to the TV and turn the dial to see what else was on TV.

What was a real challenge was to tweak the horizontal and the vertical when they decided to act up. That was done by turning little knobs at the back of the TV set. You would be watching television and suddenly the picture would go sideways which meant a vertical problem. You couldn't make out anything at all. It was like the entire picture got squeezed sideways and crunched down. The other interruption in viewing TV was the horizontal problem. The picture would become a continuous roll either upward or downward. You could see the program but it sure wasn't fun to watch. If you couldn't make it stop, it meant you needed a TV repairman.

At the TV repair shop, you might only need to have a couple of tubes replaced. That's right, tubes. No hi tech printed circuitry existed back then. If you were technically inclined, you could open up the back of the TV set and look around a bit to find the tube or tubes that looked a bit cooked. Local drug stores would have electronic tube stands and charts to help find the tubes you needed. Hopefully after you put them in it would work. Sometimes it did and if not it was time to trash your TV set.

A lot of the televisions refused to give you good reception. Some folks resorted to putting tin foil (later aluminum) at the tips of each end of the rabbit ear antenna. I don't know if it really helped that much, but a whole lot of folks did this. It became so common to go into other people's house and see the not-so-good-looking setup. You didn't think much about it. If you had rabbit ears as part of your TV setup, you probably tried the foil tactic in order to get better reception. Sometimes, a dad sent his kid to adjust the rabbit ears to get a better picture and saw that by touching them, the picture got better. He might tell him:

"Alright Jimmy. Stay right there! Don't let go of the antennae. The picture is good. Keep holding! Roger Marris is at bat, and the bases are loaded. I want see if he'll get a grand slam. DON'T YOU MOVE! "

Oh the frustration of bad TV reception. But hope was coming. The great solution to poor TV reception was Cable TV. It started way back in 1948 to allow areas where antenna broadcast signals weren't received or were poorly received. This was primarily in mountainous or geographically distant areas. Televisions hooked up to cable companies really grew in the late 60's and early 70's because it solved the problem of poor reception. The first three in the Buffalo area were Courier Cable which served the City of Buffalo proper, Amherst Cable serviced the Amherst area and Comax Cable served several of the towns outside the city of Buffalo. TV reception was much improved, not to mention the number of stations one could receive. It was a television watcher's dream come true; except it wasn't free. It was the beginning of pay TV. Not only could you get great reception, more channels, but, you could get movie channels without any commercial interruptions. The means of obtaining more and more television programming was the start of a huge industry that kept growing and growing. Comax became International Cable. They bought out Amherst Cable and incorporated their customers into International's. Subsequently, that company changed hands a few more times. The Pennsylvania-based Rigas family bought International and changed the name to Adelphia Cable. At this writing, it is Time Warner Cable.

Remembering TV Shows of Days Gone By

Baby Boomers, let's see what you remember. Here are some of the TV shows that were around in our good old days of black and white, until the mid-sixties when TV went to color.

Series and Sitcoms

The Little Rascals, Father Knows Best, I Love Lucy, Make Room Daddy, Leave It to Beaver, My Three Sons, Hazel, Mr. Ed the talking horse, Dennis The Menace, Donna Reed Show, Sci-fi Lost In Space, My Friend Flicka and The Adventures of Ozzie and Harriet featuring the Nelson family. I didn't think the Nelson show was a really great show, but as Ricky Nelson got older and began singing songs at the end of the show, I'd sometimes watch it to see and hear him sing.

Other Shows

The Three Stooges, Who remembers the short-lived show called Man with A Camera? The star was Charles Bronson. Superman and Tarzan with Johnny Weissmuller. This short list wouldn't be complete without mentioning Dick Clark's American Bandstand.

Soap Operas

Another World, General Hospital, The Doctors, The Guiding Light, The Edge of Night and Peyton Place.

Westerns

The Lone Ranger with Clayton Moore and Jay Silverheels as Tonto (real name Harold John Smith) and lived in Buffalo for a while), Wyatt Earp, Zorro and Gunsmoke (with Buffalo connection Amanda Blake as Miss Kitty), Yancey Deringer, Alfego Baca (a Disney series), Ski King, Dragnet with Joe Friday and Perry Mason.

Sports

Baseball, football, Saturday Night Fights, roller derbies, bowling, pro wrestling in the sixties from our own Downtown Aud. We loved seeing Ilio DiPaolo from Abruzzi Italy, take down the Masked Marvel, the Beast or Hans Schmidt, nicknamed The

Teuton Terror. Hans was actually French Canadian, Guy Larose from Joliette, Québec.

Kids' shows

Howdy Doody and Captain Kangaroo. The Mickey Mouse Club, with Annette Funicello

Cartoons

Felix The Cat, Mickey Mouse, Popeye, Bugs Bunny, Daffy Duck, Elmer Fudd, Porky Pig, The Flintstones, The Jetsons, Roger Ramjet and a ton of others.

Variety shows

Milton Berle, Jack Benny, Red Skeleton, Ted Mack's Original Amateur Hour, Your Hit Parade, People Are Funny, Art Linkletter Show (with segment, Kids Say The Darndest Things), George Gobel, Arthur Godfrey, Ed Sullivan, Jackie Gleason, The Lawrence Welk Show (known for his accented "En a one and a two en" as he began conducting). When I lived in Welland, Ontario in the latter part of the fifties we watched Buffalo Bandstand, a Buffalo, New York version of American Bandstand. It was broadcast from Channel 7, located on Main Street near Utica. Frank Deliusio from South Buffalo told me that he and his friends attended Buffalo Bandstand dances when he lived in the Fruit Belt area before moving to South Buffalo. I remember my older brother Jacques, and older sisters Denise and Monique, as well as some of their friends, going to Buffalo to be on the show in 1958.

Chapter Eighteen
Some Baby Boomer Influences

Rock Stars

The Baby Boomer generation was hugely influenced by a lot of what came through the fashion industry, music, television and movies. We had a ton of singers and movie stars who we looked up to and noticed how they dressed. In the fifties, a lot of new things appeared on the horizon. The music our folks listened to was way different from what became the pop music teens latched onto known as Rock and Roll. Bill Haley and the Comets launched this genre and Elvis Presley's music became the biggest thing going in the mid-fifties. Besides the above mentioned, young people influenced each other with new dress styles and hairdos for both sexes.

Rock Music

Rock and Roll music became an "evil" thing to a lot of the older generation. The term itself was used in black neighborhoods to relate to "having sexual intercourse." It (term rock and roll) was made popular in the 50's by disc jockey Allen Freed who introduced it on his *Moondog Show* and then brought it to New York City and changed the show to *"The Rock and Roll show."* With Rock and Roll, a whole lot of different dance styles appeared. For sure, there was the "jitter-bug," then things went into novelty dances like the Stroll and the Twist – (1960) made famous by a portly singer by the name of Chubby Checkers who introduced it to the world. Actually, ole Chubby began losing weight as he performed it as part of his act. It became very popular. Along with that dance style, the Peppermint Twist, then, came the Monkey, the Jerk, the Mash Potato, the Swim, the Watusi...AND...Disco in the 70s.

Movie Stars

Other influences came from the movies from stars like Marlon Brando (The Wilds Ones - a motorcycle gang movie) and James Dean (Rebel without a Cause). These were huge screen idols for the Baby Boomer generation. The media influenced a lot of what we thought, the way we spoke, the way we dressed and in many ways, shaped much of our personal beliefs and opinions. We were significantly different from our parents which birthed the phrase *"The Generation Gap"* in the '60's. Parents and teens often didn't make good connections when relating the each other. It was a time of rebellion when it seemed Baby Boomers opposed many thing their parents valued.

Beatniks

"The Beat Generation" was a cultural and literary movement in the 1950's. From that, the term beatnik was coined by Herb Caen in an article in the San Francisco Chronicles on April 2, 1958, six months after the Russian Sputnik I rocket was launched. It was part of the description of the "Beat Generation" -- and , part of that was to portray them as "un-American." The (-nik) suffix was taken from the "Russian Sputnik I rocket that was launched six months before his article.

Beatniks, were into poetry, jazz, art and living a bohemian type lifestyle. They migrated to a place in New York City called Tin Pan Alley. They were portrayed as people who didn't work much, played bongos, rolled their own cigarettes, wore sunglasses, turtleneck sweaters and berets, had mustaches and/or goatees and coined their own slang and used terms like "hay man", "cool", "groovy", "heavy", "hip", "jiv", "good and bad carma", "out of site" and so on. The beatnik culture promoted non-materialism and a *live and let live* philosophy about life. It was a "do your own thing" mentality.

Back in the sixties, two TV personalities reflected some of the beatnik traits. One was featured in the late fifties and early sixties sitcom *The Many Loves of Dobie Gillis* (1959-1963). Bob Denver played beatnik, Maynard G. Krebes. He cringed when the word "work" was mentioned. Clean-cut, Dobie Gillis, was played by actor Dwayne Hickman.

Edd (Kookie) Byrnes played Gerald Lloyd Kookson III in the 77 Sunset Strip detective series seen from 1958 to 1964. On the show, you would hear Kookie used a lot of the beatnik jive-talk and regularly take out his comb to adjust his rock style hairdo. The song, *"Kookie, Kookie Lend Me Your Comb"* was recorded during that time featuring Kookie and actress Connie Stevens.

Chapter Nineteen
Clothing styles in the Mid-Fifties to Mid-Sixties

The Girls

In the mid 50s and very early 60s girls always dressed with more self-respect and modesty. I don't remember ever seeing a girl looking sloppy. The casual dress for the Baby Boomer girls in the warm weather was cotton type pants that came to their knees, called pedal pushers. They had zippers on the side or the back. A trend for them for a while was wearing one of their dad's or big brother's white dress shirts with the tails hanging out and collars up. For school and church, girls wore dresses or skirts with nice blouses and dress shoes. For certain events, some wore nice slacks with good-looking tops.

The Guys

One of the unique things about guys in our time was that we all dressed nice as we got to a certain age. There was a certain self-respect that drove us to do so. It wasn't like today. A lot of today's kids, young adults and some adults look very untidy compared to the way we dressed. It seems as though some of the kids today dress as sloppy as they can. I don't get it. I've joked with some of the young people today that if they were to walk down South Park, Abbott Road or Seneca Street in the 40's, 50's or early 60's with their underwear showing, shirt untucked, baseball cap on sideways or wearing pajama bottoms and slippers, they might have a problem, just for looking goofy. It was about self-respect and being part of what the neighborhood was all about. We weren't rich, but we didn't walk around looking like oddballs or slobs. Looking untidy was not a goal for anyone on our strips. Today, it seems, the worse they look, the cooler they think they are. There's really something wrong with that mentality. When the Dr. Casey and Dr. Kildare medical TV shows aired in the 60s, young people started wearing doctors' scrubs. I think that only lasted one summer. They weren't that cool.

Influence from the Music Industry

In the late 50s there was a song entitled *"Black Slacks"* by Joe Bennett and the Sparkletones. Those pants became a popular thing to wear for a while. Besides black slacks, or whatever color pants we wore, we wore dressy types to hang out on the corners or wherever. In the late 50s and early 60s, gone were the dungaree jeans and tennis shoes/sneakers to go hang around the corners or the various spots we'd gather to spend time talking, going to a show, a restaurant or an event. In our minds.... jeans were for work, laborers, farmers and cowboys.

One of the styles that came in for a short while in the early 60's was skinny peg leg-fit pants. These pants were so narrow at the bottom that if you had large feet, you could barely get them on. Some guys couldn't even wear them. After you had them on, you might actually struggle to get them off. How do I know? I had a couple of pairs. I could force my feet through the bottom but when it came time to take them off, it was always a fight. I remember falling to the floor a few times trying to get them off. I was so glad when that style went out. So when bell bottoms came in style in the mid-sixties I was a very happy guy. They had lots of room. And who can forget the Madras shirts with the wild designs and large collars?

Denim pants took a break for a while, but came back really big in the late sixties and seventies. Hey! I'm sure many of you can remember the denim suits, complete with nice neat pleats and a matching vest. Speaking of dressing up, the ties in the 60s were narrow but in the seventies they got real wide. We had all kinds of ways to express ourselves in our looks. Quite a few white guys even had afros, not the huge out-of-control types, but enough to make you look twice. If a guy had straight hair, many got perms to sport the look. Some of you will remember the TV show *Welcome Back, Kotter* with Gabe Kaplan and John Travolta? Gabe had an afro but he was just a Caucasian guy with bushy hair; afro-style.

From the Movies

In the summer, a lot of the guys wore t-shirts like you see in older 40's and '50's movies. Some of the guys would roll their pack of cigarettes in one of the sleeves. That practice goes back to at least the 2nd World War. GIs did this for easier access and to keep them from being crushed in their pockets. Marlon Brando in the 1953 Wild Ones movie had a pack stashed in his T-shirt sleeve in some of the scenes.

In the warm weather in the 50's and early 60's, a lot of the guys wore a neat T-shirts along with neat looking pants. Those were the days when moms actually ironed the t-shirts, usually at the request of the young man wearing it. It was not acceptable if the t-shirt was all wrinkled. You would be mocked for it. Sad, but true. Most guys wouldn't dare go out looking sloppy. Being mocked for poor street dress was an absolute. Hey, we had an image to uphold. We weren't rich but we had self-respect.

Footwear

Although we had a shoe store in the neighborhood, many of us would get our shoes downtown on Main Street in a store called Hardy's Shoes at $7.77 a pair and no tax. We Rocks liked the Cuban-heel look. By the way, we would walk everywhere we went before we got cars. Not many got rides from mommy or daddy in those days. Our shoes wore out pretty fast and the need for a new pair came up quick.

In an effort to save our heels from wearing out too fast, a lot of us would have Louie (Louie's Shoe Shine and Hat Shop) put on steel cleats. You can only imagine the sound of a few of us walking down the street with our Cuban heal cleat-clad shoes -click clack, click clack. Weren't we cool? Louie, the owner of the shoeshine and hat shop was known by about everybody on the strip. He was a small, older, Italian gentleman with the accent to go with it. A lot of the guys got their shoes fixed there and got them shined on a regular basis. I remember when he was done shining our shoes, he'd get this little bottle of white substance, put a little dab on the tip of each shoe and do one more buffing. I asked him one day what that white stuff was. He replied; *"Is a pigeon milk."*

226

I had to ask him where he got the pigeon milk. Think about it. Did you ever in your life hear of pigeon milk? When asked, he simply said, *"Is a secret. I no can tell you."*

We never did find out where he got it from. Anyway, the shoes looked really nice when you stepped down from the two-seat perch with the metal footrests. Louie old friend, you are not forgotten. Thanks for the great shines.

Sneakers

As teens, we wore sneakers mostly for playing basketball. We paid about $2.50 to $3.50 for a basic pair back in the late 50's and 60's. For a while, we only had the black hi-top style. Keds and Converse All-Stars were a couple of the favorite brand names. Do you Baby Boomers remember when they introduced the low-cut style in the sixties? We thought they were so cool. They were still made of canvas with the rubber bottoms, though. A precursor to sneakers dates back as far as the 18th century. In 1882, the US Rubber Company manufactured a rubber sole, canvas top sneaker called Keds. By 1917, they were mass produced. The rubber-soled shoes got the name *"sneakers"* because you could walk real quiet and sneak up on people.

Today, sneakers are the primary foot gear to wear. Some kids today don't even own a pair of dress shoes. Some go to weddings and funerals dressed in a suit and, you guessed it, their sneakers. Nikes and other name brands cost more than $100 and way beyond in some cases. Some of the kids can't even conceive of the idea of putting on a pair of dress shoes. Wait till they have to go get a real job in the real world and have to grow up, clean up and dress up. By the way, back in the day, most young people only had one pair of shoes and a pair of sneakers to wear; not three four or five pairs of both items. Owning multiple pairs of shoes was unheard of.

Dry Clean Only

Our shoes were shined and our pants had pleats. We took care of our dress pants. We didn't have mom wash them in her washing machine especially, sharkskin pants. Those shark skins were brought to the cleaners. For South Park guys, it was Belvedere's Cleaners next to Precinct #15 on South Park Avenue or Cadet Cleaners at Woodside. On Abbott Road, it was perhaps, Louis's Cleaners and on Seneca Street at the Helpee Selfee Laundry and

Dry Cleaning. Dress shirts were okay for moms to put through the wash and then iron. You have to remember a lot of moms had washers that did not treat the clothes very nice. Once the washing cycle was done, then came the wringer process.

That's when moms would take the clothes and send it through a set of the wringer rollers to squeeze out the water. Most were hung out to dry on the clothesline in the backyard. If your folks had money, your mom might have an automatic washing machine with a spin cycle and then she would put your clothes in the dryer like at the laundromat.

Smoking

Living near the numerous plants that spewed out who knows what kind of pollution in many of the South Buffalo neighborhoods, we Baby Boomers inhaled a lot of nasty air. Picking up the habit of smoking fit right into our polluted life.

Most Baby Boomers smoked Lucky Strike cigarettes at first. They were only 23 cents a pack when I started smoking in the early 60's. (I quit in '75) Another favorite brand was Pall Mall, and the real tough guys would smoke Camels or Chesterfields. Quite a few of us had Zippo lighters and would do these little tricks. With one sweep against our thigh we'd open the lighter lid, then we'd slide it the other way so the striker wheel would roll to ignite the wick. Some guys would flip the lid open against their thigh, then do a snap-of-the-finger on the lighter wheel and *Voilà*, the flame would come on. Oh yeah... so cool.

Smoking was real crazy back then. It was allowed everywhere with no restrictions. In people's homes it was rampant. Children grew up breathing in second-hand smoke on a daily basis. In cars with children aboard (even newborns), unthinking parents smoked away without concern for their kids' health. People could smoke anywhere in public. Bars and restaurants were filled with smoke. In theatres, there were loges (balcony seating) equipped with ashtrays where smoking was permitted. If you rode on any of the public transportation modes including buses, cabs, trains and airplanes, it was no problem.

Some high schools even had designated places for their seniors and teachers to light up. In colleges, you could light up in most of the classrooms. I went to Buffalo State College in '73 and every class room had clouds of smoke hanging in the air. The absolute worst places that smoking was allowed were hospitals and hospital rooms where patients were recovering from operations or illnesses. What the hell were we thinking!? Today the policy everywhere is no smoking. I even heard a news story where in Belmont, California, smoking was prohibited on public streets where someone's smoke could be smelled and breathed in by non-smoking passers-by. We've indeed come a long way, baby.

Products and Hair Style

Ask young men and some young women today what teasing hair means and they won't have a clue. How about the guys with the slick hair in the 50's and 60's? There are still a few around today. It wasn't natural oil keeping that slick look for the guys who became known as *greasers*. If you styled your hair back then, the product of choice for the guys was Brylcreem. You might remember the TV ad back then: *"A little dab'll do ya."* Well, it was never a little dab for most of the guys. It was more like a *glob of Brylcreem*. Vitalis was another male hair product. It wasn't as greasy as Brylcreem. If you had a crew cut and not many did, those old boys used a waxy product called Butch Wax to keep all the hairs standing at attention; even with a 50 mile an hour wind coming at them. Speaking of hairstyles, the Rock" types had something we called a D.A. (a duck's a**) as part of the hairstyle and, a spiffy little twist of hair in front. The D.A. part of the Rock hairstyle was where you would comb the hair back at each side and bring it together at the center of the back of the head so the hair met. You would then, take the comb and run a line from the crown of the head down to your neck. You needed grease to keep that look. A lot of guys would spend more than a few minutes in front of a mirror getting the hairdo right. I'm talking guys here. A bit weird but that's the way it was.

One instrument to coif the hair was a rat-tail comb. It had regular teeth but had a handle on it that tapered off to a point. The rat tail helped control the comb for the best hairstyling possible. A lot of the guys would snip off the sharp end for obvious reasons; like it was a bit dangerous.

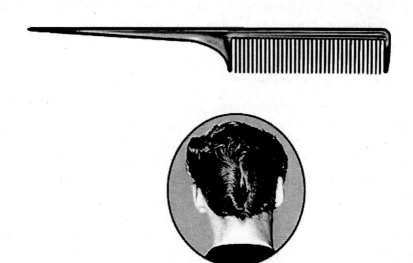

Girls' Hairstyles

Margie Weber from Altruria remembers the girls would use Spoolies as youngsters at night. They looked like a little rubber disk that snapped open. You wrapped a strand of hair around the stem portion then folded the top portion over the bottom to curl hair. They were fairly painless to sleep on. In High School girls used empty frozen orange juice cans to get the bouffant look along with lots of teasing with a rattail comb. Aqua Net was the hair spray brand of choice. To lighten the bangs (the first attempt at streaking) we used straight peroxide on the bangs.

Rocks and Squeaks

Do the terms Squeaks and Rocks ring a bell? The Squeaks or Collegiates had short hair, usually parted and combed over flat in front and wore lighter colored clothes than their counterparts, the Rocks. You can't forget the penny-loafers and the brand-name shirts the Squeaks wore; Lacoste with an alligator logo. There was a whole look to them. They were squeaky clean-cut. They sported no sideburns, no mustaches or beards and definitely no engineer boots or Cuban heel shoes with cleats.

The Rocks had the idea that the Squeaks thought they were better than them. There definitely was a difference in looks and to a certain degree, attitudes. There was an air about those Squeaks, according to the Rocks, that is. The Rocks displayed a look and attitude of the James Dean rebel; not in a bad way you understand. The whole look with longer slicked-up hair, sideburns, pack of cigarettes rolled up in the T-shirt sleeve, belt with the buckle worn to the side, the Cuban-heel shoes with cleats and all was the image of the Rock. We were just teens who picked a style to identify with.

Whether Squeak or Rock, the time spent together amounted to little more than talking about cars, jobs, a problem at school or at home, planning a party, goofing with each other, throwing zingers at people they knew who were passing by, or talking about what someone did. For sure, there were conversations among the guys about girls or girlfriends and among the girls, chats about boys and boyfriends.

It was the same for the girls but not on the corners. They usually met at someone's house. I never saw a group of girls on any of the major South Buffalo main streets hanging out on corners. It wasn't acceptable. It was a guy thing. As Latinos might say, *"Es una cosa para los hombres de la calle." "It's a thing for the guys of the street"*. A few times, there were some foolish problems between the Rocks and Squeaks. There were a few fights here and there, but the bad blood didn't last long. One reason for short feuds was that within the groups, there would always be somebody who was related to or knew someone on the other side. For the most part, it was a pretty good co-existence. After all, we were all people from the same neighborhood. After thinking about it, I reasoned that the whole thing was nonsense. We were all South Buffalonians.

Most of the Squeaks I knew were headed for college or some career in a trade or a business. The Rocks, from what I saw, did the best they could to do what they did best. Many dropped out of high school.

I don't want to leave you hanging here with a bad thought about Rocks. Most of us got steady jobs with fair to good salaries. We married, bought houses and had kids. At this writing, many are retired and enjoying the fruits of their labor. Several retired from the police force, the fire department, the steel plants, auto plants, utility companies and other jobs.

As a Rock, I along with crews I hung with, wasted a lot time on street corners. We weren't looking ahead very far. But, most of us did land on our feet later on. Personally, I worked many jobs. I was one of those drop outs but got my GED and eventually went to college earning a bachelor and master's degree in education. I taught French and Spanish for twenty-three years at Canisius High School and taught part time at Medaille College for twenty-one years.

Chapter Twenty
Changes in the mid-sixties and seventies

In the mid-sixties into the seventies, a lot of changes among the younger crowd began to make its way into daily life. We saw it all over South Buffalo and beyond. They dressed differently. They grew long hair and certain new words became part of their vocabulary. For many, their way of thinking was contrary to what moms and dads thought about life and politics. Drug use became a big problem. A large number of people got into an anti-establishment way of living and thinking. Many of their ideas were good, but at the same time, many weren't.

A lot of the changes were brought about by the Hippie movement. Hippies were younger people of mostly college age, but some were younger and some were in their thirties and even forties. It was a movement against some of the norms of society and especially against the government, *"the Establishment"*. America was in a military conflict in Viet Nam and a lot of folks believed very strongly that our soldiers had no business being there. Anti-war slogans were seen and heard all over America such as:

Don't trust the man (meaning, the government) Draft beer, not boys, Hell no, we won't go, End the war before it ends you, Make love, not war, Wage Peace, Drop acid, not bombs, Give peace a chance, Bare feet, not arms, Burn Pot Not People

Marijuana and Drugs

It was also a time of promiscuous sex and drug use. With that, another slogan became part of the hippie mentality, *if it feels good do it*. All inhibitions and morals went out the window and if you didn't at least smoke pot, you weren't cool. Some names used to refer to marijuana back then were; Pot, Grass, Weed, Acapulco Gold, Panama Red, Columbian, Gold Thai, Blond Lebanese, Sweet Jane, Mary Jane, Devil Weed, Hooch, Hemp, Wacky Weed, Juanita, Texas T, Smoking a Joint and a ton more.

Drinking cough syrup to get high and taking LSD became part of the *in things to do*. I heard a lot of the drug users back then talk about doing uppers and downers, along with LSD 25, DMT, Purple

Haze, and synthetic mescaline. A good number of people graduated to the heavier drug, heroin. Many of them were the guys who came back from Nam addicted.

The Draft

The 60's was a time when many of our young men got drafted to fight the Viet Nam War. Many of us from all over South Buffalo got drafted. As a matter of fact, most of the guys I hung with were drafted. During that time, we heard about guys who were classified as Conscientious Objectors. Some of them burned their draft cards in protest of the war and resisted going into military service. Others slipped over the border into Canada. If they returned at some point, they were arrested as draft dodgers and faced the possibility of five years in Federal prison and/or a fine up to $250,000. This was not a good time for American Baby Boomers.

Generation Gap

The sixties and seventies were some of the wildest and weirdest times the country and our local neighborhoods ever experienced as far as generation division. Little by little, many parents and young people saw a huge gap form between them as the youths adopted the new mind-set of the "hip" people. From that, the "Generation Gap" was born.

Changes in the 60's & 70's'

- Guys growing their hair long

- Guys growing mustaches and/or beards

- Young people's hip vocabulary

- Wild psychedelic music, not even close to what mom and dad ever knew.

- Guys/gals wearing tie-dyed tops and hip-huggers

- Girls going braless, mini and micro skirts, tube-tops and put flowers in their hair

- Bell-bottom pants Sandals worn in the warm and cold weather

- Bare foot young people in public places

- People asked each other *"What's your sign?"* (Meaning their astrological sign connected to the month they were born). If your astrological sign was not a good match with someone of the opposite sex, it was a negative vibe.

- Panhandling became a way to scrape up money for basic essentials or drugs

- Smoking marijuana was huge.

- Wanting to buy a VW bus or old school bus and paint it with hip designs

- Possibly head to the Haight-Ashbury area of San Francisco or other parts of California.

- Live in a commune or guys and girls living together without the benefit of marriage

- Flashing the Peace Sign

The Peace Sign Origin

The actual Peace Sign was the creation of British graphic artist, Gerald Holtom, February 21, 1958. It symbolized the objection of the people against the stockpiling of Nuclear Weapons that occurred after World War II. It was a sort of *"Ban the Bomb"* icon.

Holtom stated: *"I was in despair. Deep despair. I drew myself standing with hands palm outstretched outwards and downwards in a manner of painter Goya's peasant before the firing squad. I formalized the drawing into a line and put a circle around it."*

As radio man Paul Harvey used to say: "And now you know, the rest of the story."

Hippy Vocabulary

The use of certain words or phrases became part of daily vocabulary among hippies and young people.

"Man" was used a lot. *"Hey man, what's happening?"* *"Peace, man."* Other phrases were: *"That's far out"* *"Out of sight, man."* *"I'm hip, man."* *"That's a bummer, man."* *"That's cool, man."* *"Groovy man, groovy."* There were many more, but, you get the picture.

This began the decline of the ability to communicate intelligently. The hippie movement threw many of that generation into a dumbing down tailspin where they lost themselves in that lifestyle. Those who indulged in that way of life for a time, but had the good sense to rise above it, came out fine and became productive, proper-speaking members of society.

Unfortunately, the mentality of many from that generation was, *"I refuse to grow up."* They wanted no mortgage, no career, no future plans, no goals, no marriage, no kids and no responsibilities. Quite a few ended up living with mom and dad way beyond thirty and even, forty. Sadly, some never left the nest. I personally knew a guy like that. He died in his late 60's while still living with his mom. People like that were branded as *adultescents*. Yes, that's an actual word. Put it in your adult vocabulary. It might come in handy someday to describe adult people who still have childish or teenage interests and traits. Their bodies grew up but their minds lagged behind.

Woodstock

Anyone in the mood for being in the middle of a huge field with well over half a million people on hot sunny days and an incredible downpour soaking you to the bones? If you were young and there was going to be some of the best bands in the country, you might have said: *"Oh yeah, I'm in. Where and when, man?"*

August 1969 will be memorialized in Baby Boomer history as the three day concert called *Woodstock*. It didn't actually happen in Woodstock on dairy farmer, Max Yasgur's land in the town of Bethel, New York. The field was three miles from Yasger's home. Some people say there were well over 500,000 young people in attendance and reportedly, nearly a 1,000,000 who had to turn back because of the immense crowds on the roads leading there. Can you imagine that scene? It's mind-boggling.

Those who made it in, did all they could to have a good time and were part of a historical music event. The concert had booked over thirty bands and single performers. They had a good idea to have a rotating stage in order to be able to set up one group on one side while another group performed on the other side. The problem was the wheels on the stage fell off due to the weight of all the equipment and people resulting in huge gaps between performers. The show did go on, but much slower than anticipated. Richie Havens opened the show and his performance there catapulted his career. Jimmy Hendrix closed with a memorable rendition of the National Anthem.

My friend, Mike Pasiecznik, asked if I was going. I would have loved to. I didn't have the time or the $24 for a three day ticket. It was a once in a lifetime opportunity but it was probably a good thing I didn't go. I don't do well in huge crowds, and I definitely don't like sleeping on the ground as did thousands of those young people. More power to them. It wasn't my thing.

However, Mike, Skip Reed, Kevin Keane, John Bukowski and Glenn Echum from South Buffalo went, saw it, enjoyed it and returned to their cozy homes.

Mike told me:

"We had a stretch of heavy rain, but it didn't last. Most of the time, it was sunny. We had a great time."

On the down side of things, the concert started late, there were many drug arrests, way too few Johnny-On-The-Spot toilets and an incredible downpour of five inches in three hours that turned the entire place into a mud field with ponds. It was reported that several women suffered miscarriages and, a mother had to be flown by helicopter to a hospital to deliver her baby. The U.S. Army was brought in to assist both concert-goers and performers with food supplies, medical assistance and transportation issues. Two people died during the concert; one from a drug overdose and the second, a guy who was run over by a tractor he didn't hear coming through the field while he was sleeping on the ground.

The promoters were in debt over a million dollars after the concert. It took them years to clear the debt and make a profit through the audio and video recordings sold.

Chapter Twenty-one
Baby Boomers and Cars

Gas Stations

Before any Baby Boomers ever got a car, we got to ride in our parents' car and see firsthand what it was like to drive; starting the car, checking the rear view and side mirrors, putting on the turn signals, putting it in gear, holding on to that huge steering wheel most cars had back then, taking off, stopping and parking. For sure, we got to see what happened when dad pulled into the service station.

When dad went to a gas station, they were full service. There were no snack shops back then. There was air for your tires, oil for you engine or oil changes if the car needed it, gas, and engine repairs. Today it's like going into a mini supermarket. They sell all sorts of things. Back in the day you got service. You'd pull up and an attendant would come out and ask you:

"What'll it be today, sir or ma'am?" You'd answer: *"Give me $2.00's worth, please."*

Understand that back then $2.00's worth of gas would give you around 8 gallons of gas. Many of the eight cylinder cars held 18 to 20 or more gallons per tank. A lot of those big cars only got about 15 miles to the gallon; some even less. If you're tank was low, you might have said to that friendly attendant:

"She's real thirsty. Fill her up, please."

239

If the tank were near empty, you could fill up for less than $5.00. What does it cost someone today with a Hummer or big old eight cylinder Ford 350 at $2.30 per gallon?

During a full tank fill up, the attendant took time to clean your windows, check the oil level, check your tire pressure and add air to your tires if needed. Some patrons would even tip the attendants for service. In the good old days, no one had to get out of the car, ever. As a matter of fact, you weren't allowed to serve yourself. Today, the gas stations that only sell gas may have an attendant on hand, but all he'll do is pump your gas and nothing else. Cleaning windows, checking the oil and tire pressure is all up to the driver.

A lot of the older cars burned oil and needed to be topped off from time to time. Back in the sixties, I could buy recycled oil for half the price of brand new oil. I got my recycled oil at the cut rate gas station at the corner of Hopkins and Tifft. It came in glass bottles with spouts. For guys with tired old cars that burned a lot of oil, that was the way to go.

Owning a car was a responsibility. You needed to stay on top of things to keep the car rolling. It might have been changing the spark plugs, rotor and rotor cap (when the engine didn't run right). Maybe the timing needed adjusting or the brakes needed brake shoes. There were no disc brakes then. In those days, muffler systems weren't made to last. They corroded faster than you'd like them to, especially with the salt in the streets during Buffalo winters. They were made of regular metal, not stainless steel and there were no catalytic converters or emission control units. Also, there was a time when all cars had rubber tubes in the tires. Tubeless tires were a good invention. As with the recycled oil, I remember buying re-cap tires. For local driving, they were fine. On long highway trips at high speed on hot asphalt, well, that was a crap-shoot. Tires were known to come apart at the seams. Thank God for spare tires, hopefully in good shape.

Now, we get to the business of getting legal and more independent by getting a driver's license and our own car.

Driver's Permit/License

Getting a car for getting around and going downtown or wherever, was definitely one of the things on the minds of most of the guys as they turned sixteen. First, one needed to go through the process of obtaining a driver's permit. How many of you remember the whole process of getting your license? I remember a lot of South Buffalo guys talking about getting legal by getting their driver's license.

We couldn't wait to turn sixteen so we could get our driver's permit at the DMV in the Ellicott Square Building. That was a special time. It was a grown-up thing. The Ellicott Square Building is a classic old building with revolving doors. For those who went there to take the written permit test, can you remember walking in, from either the Main Street entrance or the Washington Street entrance? Once in the building, you'd find yourself walking into the big open space from Main Street and looking up to your left to find that elegant staircase and seeing the sign that read New York State Auto Bureau. Up you went and approached the counter to ask for an application for a driver's permit. You were handed the paperwork along with a little booklet to study for your written test. You took it home and studied until the day finally came when you'd go for it.

You went to the Auto Bureau, walked up those same stairs, approached the counter, and were directed to go sit at a desk where you took the test. Many were scared to death that they would not pass. It was corrected right after you took it, and you were either, elated or demoralized. If you passed, you got your permit right away which would be good for six months. Within that time, if you felt confident enough in your driving ability, you could set up an appointment for the road test.

After obtaining the driver's permit, you would boast to your friends that they might see you behind the wheel of your dad's or big brother's car. In the back of your mind, you would think a lot about the real payoff; actually getting your driver's license. Now, that was really grown-up. I mean, you could go off in dad's car, all by yourself. How much cooler could you be?

In time, you would set up that drivers test. At the time, everyone I knew went to the Williams Street testing site near South Ogden in the East Lovejoy area (The Iron Island). McKinley Parkway, next to the Park Edge Market was another site for testing at one time. When the moment finally came for your road test, you were sweating bullets. It wasn't necessarily because you weren't ready, but because you had heard about other people who flunked, some once and more than twice. Your mom, dad, big brother or a friend would drive the car to the site. You waited your turn for the examiner or inspector to approach the car. You would give him your driver's permit and appointment confirmation form. The driver got out, you slid behind the wheel and the inspector got in the passenger side. You waited for directions and prayed you wouldn't screw up... Think back folks. As the man gave you multiple directions for your little trip, did you not get a little pale? The directions might have gone something like this:

"You will be going straight until you come to the first street, make a left, go two blocks, make a right and then another left. Then, go two blocks and pull over to the curb."

In those days, you could fail the test before you actually drove if you failed to put on your left turn signal and signal with your left arm as you pulled away. You had to do both.

If you could actually manage to remember the initial directions until you pulled over to the curb, then you worried about the next two maneuvers. You knew those were the most feared maneuvers of the test: the three-point turn and the parallel park; especially, the parallel park. With either one of these, if you hit the curb, you would fail on the spot. If you really botched up your test, the inspector might cut the test short and tell you to go back to the starting point, that you weren't ready. Plenty of guys and girls came away teary-eyed, only to try again, and for some, try, try again another day. I'm proud to say I pass on the first try.

Dreaming of Getting a Car

As high school students, possessing a driver's license and getting a car was another whole process. It meant getting a job and saving up for one. Probably 99% of us came from "blue-collar" families and getting junior his own car wasn't in mom and dad's budget. It was up to us young hopefuls to work at getting that first car. All the guys looked forward to the day they'd get one. I mean '55 Ford, '55, '56 '57, 58 Chevy, and so on. Hey, even Eddy Ish's 50's station wagon was cool. For a lot of us it didn't matter what we had to drive. When we finally got a car, as long as it got us around, we were happy, very happy.

Not many actually had their own car in High School. As a matter of fact, very few did. I remember Eddy Funeziani, a South Buffalo guy, I believe had a '61 Chevy convertible. I worked with him at the Bocce Club Pizzeria on Clinton and Adams. Yes, we were envious. Most of the guys I hung out with didn't get a car until they got real jobs. One of the problems with the real jobs was not many paid big money, so paying for everyday expenses and saving up for a used or new car was really hard. Most of us could only hope to buy something used. My first car was a raggedy eight cylinder '55 Ford I bought from Jimmy McCrory who lived on Mariemont. It had a lot of rust, no heat, no radio, and people in the back seat could see the asphalt through the floorboards as I drove. Hey, what do you want for $85? The cool thing about the car was that it was a three speed on the column model or three on the tree, as they used to say. I could lay rubber in all three gears. Of course, I never sped. Yeah right.

As you may have noticed, I mentioned only guys going for their driver's license and getting their own cars. I didn't know any young lady age 16 to 18 who talked about getting her license, let alone, buying her own car. It wasn't the norm back then. Most young ladies more or less depended on their boyfriends to get one. More than once, young men would ask their girlfriends for money for gas or repairs. In some respects, they both shared the car. A lot of the guys had car payments and other maintenance expenses or mechanical repairs that only garage mechanics could do. As the ladies got jobs in the mid to late sixties, they got their license and eventually got cars. I remember my own sisters taking busses to go to work downtown, and after saving a few bucks, they bought used cars. Having a car back then was something people appreciated a lot. For many, it was a luxury.

Baby Boomers, dare I even go into modern cars? The mechanisms in new cars have come such a long way and the prices, well, in some cases are extreme. I can remember in 1956, a Volkswagen bug was between $1,300 and $1,500. Today, the price for the same basic car is $20,000 plus. Midsize cars went from $2,500 to $3,500. A brand new 1966 Mustang 2 door hardtop went for $2,370.

Need a Mechanic?

There were a ton of guys who were very good mechanics. Some could take an engines apart in the morning and put it back together so they could drive it at night. Today, tinkering with what's under the hood of your new car could result in a whole lot of grief. In some cars, you're lucky you can get a wrench in to try to fix or adjust anything.

In the good old days, I can remember some of the local guys like Mike Pasiecznik, Billy West, Butch Wilson or Joe Masullo, beefing up their cars and hearing terms like high-performance carburetors, four barrel AFB, fuel-injection, 411 rear-ends, Jack's Custom Traction Master, Muncie Four Speed, synchro-mesh transmissions, something called posi-traction, three on the column, four-on-floor Hurst Shifters, tachometers to keep an eye on the RPM's, dice on the mirrors, hand-rubbed lacquer paint jobs with maybe twenty coats or so of candy-apple red or metal flaked blue paint, or how about no color at all, just '55 Chevy black primer? How about hood-scoops and skirts, Hollywood mufflers, glass-packs, Continental Kits, chromed-reverse wheels? And, those classy white wall tires and curb-feelers some guys would put on to help prevent them from scuffing those white-walls.

If you were really cool, your steering wheel had what they called, a suicide knob on it. I had one on my '55 Ford. Not many of our cars back then had power steering. The suicide knob made it much easier to make those turns, especially when a guy had his girlfriend close to him on the bench seat with his arm around her shoulders. Do you remember that guys? Oh, how we loved those bench seats. Cars back then could easily fit six passengers, maybe seven. That would be three in front and four crammed in the back seat. While I'm speaking of what cars had, let's not forget what the interiors were made of. A lot of us remember real well, the metal or leather dashboards and door panels. Cars back then also had the high/low beam foot-switches on the left side of the floor. Today, they're on the steering wheel column cluster of electronics. They were easy to activate; one click for high beams and another click to go to low beams. Another great thing we had was a regular size spare tire in the trunk, not one of those ridiculous doughnut tires they put in there today. If you got a flat back then, you'd put on the spare, and it matched all the other tires. No need to take it easy on the spare.

With a doughnut tire, you need to be careful not to drive on it too fast or too hard for any length of time.

In the 40s, 50s, 60s and 70s, when you saw a car, you could tell right away what it was. There was no mistaking the '49 Ford Coupe, the '57 Chevy, the '58 Rambler, the '62 Plymouth, the '63 Mustang or the '65 Chevy Nova, 70 Lincoln or Cadillac. Those were the days when we had cars with great distinct looks; real chrome bumpers and little vent windows. I loved those vent windows. Speaking of bumpers, back then, you could actually hook up a rope or a chain to them to tow a car. If you try to do that with today's bumpers, you will cause a lot of damage if you can even find a place to hook up. Today's bumpers are not practical. They are there strictly for show. Another great thing they've taken away from our cars are those strips (gutters) at the edge of the roof that stopped water from falling into your car when you opened your windows in the rain. Today, if you open the window when it's raining, you get a stream of water rolling off the roof and pouring inside the car. That's one great idea they threw away. They were also used to tie down roof racks. Detroit, please bring back the vent windows and rain gutters. What the heck were they thinking when they decided to discontinue those?

Local Motor Men

A few of the older guys took regular cars and souped them up to give them more horse power. Not only was power important, but looks and sound were as well. I wondered what Baby Boomer from the old neighborhood might know who had what car back then. I remembered Butch Wilson was one of those car guys. He gave me a lot of information on who owned what car back in the day. I was completely amazed that he knew the owner, the year, make and even the engine size of the machines. He started with:

Sam Fassari's '62 Chevy 409. Then, he kept giving me names and cars; Jim Morgan's '57 Ford, Doug Alessandra's '57 Chevy and '62 Chevy Nova II, Joe Avolio's '65 Chevelle, Steve Moscato's '61 Dodge CONY 383 engine and four speed (on the floor of course) Dick Woolgar's '63 Chevy 409, Gary Schintzius' '63 Tunnel Ram Chevy Nova and '64, 409 Chevy Impala, Ron Wendtland's '66 Chevy Nova, Billy West's '56 Chevy called the "Vengance." West did take his machine to local racetracks to compete. And, Butch Wilson himself with a '59 Chevy (big fins), a 348 W/block and a 4 speed Hurst shifter.

Those were from the general area where I lived. There were several other machines from Seneca and Abbott that were around and would often test their horse power against any takers from South Buffalo at the Tifft-Ohio Street Drag Strips.

At that time, you had to have four on the floor equipped with a Hurst speed shift or you weren't cool. Speaking of shifters, all of those old boys can relate real well to the three speed on the column.

According to Bob Regan, the Lasker brothers, Tommy and Jimmy had a white '53 Olds with a Cadillac engine in it. Carmen Nappo from Sheffield Ave remembers the '59 Chevy, the '53 Olds and the '53 Ford he had. And Frank Daluisio, also from Sheffield Ave, had a few classics; '58 Chevy, '61 Chevy Impala, '64 GTO 389, '66 Chevy Biscane and a few others.

Today, you can only see those magnificent classic cars at various locations on Cruise Nights during the summer months. They are things of beauty. What was your favorite back then?

Sam Fassari's Crew and Cars

Sam Fassari told me that he and his friends hung out on Lockwood and South Park at Parson's and Judd Pharmacy during his early to mid-teens. Jim Morgan was one of his close friends. From his mid-teens to early twenties he hung at Deco 22 and Sperduti's Tavern. His crew was into cars and they even had a car club called the Gear Grinders. It later, became the Torid Torquers. They would cruise together to car shows and drag strips in the early 60s. He mentioned the Dunkirk and Erie, PA drag strips, Cayuga Drag Strip in Canada and finally, the Niagara Drag Strip that opened in the mid-60s. The latter, became their main drag strip. He also mentioned the illegal drags that were held at the foot of Tifft and Ohio streets. Some of the guys he remembers were:

Butch Wilson, Paul "Butch" Tara, Marty Hockey, Larry Courtney, Roger "Butch" Bohn, Dick Woolgar, Steve Muscato, *Jim Anthony, Ray Zielinski, Doug Allesandra, Paul Toms, Bobby Ulrich, Bill Cook, Doug Kroll, John Messore from Whitfield, Bob McDonald from Choate, Ray Berst from Eaglewood and Dick Grangle from Alsace.

*Jim Anthony *worked for the Buffalo Fire Department. He retired around 2001 and relocated in Paducah, Kentucky with his wife Mary, to be near family.*

Here's what he had to say about a part of his time in South Buffalo and the car scene.

"The 50's and 60's were magical; possibly the best time of my life. We were running souped-up Ford V-8 engines and could outrun the 6 cylinder Plymouths the cops had at Precinct 15, at the time."

The Drag Strips

Now then, these fine law abiding Baby Boomer car owners with their beefed up engines, as mentioned before, tested their horse power against each other from time to time. Butch Wilson talked about testing these machines at night on Tift Street near Fuhrman Blvd. This was pre-Ohio Street drag races. So as to not accuse anyone of speeding, we'll say they revved up their engines as close to the red line as they could. A few guys pushed beyond the red line and blew their engine. I don't know how all those tire marks got on that stretch of Tifft Street.

There was a little game some of the fast car owners liked to play. They'd have a guy sit back in the passenger side of the car. The owner (driver) would put a ten dollar bill on the wide dashboard near the windshield and bet the passenger that he couldn't snatch the bill when he (the driver) said "Go." Once he said "Go" he'd hit the gas and the passenger, try as he may, if the timing was right, could not grab the bill. That was most of the time. The acceleration force was so great in some of those cars that it would pin the passenger to the seat and not allow him to get the prize. Too bad.

Blizzard of '77

The biggest news item for 1977 was the Blizzard. It started on January 28 and lasted until February.

Buffalo was hit with a very severe blizzard that made news around the world. All Buffalo areas were shut down tight. There was a strict driving ban. No one was allowed on the streets; not that anyone really wanted to be outside in the bitter cold. The city and outlying areas were complete disasters. Over twenty people died. Some were literally buried in their cars under massive snowdrifts caused by 70 mile per hour winds. Some snow drifts were as high as

30 feet. Many individuals were rescued in time, but unfortunately, some were not. A few froze to death or were asphyxiated from carbon monoxide after having to stop because of the zero visibility but leave their cars running for warmth. They were trapped, with little hope of being found. It was horrendous. Buffalo was declared a State of Emergency. Besides being known as the Queen City, Buffalo also became known as "The Blizzard City."

A Parting Note...

After several years of hanging around with friends, dating, playing around with cars, racing, hopping bars, checking out different bands in numerous night clubs, the majority of the guys settled down and began to live the kind of life their parents lived. They got real steady jobs, got married, had kids, and a mortgage. It's the cycle of life. What goes around comes around. It's not only what a lot of hip people would call karma, it's the way life is. The Baby Boomers had their youth and did all the things young people do; many had a blast doing it. Now, they've become like their parents. That's not a bad thing, by the way.

So ends our trip down memory lane as we ride our '49 Ford, '55 Olds, '60 Chevy or '70 Mustang down the road. Happy trails.

Closing Remarks

I hope the contents of this book brought you great memories of the way it was during the hay days of the Baby Boomers of the 40's, 50's, 60's and 70's. There's a good amount of information that a lot of folks may have never known about our great area called South Buffalo. I'm sure most of you who are South Buffalonians were able to make connections with a lot of the people, places and events mentioned in the book.

May this work be a source of reference to remember what Baby Boomers experienced in their younger days. So many grand-parents and parents have never taken the time to share with their children what it was like living during their youth. By the time they leave this earth, and have not passed on much information or any at all, it's too late. It's all gone. Many children will ask about their parents' and grandparents' past as they get older.

You who are parents and grand-parents are a wealth of information. Do take the time to pass on stories and experiences of your life and your family's past. In doing that, you'll find that your children and grandchildren will feel better connected to you and have an appreciation of both the good and bad times you lived through. You may not realize it, but most of you have so much you could talk about with the next generation.

The Baby Boomer Generation's children will leave behind some kind of legacy. We had the "Greatest Generation" of people from World War I, World War II and the Korean War, who brought the Baby Boomer Generation into the world. What shall we call the children of the Baby Boomers? Can we hope to maybe call them the "Enlightened Generation, the "Intelligent Generation," the "Great Achievers Generation" or the "Peaceful Generation?" The last two would be very nice. What will their legacy be all about? What will they leave behind for their own children and grandchildren?

"It was great living in South Buffalo. A lot of the memories of the people, places and events have not faded with time. Many have become more solidified in the hearts and minds of those who experienced them."

I sincerely hope I've done a good job bringing many of you back to a time when life was simpler, friendlier, safer, exciting and perhaps, more fulfilling. God bless.

Roger Roberge Rainville

About the Author

I was born Magog Québec, Canada in 1946; fifth of ten children to parents, Léo Paul and Lucette Roberge Rainville. My first language was French. Our family moved to Welland Ontario in 1955 where my siblings Gilles, Jacques, Denise, Monique, Lise, Suzanne, Francois, Carole and Louis.and I learned to speak English. We move to 180 East Abbott Grove, Orchard Park on April 15, 1959. My dad worked at the Ford Plant and mom worked as a waitress at Colonial Kitchen in Blasdell. In April of 1960, we moved to to 72 Altruria Street, South Buffalo. The house number was later changed from 72 to 172 Altruria.

Although not originally from South Buffalo, I'm proud to tell people: *"I am a South Buffalonian."* When asked what nationality I am, I always answer *"I'm not a Canadian, I am a French Canadian,"* with the emphasis on "French". As with people who are proud of being South Buffalo Irish, Italian, Jewish, Polish, Hungarian, German, Puerto Rican, or representing any other nationality, I'm also proud of my roots and still maintain ties with my relatives in Québec. I tell folks that South Buffalo is where I spent some of my best years from age thirteen to adulthood. I came to have a great fondness and appreciation for the people and places in the South Park area, as well as, McKinley Parkway, Abbott Road and Seneca Street.

I attended school #29, Holy Family and South Park High School. I was not a good student and came to realize later in life that I had learning difficulties. Still, I went to college at age 38 which was very difficult but I succeeded. I studied at Buffalo State College to earn my bachelor's degree in secondary education French and Spanish, graduating with a 3.2 average. I attended UB for my master's degree and graduated with a 4.0 average (sigma cum laude.) After college, I worked as a French and Spanish teacher for the next twenty-three years at Canisius High School, and taught part time at Medaille College for twenty-one years.

I'm married to Donna Aures and am blessed with two children, Linette and Christian; four grandchildren; Saralin, TJ, Isaac and Evan as well as two great grandchildren Emma and Ethan. I sing and play rhythm guitar. I've also written many secular and gospel songs, one of which was recorded by gospel singer Jackie Davis. I've written a 152 page autobiography for my family, and another book, based on the story found in Luke 15 on the Bible entitled "*The Prodigal Son and The Love of a Father*" (*available on Amazon*), *ISBN 978-1935018-98-8*

Starting in 1981 I was involved in prison ministry in such facilities as: Attica, Collins I and II as well as Gowanda Correctional and a biker ministry.

I've practiced and taught Isshin-Ryu Karate since 1969 and have achieve the rank of master 7th degree black belt. I've also been an avid motorcycle rider since 1972 and presently ride a Heritage Softail Harley Davidson.

Acknowledgements

Anthony Jim

Accordino, Sam

Angie at Mazurek's Bakery

Aures, Kathy (Byrnes)

Batchelor, Ralph

Bohen, Timothy

Banko III, Steve

Best, Tom

Benjamin, Art, Nick Kobseff and Lou Sabella

Caffery, Kevin

Caruso, Dave

Castillo, Kevin

Concheiro, Dan

Colpoys, Ray

Concheiro, Dave and Bernadette

Cudney, Ed and Lori

Daluisio, Frank

Dargavel, Dennis

Dickman, Tim

Dingledey, Lou

Dolan, Chris

Domzalski, Bob

Donnelly, John (Jackie)

Dunlop, Rich

Fitzgerald, Tim

Fassari, Sam

Fitzgerald, Ann (Kenefick)

Paul F. Gannon

Erin Gannon

Greene, Bob

Golden, Rich

Guido, Anthony "Chuck"

Held, Bill Sr.

Hermann, Pete

Heitzhaus, Jack

Hyde, Bert (Guise)

Kelley, Tom

Kraengle, Maryjean

Leahy Clan...Tom, Peg, Eileen, Pat,

Bill, Dan, Susan and Kim

Liberti, Joe

Lovern, Pat (Greene)

Lowman, Hanna

Lucenti, Joe

Mahoney, Jim and Diane

Mattingly, Ray

McEwen, Billy

McLaughlin, Art

Miller (Crystal Ave) Jimmy

Miller, Edward, Iva (wife) and Iva (daughter)

Mulvaney, Chris

Murtha, Larry

Nappo, Carmen

Neaverth, Dan

Nicholson, Bill

Nightengale, Pat

Nolan, Kevin

Overdorf, Peg

Parisi, Joe

Pasquarella , Roger

Pasiecznik, Mike

Petrili, Adele

Pierro, Lorraine

Pugh, Jack

Ralston, Jimmy

Redmond, Mr.

Redmond, Dan

Regan, Bob

Regan, Gerry

Richards, Margaret (Nash)

Rodriguez, José

Rohloff, Alan

Rohloff, Rose Mary (DiTondo)

Salomon, Lynn

Sanly, Robin

Scahill, Joan Graham

Scaccia, Tony

Scaccia, Maria (Gawronski)

Schintzius, Gary

Seifert, Ken

Shanahan, Terry and Joan

Shea, Dan

Shea, Jerry

Shea, Jim

Sitarski, Carrie

Starzynski, Marge

Starzynski, Tony

Szczygiel, Peggy May

Tutuska, George

Vaughn, Greg

Wagner, Jack

Weber, Marge

Wilson, James "Butch"

Williams, Bob and Jeannette

Wojciechowski, (Smokey) Dennis

CPSIA information can be obtained
at www.ICGtesting.com
Printed in the USA
FFOW05n0943190717